ESCAPE FROM THE SHADOWS

ESCAPE FROM THE SHADOWS

ROBIN MAUGHAM

His autobiography

HODDER AND STOUGHTON
LONDON · SYDNEY · AUCKLAND · TORONTO

For
HONOR and DIANA
with my love

I know my heart, and have studied mankind: I am not made like any one I have been acquainted with, perhaps like no one in existence . . . I at least claim originality, and whether Nature did wisely in breaking the mould in which she formed me can only be determined after having read this work.

JEAN JACQUES ROUSSEAU,
The Confessions

Preface

———

THE NEW-FOUND LIBERTY AND THE NEW LICENCE WHICH
have been granted to writers in the United States and in
England, have been used to the full by various novelists. But
many biographers are still oddly reticent, and so are almost all auto-
biographers.

Yet the main impulse which moves a writer is the desire to tell the
truth—the desire to reveal the anxiety and pleasures of his mind, to
express the pains and joys of his spirit, the meanness and nobility of
his life, and thus to purge himself by placing on paper once and for all
the passions of his body and the inclinations of his heart.

Surely the new dispensation afforded to writers should extend not
only to novelists but to those who feel impelled to tell the true story
of their lives? Certainly the young reject the conventional hypocrisy of
even a few years ago. They demand the truth—bare and ugly though it
may be.

In this autobiography, accordingly, I will try to use the same freedom
of expression as a novelist enjoys today. I intend to reveal the whole
truth about myself, about those whom I knew well, who are dead, and
subject to the dictates of discretion and to the laws of libel—about
those who are alive and whom I know well. On the few occasions when
these two dictates interfere with the true story of my life, I have either

7

altered a character so that the person concerned will be unrecognisable, or I have fused two characters together. But the truth has not suffered.

Let me explain.

Both in my novel and in my play, *The Servant*, all the four main characters were, in fact, partly based on people who existed in real life. But I took traits from other people I knew, and I changed the external appearance of all the real persons involved so much that they did not even recognise themselves. But the essential truth of their relationship with each other and with me has remained.

Most writers wait till they are sixty or seventy before writing their autobiographies. I am fifty-five. I am beginning the story of my life *now* for three reasons. First, because I feel an intense desire to rid myself, once and for all, of the ghosts from the past which still haunt me. Secondly, because I have longed to explain my true character and how it came to be formed. Lastly, because I believe that memory fades far quicker than is generally supposed. But in this respect I am lucky, because ever since the war I have made notes and kept a diary. Moreover, I have used many incidents from real life in my novels, so I have only to re-read a novel for incidents from my past to come flooding back into my memory. I have made considerable use of this material and of material from my book *Somerset and All the Maughams*. I know I shall be accused of repeating myself in the various passages from my 'family book' that I have used. But how can I omit essential scenes from my life? How can I write them in different words and with different dialogue? If my father, for instance, made a certain remark in 1945 and I reported it in 1966, how can I possibly change his words in 1972? I must repeat myself for the sake of the truth.

I am calling this book *Escape From The Shadows*. Two of the shadows are those of my father—a former Lord Chancellor of England—and of my uncle, William Somerset Maugham—perhaps the most successful writer of this century. For the last forty years I have been trying to escape from the shadows of their fame. I hope that this book will at last release me from their ghosts. The third shadow has been more dangerous; I will try to describe its nature in the course of the pages that follow.

*   *   *

My story begins as a very lonely child with elderly parents. As I grew up I entered the quite natural phase of being more attracted towards my own sex than towards girls; yet I was so imbued with the strict upper-middle-class moral conventions of my family that I was stricken with guilt by my apparently perverse inclinations and tried to make myself 'normal'—and at times succeeded. The war years between 1939 and 1945 made me realise that I was predominantly homosexual. The anxiety of that realisation turned me to drink. Perhaps it was fortunate that I did not suffer from the same delusion as my Uncle Willie, who told me in his old age that his greatest mistake had been to persuade himself that he was three-quarters normal and only a quarter queer— "whereas really it was the other way round". But though I came to accept my own similar nature—that I was mainly, but not wholly, homosexual—the torment and the guilt remained.

Overshadowed, queer and alcoholic, I should have been a complete failure. To this day, I am still surprised when the critical or financial success of one of my novels, plays or films—in various countries—would seem to suggest that I am a success. But I am not a success in my own eyes for reasons which this book will certainly reveal.

ACKNOWLEDGMENTS

I have dedicated this autobiography to my sisters Honor and Diana. To them, and to our beloved and mourned eldest sister Kate, I owe much of the encouragement and wise advice which has sustained me as a writer and guided me throughout my life.

Here, I would also like to express my gratitude to those who have helped me with this book and to others who have allowed me to quote from their work or make use of material from my own published writing—particularly, in this last instance, Longmans and Heinemann, joint publishers of *Somerset and All the Maughams*; Heinemann again, who published my novel *The Man With Two Shadows*; Chapman and Hall, who published my war book *Come to Dust* and my travel book *Nomad*; the editor of *The People* newspaper, for which I have written many articles over the years; and Andre Deutsch who included my tribute in their book *Gilbert Harding, By His Friends*.

For permission to quote from the work of others I am especially indebted to Mr. Beverley Nichols (*A Case of Human Bondage*), Mrs. Cherry Anderson (*New Light on Survival*, by her father, Roy Dixon-Smith), Mr. R. F. V. Heuston (*Lives of the Lord Chancellors, 1885–1940*), Mr. Nigel Nicolson and the estate of Sir Harold Nicolson (Sir Harold Nicolson's *Diaries*), Sir Noël Coward for his version of *Let's Do It*, Lloyd's Register of Shipping, for permission to quote from the Register.

I would also like to thank my dear friend Gillian Dearmer—now Mrs. G. M. Warr—for allowing me to read and use my letters to her; and Mr. Michael Davidson, for permission to quote from *The World, The Flesh and Myself* and for all his valuable advice.

And I gratefully acknowledge the editorial, research and secretarial help of Mrs. Nancy Hosegood, Mrs. Jeanne Francis, Mrs. Kathleen Osborne, Mrs. Renée Barber, and Mr. Timothy d'Arch Smith. My thanks are also due to Derek Peel for checking the proofs and making the index, and especially to Peter Burton for all his assistance during the writing and preparation of this book.

Robin Maugham,
Ibiza, 1972.

Contents

———

Illustrations

———

KEY TO ACKNOWLEDGMENTS

1   Peter Burton   4   Miguel Sanchez Marco
2   Now in the possession of Winifred Durnford 5   Cole Lesley
3   The *Daily Mail*   6   Peter Madock

PART

ONE

IN FRONT OF THE OLD HOUSE, WITH ITS BATTLEMENTS and stone porch, the lawn stretched out like a lagoon around the ancient mulberry tree. A local legend was that a Cavalier had hidden in the thick leaves of the tree as long ago as 1643, after the battle of Lansdown, while Cromwell's soldiers searched the garden.

The evening was pleasantly warm. I was playing rounders with my sister Diana and the Sparrow children from the farm next door. I was fond of Diana, but slightly afraid of her because she was sixteen—eight years older than I was. From the shadow of the mulberry tree creeping across the lawn I knew that Rose, my governess, would soon come to collect me to take me to supper in the nursery. I knew also that in her wonderful kindness she enjoyed watching me playing and would wait patiently until the game was over.

For a moment my attention slipped away from the game, and I turned to look at the hayfield beyond the house. Suddenly I stood still in wonder. Hal, the twelve-year-old Sparrow boy, was riding their largest cart-horse, which had just been unharnessed from the haycart. It had been hot in the fields—so hot that both rider and horse were sweating. Dark patches of sweat showed through Hal's singlet. Dark patches stained the sleek chestnut flanks of the cart-horse. The horse was broad in girth, and Hal's slender thighs had been stretched wide to straddle him. Hal's legs were bare. He was very lean. His matted hair hung down over his forehead. With his blue eyes and sunburned skin I thought he was the most beautiful person I had ever seen. I longed to be old enough to know him; I longed to be like him, and as I stared up at him in adoration I felt a stab of pain in my heart so keen that I nearly fainted.

Alas, I have known this feeling on many occasions since that day. I had hoped that the intensity of the pain would grow less as I became older. It hasn't.

Hal saw me and smiled. I smiled at him and then turned back to the game because—though I was innocent—I had experienced an odd feeling both of guilt and embarrassment while I was staring at my hero.

Presently my absorption in the game was distracted by another apparition. Down the drive that led past the lawn to the house there came an open 'tourer', bright yellow and glittering with windscreens, both in front and at the back. Driving it was a man in a check cap and thick motoring-goggles. The tourer was the longest car I had ever seen—and the strangest because its wide mud-guards were strapped flat to its sides with bits of string and leather bands, like skis. The driver's build seemed somewhat familiar. Then Diana and I recognised him.

"Daddy!" we cried a little uncertainly, but the goggled man waved back to us so we knew we had guessed right.

"Hullo, children!" he called out in his hollow voice.

To explain the reason for my father's advent in this strange car I must recall the explanation that my mother gave me some years later.

*   *   *

My father at the time was one of the leading barristers in England. A conference which he had attended that day had ended four hours earlier than he had expected. Idly my father strolled through the London streets, wondering which train he would take to Bath where King, our chauffeur, would meet him in the Crossley. At that moment my father happened to pause in front of the glass windows of an obviously respectable shop that sold new motor-cars. Nearest the window was a large Fiat tourer. Its long bonnet gleamed in the sunshine. It had two 'occasional' seats so that the car could convey six people. My father had a wife, three daughters and a son. The car could carry the whole family. Moreover, the chauffeur was sometimes overworked, driving one or other of us about. A second car was obviously needed. The price was high—but not exorbitant. And growing like a splendid orchid in my father's mind was the idea that if he bought the

18

Fiat now he could drive it straight down to Hamswell House below the Lansdown Ridge. My father glanced at his watch and calculated that he would arrive at the moment when at least two of his children would be playing on the front lawn.

"Who is that strange man in that strange car?" he could imagine us saying. Then would come the joyful recognition. "Daddy!" we would cry as we ran towards his immaculate vehicle. "It's Daddy." And then he would wave his hand towards us—"Hullo, children," he would say calmly.

My father opened the door of the motor dealer's shop and walked in. The fact that he had never driven a car before did not deter him in the least, for my father throughout his life clung firmly to the theory that if you had a first-class brain—and he knew very well that he *did* have a first-class brain—then you could master any task or science to which you applied yourself.

The head salesman now approached my father who was examining the Fiat through his gold-rimmed monocle.

"Is there anything I can do to help you, sir?" the salesman asked.

My father put a finger on the Fiat's bonnet.

"I will take this one," he said.

"Certainly, sir," the salesman said, disguising his slight surprise at the speed of my father's choice.

"Can I take you for a trial run?"

"I presume the car moves," my father said, "and is guaranteed to be in mechanical order."

"Certainly, sir."

My father took a cheque-book from his pocket.

"I will write you a cheque," he said, "and you will telephone my bank quoting the cheque number to make sure that I am no impostor."

"Certainly, sir."

"However, there is one clause I must insist on inserting in our contract."

"Is there, sir?" the salesman asked nervously.

"You will send an expert car-driver with me as far as Reading," my father continued firmly. "By the time we reach Reading I shall have mastered the art of driving the car, and I shall send your man back to London by train, first-class."

"Certainly, sir."

"We shall stop at my London house en route so that I may change into appropriate clothes."

"Certainly, sir."

*　　　*　　　*

Half an hour later, my father having changed into appropriate clothes at his town house—3 Rutland Gate—was sitting beside a nervous young mechanic who was driving the Fiat down to Reading. My father sat in silence, but he was observing acutely how the mechanic changed gear and how he moved the steering-wheel to avoid the on-coming traffic.

The mechanic stopped the car outside Reading Station.

"Thank you very much," said my father, fumbling in his pocket. "Here is the money for your fare to London—and here is a small remuneration for your kind service."

The mechanic looked at him doubtfully. "Thank you, sir," he said. "But are you sure I oughtn't to take you a bit farther? I mean, after all you've never driven a car before."

"I am grateful for your concern," my father said, "but you need not be worried. I have acquired all the knowledge that is needed for the craft of driving. Goodbye, and thank you."

With which words my father drove slowly but steadily out of the station yard and turned left towards the road to Bath. Unfortunately, a few yards along the road there was a large lorry parked correctly on the left-hand side. There was also a car approaching. My father in his determination to avoid the on-coming car pulled the steering-wheel a little too much to the left and ran straight into the off-side of the lorry, removing the whole of the Fiat's left mud-guard. The lorry-driver popped out of his cabin like a jack-in-the-box.

"What the hell do you think you're doing?" he shouted.

My father, who was always courteous, took off his cap and nodded politely to the lorry-driver. "I must apologise," he said. "My judgment of the distance between your vehicle and mine was a trifle at fault. I will give you the name of my insurance company. I will accept full responsibility for the accident, so that you will be amply rewarded for the slight damage your lorry has sustained. Meanwhile, may I ask your assistance in helping me to strap on my mud-guard, which seems to have been separated from the car."

A lesser man than my father might have given up his ambition to reach his house that evening. He might have driven to a garage, and at a later date taken driving lessons. But twenty minutes later the yellow Fiat, with its mud-guard strapped to its side, was moving steadily along the Great West Road, as it was called in 1924, and three hours later—after a few minor mishaps—my father reached Bath. Now, the hill out of Bath is steep; and in those days many cars could not ascend it in first gear, so they would turn and mount in reverse, which was the lowest gear. But my father, who was by now confident of the Fiat's power, only made this decision half way up the hill; and in his efforts to turn the car and change gear at the same time, unfortunately he swerved into a large car that was coming *down* the hill, and took off his right mud-guard.

Once again his courtesy prevailed over the wrath of the driver whose car he had damaged. Once again he took off his cap, claimed full responsibility in writing, and gave the name of his insurance company. And soon he was steering backwards up the hill, and at last he reached the Lansdown ridge. His great moment was not far away, and presently it came. There he was in his Fiat advancing proudly down the drive to his house, and *there* were two of his children playing with their friends on the lawn.

"Daddy!" we cried. "It's Daddy."

Here was his great moment. He waved with a gesture so casual that one might have thought he was used to driving yellow Fiats every day of his life.

"Hullo, children!" he called and waved once again.

And still waving, he drove the car straight into the stone porch of the house.

*   *   *

My laughter at seeing the car wedged into the stone porch was restrained by fear. For although my father had never beaten or ill-treated me, I was very afraid of him. He was fifty when I was born; and when I was eight he seemed extremely old.

My earliest memory of him was of a pallid-faced, strange man who came into the nursery shortly after I had been given my supper by my first nanny, whom I had secretly christened 'Crosspatch'. I stared at the stranger nervously.

"Say 'Good evening, Daddy'," my horrid nurse prompted in a whisper.

"Evening, Daddy," I muttered.

"Good evening, Robin," my father said in a weary, hollow voice.

For a few alarming moments there was silence.

"What did you do this afternoon?" the man asked in a stern, accusing voice.

What indeed had I done? What misdeed had I committed within the last few hours that he had discovered? I had picked my nose, and Nanny had slapped me hard.

"We went for a walk in the park, didn't we?" Nanny prompted in the falsely cheerful voice that she always used when grown-ups were present.

21

"Went for a walk," I mumbled.

During the silence that followed, my father fumbled in his pocket and produced a tuppenny bar of milk chocolate, which he examined with such care that for a moment I thought he was going to eat it. Then with a quivering hand he held it out to me.

"Here is a present for you, Robin," he said.

I gazed up at him in surprise. Evidently no misdeed had been uncovered.

"Now what do we say when we're given a present?" Nanny asked, smiling archly. "We say 'Thank you', don't we?"

"Thank you," I mumbled.

My father looked gloomily round the room. I suppose he was trying to think of something to say.

"May I eat it?" I asked.

My father glanced at Nanny, who beamed confirmation.

"Now?" I asked, unwrapping the silver paper that enveloped the bar. Nanny sent out another beam of approval.

"If you want to," said my father.

"But not all at once," Nanny added warningly.

But her command came too late. I had swallowed the lot.

"What do you intend to do tomorrow?" my father asked in his accusing tone of voice.

I was silent. The last thing I intended to do was to betray my plans to this stranger.

"After our morning lessons we're going to see the ducks on the Round Pond, aren't we?" Nanny said merrily.

"Yes," I answered.

"How are the lessons going?"

Again I was silent, for each lesson was an ordeal for me. I had wept that very morning; and the strain of the man's inquisition, combined with the large piece of chocolate I had devoured, was beginning to make me feel sick.

"They're going very well," Nanny said swiftly. "We can do our multiplication table right up to ten."

"What are five times seven?"

"Thirty-two," I said after a pause.

"Now that's not right, is it?" Nanny laughed brightly. "We know better than that, don't we? We know what five times seven make, sure enough! Five times seven make . . ."

But she never finished her sentence, because at that moment I was sick on the floor.

*   *   *

When my parents were in London I was very lonely, for each afternoon, after I had left the day-school I attended, I would be alone with my nanny. My three sisters were much older than I was, and my mother was usually so busy running a large household and entertaining her own friends and the celebrities from the law-courts whom my father knew, that she seldom visited the nursery. Besides, I had heard her tell my sisters that she did not *like* little boys. During the early years of my life, my mother was unwell. My sister Honor tells me that, as a result, my mother was often irritable and impatient with me. ("As a child you were pathetically docile," Honor told me. Then she smiled. "But thank heavens you've made up for it since," she added.) Gradually, I learned to entertain myself in the nursery. I made houses with toy bricks; I constructed railway lines; and once with old sheets I arranged a whole mountain of snow for my train to run through.

I also invented stories for myself, and I cherished my own fantasies.

One of my fantasies was connected with the play *Peter Pan* to which my mother had taken me. To me, Peter Pan was not an actress on the stage dressed in the guise of a boy; but a real boy who existed in real life, a boy who was a few years older than I was, a boy who had learned to fly. And each day this boy became more and more real to me until I knew for certain that he would come to rescue me from the constrained life I led. He would appear at the windows and take hold of my hand, and together we would fly over the roof-tops of London and reach an abode where there were no nurses, no lessons, no masters and no rules. And there we would live together, ageless, for ever. So real to me was this fantasy that one evening I believed the boy was there, standing on the sill of my bedroom window. It happened thus.

Nanny had put me to bed several hours ago, but I could not sleep. I lay in bed, staring at the gap between the blue chintz curtains, which had been only partly drawn to let in air through the open windows because it was a hot summer night. In the nursery next door I could hear Nanny talking with Mabel, the head housemaid. They spoke softly, thinking I was asleep, and only fragments of their conversation reached me. "And I said to him I said, 'If you think that I'm that kind . . .'," Mabel was saying. Then I heard Nanny's voice: "Well really! Who'd have thought it! And him a sergeant and all."

I didn't listen attentively to the few phrases of their conversation, for they seemed very dull. As far as I could gather, they always seemed to be talking about other people, whereas I would have thought it was much more interesting to talk about themselves. Besides, I didn't much *like* Nanny, and *her* attitude towards me had changed since an event which had taken place only a fortnight ago. I had kissed her goodnight more affectionately than usual because I had seen that she had a toffee concealed in her hand, and I expected that she would give it me. After I had kissed her, she stood beaming down at me. Then she asked me the question:

"Who do you love most in the world, ducky?"

I knew that my response should have been to kiss her again and say, "*You*, Nanny darling." Then the toffee would have been mine. But honesty won.

"Myself," I had replied; and muttering, "Talk about ingratitude", Nanny had promptly left the room to join Mabel with her thick black stockings and shiny boots in the nursery next door. The following day Nanny was a crosspatch again, so it was more important than ever that the boy should fly into my room to take me away. Each night I prayed that he would arrive. I could imagine him perfectly. He looked a little like Hal from the farm next door at Hamswell, but his eyes were a deeper shade of blue and his skin was more smooth and his shoulders were broader.

So now I lay in bed, longing to hear the gush of air as the windows flew apart and the boy appeared. I knew all that he would say to me and all that I would say to him. Then, quietly, so that Nanny should not hear, he would teach me to fly. Then he would take my hand, and together we would float through the window, leaving the room with its silly frill of lambs round the walls, and soar over the roof-tops into the starlit sky.

All the other nights I had lain in bed, waiting for the boy to come, I had somehow known that in fact he would not appear. But this evening for some reason I was certain he would arrive. My eyes were fixed on the gap in the curtains. The clock on the landing struck ten. It was old and rusty and croaked dismally as it chimed. The boy must come tonight. Why did he delay so long? In the nursery next door, I heard my nurse saying: "And I said to him I said, 'You won't carry on like that with *me*, I'm proper and don't you forget it.'" Her voice faded away. Then there was silence. The two of them must have left the room. The night was very quiet. I could hear not a sound. The room was completely still. I felt hot and strangely excited. Why didn't he come? Then, a few minutes later, I knew somehow that he was approaching. At the same time I was worried because the two women had left the nursery, for I was aware that it was not only the boy who could fly. There were evil people with long wings like bats; there were witches and demons. Then, suddenly, I heard a faint tapping at the window, and I seemed to see a form—a dark form—standing on the sill between the two curtains. The sound of tapping continued. I was frightened. Why didn't the boy call out to me softly—as he had in my dreams of him? Perhaps it wasn't the boy. Suddenly I was certain that it wasn't the boy framed between the two curtains. There was something evil standing there. Then the figure moved.

"Nanny!" I called out. "Quick!"

A moment later Nanny came bustling into my room.

"Quick," I said to her. "Please, quick. There's someone at the window, trying to get in."

"Nonsense," Nanny said. However, she went to the windows and bolted them and drew the curtains.

"You've had a bad dream," she said. "Now you just be still, and I'll go and boil up a nice glass of milk for you. I'll leave the door open. I'll only be in the next room."

I lay back in bed. I was convinced by now it had only been my imagination that made me think the apparition at the window had been evil, and as a result I had made a ghastly, irrevocable mistake. The boy had indeed come to see me, but I had frightened him away. The window had been bolted against him. The boy would never visit me again. Never. I had lost my only chance of happiness.

Next door I could hear Nanny saying querulously to Mabel: "He ate his tea far too quickly. I must see that it doesn't happen again."

No, I thought to myself, it will never happen again. I shall never find the boy who will take my hand and fly away with me for ever.

I was right. I never have.

*   *   *

When Nanny became such a crosspatch that she grew violent in her rages, my mother decided it was time for her to go, and a French governess was installed so that I should learn to read in French as well as in English.

Mademoiselle Vogne from Dijon was a tall, thin lady with a long nose which dripped like a tap in cold weather. She had large, grey, mournful eyes and a receding chin. But though her aspect alarmed me, she was a kind person and an excellent teacher. Her trouble was that she had a sad disposition. To Mademoiselle Vogne the world was an evil place full of wicked people—most of whom would do her a bad turn if given a chance. Moreover evil influences could enter into inanimate objects. Wicked spirits could knock the teacup out of her hand or trip her up or give her a cold in the head. But over the years she had learned to accept the malevolence of the world.

"Ah, c'est la vie!" was her constant lament. "C'est la vie!"

Mademoiselle Vogne was not a merry companion, but I shall always

25

be grateful to her for her patience with me. Quite soon I found I could speak French almost as easily as English. On the few occasions that I was allowed in the drawing-room when there was a party, a grown-up, who wished to say something to my mother which was unsuitable for a child's ears would say it in French and I would understand most of it. Then my mother would catch my eye and give me a secret wink.

I adored my mother—as did my three sisters; and so much of their veneration communicated itself to me that I thought of her more as some remote goddess into whose presence I was daily summoned for a short while rather than as the parent whose child I was. My mother's attitude towards me when I was a child was affectionate yet aloof. Her love for me increased as I grew older. But as an infant I sometimes irritated her. I have a feeling that in 1916, when I was born, she did not want another child. My sister Honor told me that when I was a baby my mother used to roll me down a grassy bank because it amused her poodle to pounce after me. However, by the time I was seven or eight there existed an odd psychic relationship between us. For instance she would write down a number on a piece of paper and I, from the other end of the room, could tell her what the number was. I had, at that time—and at moments since—this odd psychic gift, which at the period seemed perfectly natural to me. To amuse her house guests my mother would turn upside-down the stack of letters which the postman had brought that morning, so that I could not see the writing. I would place my hand on each letter and announce, correctly, from whom it came. I can remember that I thought there was nothing unusual about this. It was merely a boring chore to do before I could eat my porridge.

*   *   *

I had often heard my sisters talking about my uncle William Somerset Maugham. I knew that Uncle Willie was famous because he wrote stories and plays. I had vague memories of a well-dressed, attractive man with a skin the colour of parchment, who came to visit my mother. Willie, as I called him from the time I was seventeen, was devoted to my mother. She was one of the very few women about whom he never said anything unkind or bitter. And so fond of her was he that when I was seven or eight he asked her to bring me to lunch with him at the Savoy. I was entranced at the prospect of going to a place that sounded rather like a palace.

"What happens at the Savoy?" I asked Mademoiselle Vogne.

"The Savoy!" she cried. "Will he then take you *there*?"

"Why shouldn't he?" I asked.

26

"Because the Savoy is a *mauvais lieu*," she answered. "It is a wicked place where wicked men take wicked women."

"What do they do there?"

Mademoiselle Vogne sighed. "*Ah, c'est la vie!*" she said.

"But what do they *do*?"

Once again she sighed. "They eat oysters," she replied, "and they drink champagne."

Her words impressed me greatly. I realised that with my mother present I hadn't a hope of drinking champagne, but I was determined to eat oysters.

The day came. I was dressed in my best suit. In the car my mother pinched my cheeks, because she said I looked sallow. We walked into the hotel, and there was Uncle Willie—even sallower than I was—waiting to greet us. He led the way to a table in the restaurant. The head waiter handed a large menu card to each of us. I looked at it intently but I could see no mention of oysters. Then I noticed—at the very bottom of the list of *hors d'oeuvre*—the magic word 'Oysters'. Beside the word was written 'Special Supplement'.

"Now, Robin, what would *you* like?" my Uncle Willie asked after my mother had ordered. "*Hors d'oeuvre* to start with?"

"Thank you," I said nervously.

So he began to read out the list. "Smoked salmon or potted shrimps?"

I made no reply, but I looked at him hopefully. Patiently my uncle, who had begun to stammer slightly, read out the list to the very end. I remained dumb.

"Oysters," he suggested at last in despair.

"Yes, *please*," I cried.

Uncle Willie took out his monocle, fixed it into position, and stared at me in gloomy silence. Then he spoke.

"You would be unlike the rer-rest of the younger members of your family," he said sadly, "if you did not prefer the most expensive." Suddenly he smiled at me, and I knew I'd got my oysters.

*   *   *

I was always happier in the country than in London because at Hamswell there were Kathleen and Doreen Sparrow to play with. They were about my age. Kathleen was quiet, gentle and very beautiful. Doreen was high-spirited and full of vitality and laughter. I was very fond of them both; I envied their freedom and self-assurance; and I loved their soft Somerset accents which one summer I adopted with some success. Another source of joy to me was that Mademoiselle Vogne had returned to Dijon, and Rose had taken her place. I liked

27

Rose as soon as I saw her. She was in her middle thirties. Her pale blue eyes and gentle smile exuded kindness, and she had a wonderful gift of sympathy. When we played draughts or snakes-and-ladders together she did not play as a grown-up playing with a child, she *became* the same age I was, and we were equally excited by the game. At last I had found a companion, and soon I loved her deeply.

Moreover, my mother could spare more time to spend with me when we were in the country. In Bath she had found an old song-book which contained one song that delighted us both, and she would play it on the piano and sing me the words. I can remember the first line:

"Now Tommy was a naughty boy, as naughty as could be."

Then followed a list of Tommy's misdemeanours which were considerable. He teased girls and pulled their hair; he threw things out of the window; he broke his sister's dolls. He was a thoroughly bad type of juvenile delinquent. And he fascinated me. The recital of his misdeeds in the song was too short. I begged my mother to tell me more about him, for I was convinced he was a real person. My mother had a splendid imagination, and I think she was amused by my eagerness. As a reward, if I had not been tiresome all day, she would come and sit by my bed after Rose had tucked me up and tell me stories about Tommy. His behaviour was flagrant. Against the direct orders of his father he had climbed up a gigantic tree and slipped, and had been saved from death only by falling into a hammock. While staying with his parents at Worthing he had stolen a small sailing boat and put to sea with the intention of reaching France, but a violent tempest had arisen, and he would certainly have been drowned had he not been rescued by a passing destroyer. Tommy had also been caught poaching by a huge game-keeper who decided to hand him over to the police, and had only just managed to escape in time by kicking the man hard on the shins.

I realise now that a conflict must have arisen in my mother's mind between the moralist who felt that retribution should follow wickedness and the artist who wanted her story to be a success. But there was little hope for the moralist, because I was so devoted to Tommy that if I heard he was going to be punished I would burst into tears and sob throughout the night until I was told authoritatively that the punishment had been cancelled and that Tommy was well and happy again.

Sometimes a tinge of wistfulness would seep into the stories my mother made up. Perhaps Tommy was the kind of son that secretly she had always wanted. He was certainly very unlike me—not that I was good, I was tiresome; I did stupid things like painting noughts and crosses on my bedroom wall and crying whenever the old Crossley back-fired; I was always nervous and sometimes petulant or sulky. But

I was never really wicked. ("You were such a *good* little boy," my beloved Rose, now aged eighty-three, wrote to me the other day.) And I was never brave, I would never have dared to climb a tall tree—especially if my father had told me not to, for I was more frightened of my father than of anyone I had ever met. I would never have stolen a sailing boat or kicked a gamekeeper. But Tommy wasn't frightened. My mother was there to prove it. Tommy defied his father and even answered him back. Tommy was three years older than I was. No one of my age could have been quite so tough. But I knew that even at the age of eight or nine he would never have dragged his feet and stammered when strangers spoke to him. Gradually Tommy became the embodiment of all the things I could never be. He was strong and ruthless, good at games and a crack jockey, as well as a fearless swimmer and an intrepid mountaineer. He was insolently brash and never felt a twinge of nervousness in his life. I use the word 'embodiment' because he was so real to me that I could see him and touch him. When Rose had gone to her supper and I was alone in my bedroom on the top floor he would come in and lie beside me and comfort me. I could sense his presence rather than see him. In my imagination he had curly brown hair—mine was dark and straight—starry blue eyes, a snub nose. Sometimes he looked like Hal Sparrow when he came back from the hayfields.

I used the character of Tommy in a book of mine called *The Man with Two Shadows*. I have used him in this autobiography because he became a vital part of my life.

I was happy that summer, but there were premonitions of disaster. I had been warned that in the winter term I was to go to a preparatory boarding school—Highfield School, at Liphook in Hampshire. And I dreaded the moment. I had read *The Bending of a Twig, Tom Brown's Schooldays*, and *The Holiday Annual*. I could not identify myself with a single character in them. I seemed to fit into no category. Certainly I could never hope to be Harry Wharton or Bob Cherry. And I would never stand up for a fight. The boxing lessons my mother had made me take in a London gym had been a great failure, for though adroit at defence I would never attack.

The day came nearer. Rose and I were sent up to London—to 73 Cadogan Square where we now lived—to buy my school things. This had to be done in advance for tabs bearing my full name had to be sewn on each garment, each handkerchief, each sock. Rose and I also bought a parrot in the King's Road. On being taken home it remained obstinately silent, but let out from its cage it flew smartly to the carved wooden head of my bed and devoured it between the hours of five and eight. My mother, who came up to town a few days later, made us take the parrot back the next day. We bought budgerigars instead. Rose and I then decided that inasmuch as I dropped things continually and might have them snatched from me by naughty schoolboys, I should buy clips to attach each object to me. Thus we found a screw-clip that fitted into my straw boater and was attached to my stiff Eton collar, a fountain-pen clip that clamped my pen firmly into my breast pocket, a watch-chain for my old half-hunter, which seldom worked, with a leather end secured to one of my trouser buttons, and a clip for my school tie.

Then came the farewell presents. My mother gave me a lovely Chinese lacquer pencil-case, and Rose gave me a set of coloured pencils. I was also given several toys to put in my play-box.

My mother took me to Highfield School, Liphook, with King driving the new family Rolls. My mother greeted the Headmaster, the Reverend W. Mills, and his wife, and then left me in the school hall, standing beside my play-box with my name—R. C. R. Maugham— painted on it. Presently I was taken to the lower classroom. That first afternoon at Highfield there were no lessons. The boys in the classroom gathered round me examining me in a silence broken only by brief titters. My hair was long; I was small for my age and very slim; my pale skin and delicate appearance were certain, I now realise, to have excited the instinct for cruelty which smoulders in most schoolboys.

"Can you speak?" the tallest boy asked me.

"Yes," I answered. I could feel myself blushing.

"What's your name?" the boy asked.

"Robin Maugham."

"Can you repeat a sentence you hear, Maugham?"

"Yes."

"Then repeat after me. I one my mother. I two my mother . . . Go on, repeat it."

In confusion I continued uncertainly, until I heard my voice saying: "I six my mother." Then I stopped.

"Go on," the boy said.

"I seven my mother," I continued. "I eight my mother. . . ."

And at that all twenty of the boys broke into wild yells of triumph. "He ate his mother!" they screamed in derision. "Maugham ate his mother!"

As I listened to their laughter, I tried to smile. But even as I made the effort, I felt that in some terrible way I had betrayed my mother's confidence in me. But it wasn't the feeling of guilt which upset me, it was the expression on the boys' faces as they stared at me; for I suddenly became aware that, for some reason I could not understand, they disliked me. They were all hostile to me, and I had never met with hostility before. At Hamswell they were all fond of me—even Mr. Jenks, the gardener, whose peaches I stole. The realisation that, at the age of nine and without any bad behaviour on my part, I was disliked filled me with a kind of sick fear. I felt trapped. I couldn't move. The largest boy came over to my desk. He picked up the Chinese lacquer pencil-case. Then he took out each coloured pencil one by one, and broke it. I remained motionless, watching. Then he took up the case again, and I knew that he intended to destroy it as well as the pencils. While I watched him, I felt a dizziness in my head, and my whole being seemed in turmoil. For a moment—only for a second or two—I lost consciousness. It could only have been a brief period of unconsciousness, for when I recovered the boy was still watching me and he was still holding the pencil-case. Then, for the first time in my life, I heard Tommy's voice.

"Don't move," Tommy said. "Sit still and try to pretend you don't care what they do. And don't worry. I'll be close to you to protect you."

At that moment the large boy broke the case over his knee, and in the same instant, as I saw it lying shattered on the floor in two jagged pieces, something inside me snapped in half also, and in a strange way I suddenly became two people—the sensitive, frightened boy who suffered and the callous person who belonged to Tommy and who, as the school years went by, gradually became part of me. It was this other self which I presented to the classroom.

This split which I kept hidden from everybody—even from Rose—was to have dangerous results later in my life.

*   *   *

I loathed Highfield School. Misery hung around me like a fog, muffling my emotions. Only now and then would the fog lift in gratitude for some unexpected trivial act of kindness; and then, with the first act of subsequent brutality, the pain would have been unbearable—except for Tommy's presence.

I lived in a world whose fabric was strange to me, whose rules I did not understand, and which was without any logic—like a nightmare. And much of what I had been taught at home seemed to be wrong. Thus the Maths master, who also taught French, gave us ten nouns to learn. One of them was *soldat*—which he pronounced as if it rhymed with bat. Without thinking, like an idiot, I corrected him. This aroused his fury and the merriment of the class. "*Soldat!*" they shrieked as they crowded round me later in the playground, "*Soldat!*"

I was hopelessly ignorant about sex. Before I left for Highfield, my mother took me for a walk round the garden. For once, she seemed embarrassed and her sentences had been rambling. I must realise, she told me, that I was quite an attractive little boy—though I would be more attractive if I washed my face and hands more often. However, without in any way being conceited about it or taking advantage of it, I must appreciate that I was lucky enough to have charm of manner. Moreover, my thick hair and huge brown eyes and delicate face were very pleasing, and there was nothing wrong about that at all.

"You are fortunate to have been born without a blemish," my mother said. "However, when you go to Highfield, you'll meet boys much older than yourself, and some of them will tease you because you're attractive —and they're jealous. And among these boys there may be one of them who will try to persuade you to let him be all alone with you—perhaps when you're out for a walk in the woods. And then this older boy may tempt you to commit with him an act which in the Bible is called 'fornication', and is forbidden by God because it is very wrong and very evil. And if this happens, then you must tell the boy that you will never agree to the act and that you've been advised by your parents to tell the Headmaster if the boy ever suggests doing such a thing again."

I was astonishingly innocent, and I did not discover the true meaning of fornication until I reached Eton. But I formed a romantic love for a boy called Haines. I was only ten years old then, and he was almost twelve. Less than five years later I wrote down what I could recall of a particular half-term holiday which we spent together, and I entered it in a diary. Looking back on the entry I find it accurate and vivid, so I will place it here—slightly amended—because here is the place into which it fits.

*   *   *

I am lying on an iron bedstead, listening to the sounds of breathing in the dormitory. It is my third term at Highfield School, and I am just ten years old. It is half-term; my mother has driven down from London and has taken me out for the day; and I'm suffering slightly from indigestion after three large helpings of strawberries and cream.

Half-term at Highfield begins on Friday at noon and ends with Chapel on Sunday evening at six. For the last fortnight little else has been discussed. Now, two of the days are over.

I turn listlessly on my back. As I wonder whether I'll be sick, a terrible thought occurs to me. If I'm sick tonight they may not let me go out tomorrow. I begin to pray: "Please God, don't let me be sick."

32

For a term and a half I have worshipped Haines, and tomorrow I'm taking him out—Haines, who is nearly twelve years old and plays in the second XI, both at cricket and at football; Haines, with his stern face and broad, tight-skinned back with a mole on the left shoulder-blade, a mole which always fascinated me.

At Highfield there is a convention that a boy's parents can take out for the day any boy whose family can't come down to visit him. Neither Haines's father nor mother has been able to leave Wolverhampton, so he's been taken out by various parents on Friday and Saturday, and I had thought that someone would be inviting him out tomorrow, Sunday. But while we were undressing in the dormitory this evening, a boy said to him, "I say, Haines, who's taking you out tomorrow?"

"I was to have gone out with Ranger," Haines replied. "But his people have to get back before lunch."

As I began to brush my teeth, I was trembling. Did I dare to ask Haines out? I was almost sure my mother wouldn't mind. But he was nearly two years senior to me, so would he think it impudence? I began to speak but couldn't. If I was to ask him tonight I must ask him soon, for I knew the bell for prayers would sound in a few minutes and afterwards talking was forbidden, and I couldn't whisper because he slept at the other side of the long room. Besides, if he laughed at me all the others would giggle. I could hear them the next day saying: "Have you heard the latest? Last night Maugham asked Haines to go out with him. Yes, Maugham did." But I had to ask him. I clenched my hands and walked over to his bed.

"Haines," I said. "Could you, I mean, will you come out with my parents tomorrow?" I wasn't going to tell him that my father wouldn't be there.

"Thanks awfully," Haines replied. "Are you sure that's all right?"

"Oh, perfectly sure."

"It's terribly decent of you."

I walked back to my bed. I wanted to shout with joy as I listened to the others telling about the grand time they'd had that day. Presently the bell sounded for prayers.

The Headmaster has just called down God's blessing on us all.

I'm glad my father is in the middle of a big law case, so that he hasn't been able to come down for the weekend. There will just be the three of us—my mother, Haines and myself. I hope my mother won't say anything shaming . . . At all costs I mustn't be sick. I listen to the sound of voices floating up through the wide-open windows from the cricket ground below, where some masters are strolling round for a walk after their dinner. At that moment I hiccup and feel better. Soon I shall fall asleep.

The next day Haines and I are standing outside the school with the other boys who are waiting for their parents to arrive. Haines's mother is very young and pretty, and I am afraid he will think my mother is old. Then I am ashamed of my disloyalty. Presently I see my family's dark green Rolls sweeping round the corner with King at the wheel.

"There it is!" I cry.

"What a lovely car!" says Haines, whose parents are rather poor. My heart lifts with pride.

King draws up the car opposite to us and gets out to open the door. I give him a wink and he winks back. My mother steps out of the car and kisses me. I feel embarrassed and hope that Haines won't tell the rest of them. Boys' mothers oughtn't to kiss them in public. It isn't form.

"Oh, Mother," I say—for I'm not going to call her 'Mummy' in front of him. "We're taking out Haines, I hope you don't mind?"

"No, of course not," she replies. But I have an idea that she does mind—just a bit.

"Will you go in and get permission from the Head?" I ask.

A few minutes later we are sitting in the Rolls, driving out to the country hotel where my mother is staying, and my fears have left me. My mother isn't being a bit embarrassing. She is talking charmingly to Haines. I was obviously wrong. She doesn't mind at all, and I feel wonderfully happy. Haines and I play about on the swing and run races in the hotel garden during the rest of the morning, while my mother looks on. I can see that Haines is enjoying himself, so perhaps he will become a friend of mine after this.

When we settle down to an enormous lunch in the restaurant, I notice that he is impressed by the menu. Suddenly my mother says: "By the way, Robin, I forgot to tell you—Nanny sent you her love."

There is an awful silence. She has uttered the unspeakable. Haines will never realise that my parents have kept on Rose to do sewing and mend clothes. He knows I'm the youngest of the family. The rumour will go round the school that Maugham still has a nurse. I feel myself turning crimson. I hate my mother; at that moment she seems to me almost old and plain. I don't dare look at Haines; I stare miserably down at my plate.

"And kind King has fixed up nets for you on the lawn behind the greenhouse so you can practise bowling there."

That's better, but the harm has been done.

"Did I tell you that we've all definitely decided that Diana should be presented at Court next year?" my mother continues.

"I'm glad," I mumble.

I say little during the rest of lunch and barely answer when my mother speaks to me. I loathe her; I wish she were dead. I must get Haines alone before we go back to school so I can explain. An idea comes to me.

"Haines," I say brightly, "let's go for a walk after lunch."

My mother begins to speak and then stops.

"Yes, let's," he answers.

"You two boys go out for an hour," says my mother. "I've got some letters to write and my packing to do." Her voice sounds rather strange, but I don't stop to think about it.

"Come on, Haines!" I cry, and we rush out together. At last I am all alone with him.

"Let's go down to the golf course—they've got some good players down there," Haines calls out.

"It's a bit of a way, isn't it?"

"Gosh, no. Not if we hurry."

I find it easier explaining to him about Rose than I'd imagined. We reach the golf course and follow the pro round for a while. Then we find an old golf ball and begin playing catch. I'm happy. This is the kind of afternoon Tommy would have spent. Suddenly I look at the wristwatch my mother gave me for Christmas and see that it is half past four.

"We must rush back," I say, beginning to move off.

"Must we?" Haines asks.

"But don't you see? We shan't be back till five anyway, and we'll have to start back for school at five-thirty."

"There's plenty of time," Haines replies, beginning to saunter very slowly in my direction.

"No, there isn't. I've hardly seen Mummy—I mean my mother— at all today."

"It's fun out here."

"Oh hurry, please hurry," I beg, almost in tears. I begin to run, but Haines still loiters.

"You must come."

"No, I mustn't. You go on ahead if you want to. I want to see the pro play this hole. Look, he's over at the thirteenth. He'll be here in a jiffy."

I think of running on ahead, but it will be difficult to explain to my

35

mother if I arrive alone. Besides, in my confusion I can't quite remember the way.

"Please, please, Haines, come on."

"All right," he says. "We'll go back to your Mummy."

I know he is cross, but all I want to do is to return to the hotel as quickly as possible. I begin to run. Haines strolls slowly along. "Don't be a silly," he shouts after me. "There's plenty of time."

And all the time I'm thinking: "I shan't see her again for six weeks. I've hardly seen her all day, and we haven't been alone together once."

I try hard not to cry. I look back. Haines is still ambling along far behind. Misery gives me courage. "Hurry up!" I shout.

"Why should I?"

"Because I want to get back." I can't explain my agony of mind to him. He'd never understand.

The distance to the hotel seems interminable, and with each step I'm saying to myself: "She's waiting for me, and I haven't seen her alone all day."

Suddenly I realise that she has driven all those miles only to be with me. For some reason I hadn't thought of that. I feel mean and horrible. I have hurt her, and she must have been waiting for me for the last hour. I can see her lined face watching the clock in the lounge. The hotel is still far off. Haines is still dawdling some way behind. Then something breaks in me. I wheel round and shout at the top of my voice, "Hurry up, you blasted swine, or we won't take you back!"

I begin to run. I look back. Haines goes on walking for a moment, then begins to run too. We arrive breathless at the hotel and find my mother sitting in the lounge. "What happened to you?" she asks. "I thought you must have been run over or something."

"I'm terribly sorry," I mutter. How can I explain in front of Haines?

"It doesn't matter. I suppose we'd better be leaving."

"You'll stay for Chapel, won't you?"

"No, darling, I can't. I must be in London in time for dinner. As it is, I'll be late."

"Please, can't you stay?"

"No, really I can't. Your father would be furious with me."

On the way back to school, I can't speak for fear of crying. I keep hearing a voice saying: "You won't see her again for another six weeks, won't see her again."

Haines sits sullenly gazing out of the window. Neither of us talks. At last my mother says: "What's wrong with you two? Have you had a row?"

"No," I reply. "We haven't."

36

Haines still says nothing and just stares out at the fields passing by. I pray that I will have a moment alone with my mother so I can explain to her. The car draws up at the school. All three of us get out, and my mother shakes Haines by the hand. "Goodbye," she says to him while I say goodbye to King.

"Thanks very much, Mrs Maugham," he mutters. "Thanks for everything."

Then she turns to me. "Goodbye, Robin," she says, and kisses me lightly on the forehead. Now is the moment to explain. But I look round, and Haines is still standing there.

"Goodbye, Mummy darling," I whisper. "Thanks for a lovely time."

She steps into the car; King settles the rug over her knees, and she waves to us as the car moves off. I watch it disappear down the drive. I mustn't cry; I've got to survive the evening service in Chapel. The bell is already ringing, and I'll be late if I don't hurry. I catch a last glimpse of the car through a gap in the trees. When I turn back to the boys' entrance, Haines has vanished.

We are singing a psalm, and I stand in Chapel feeling miserable. I won't see her again for six weeks—forty-two days. I'd been cross at lunch; I'd left her alone and gone out with Haines; I'd kept her waiting, and then I hadn't been able to explain. I had hurt her, and I hadn't even made friends with Haines.

The Headmaster has announced the number of a hymn.

"The day Thou gavest, Lord, is ended," we are now chanting. "The darkness falls at Thy behest." And it's true. The day has ended, I realise. It's all over. It'll never come back. I can't have this day again . . .

If only I hadn't asked Haines out, I'd have been alone with her and perhaps we'd have played draughts after lunch and then she'd have talked to me and told me stories, and we'd have been happy. But instead of that, we hardly talked together for a moment. And all the time I was playing down on the golf course with Haines, she was probably thinking about me and wanting me to return, and then we were more than an hour late, and I wasn't even happy on the golf course. I'd have been lots happier with her—heaps happier—and there she was worrying because we hadn't come back. If only I'd had the sense to think of that. I love her—miles better than anyone else in the world—hundreds of miles better.

We are kneeling now, and the Headmaster is reading the prayers.

Perhaps she thinks I don't love her because she's older than other mothers are, and not so pretty. Oh God, please don't let her think that. Gentle Jesus meek and mild, please listen to me. I love my mother best in the world, apart from Rose. Please let her know it. Please, I beseech you, don't let her think I don't. And please listen to this. I can't tell her myself now, I can't say it in a letter home, and today's over. So please don't let her think I don't love her. If you do this for me, I'll be good for ever and ever. Amen.

"The Peace of God, which passeth all understanding, keep your hearts and minds in the knowledge and love of God . . ."

The service is ending.

That night as I enter the dormitory, they all chant in chorus: "Maugham's got a Nanny . . . Maugham's got a Nanny."

I will mind that later, but now the agony is too great for it to matter. Somehow I can't even cry.

I am awake long after the rest of them are all asleep. The light of a full moon shines in from the open window. The night is very quiet. I hear the Chapel clock strike two. I begin to pray again. I turn and look at the picture of my mother behind my bed and begin to cry. I sob quietly into my pillow for a while, and then . . . And then the door of my memory swings shut, so I must have fallen asleep. But the misery of my guilt continued for a long while.

*   *   *

Evidently I had already learned to disguise my feelings and to present a false façade to the world. I am certain that despite our close relationship my mother had no idea of the sadness I suffered on the drive back to school that day, for Tommy had protected me.

Some forty-six years later it is interesting to read the entry for that day in my mother's diary. "Drove down to Highfield. Robin looks splendid. Dine with Willie at Savoy."

*   *   *

Each term at Highfield seemed endless. I was desperately homesick and unhappy, but I never dared to tell this to my mother because I knew how much she wanted me to be good both at work and at games. She wanted a robust, popular son; she had got a nervous, over-imaginative little boy who was happy only during the few wonderful hours each week that we were allowed to spend in the school library.

I was not bad at lessons; I was not bad at games. But I excelled in neither. I had made a few friends—most of them misfits like myself. Each morning when the school bell rang I awoke to sadness. Though I never dreamed of telling my mother, Rose knew. Swearing her to secrecy, I would write long letters to Rose, and the letters she sent me in return encouraged me somehow to survive. I had only to hold her

38

letter clutched in the palm of my hand, and I would forget the sodden grey playing fields and the sadism of my form-master, Mr. Grove, with his ginger moustache and his sleek, thinning hair which was plastered on to his forehead like a shiny wig.

Only the Headmaster was allowed to cane us, and Mr. Grove was very careful not to use any form of physical violence. He made us suffer by crude sarcasm and by the fact that from his personality there came a spirit which I can only describe as being evil and frightening. He had served as a sapper in the Great War, and his military service appeared to have become an obsession with him.

"Stand up, Maugham," he would suddenly bellow. "Stand up and stand straight." For a moment he would pause while his small blue eyes glared at me and his chin jutted forward. "Now then," he would say, "what was the last thing I said? I'm waiting. Repeat it. I want you to tell me the last thing I said . . . Exactly. You can't? And shall I tell you why you can't? Because you weren't listening—because you were staring out of the window. *Do* you think I fought in the trenches of Flanders—*do* you think I waded through gore and mud in order to sit in a classroom teaching Latin to a little idiot like you who hasn't got the manners even to listen to a word I say? Now go and stand in the corner. You'll stand there—to attention and without moving—until the end of the class."

I know that none of the heroes in the books about school that I had read would have been disturbed by Mr. Grove, but I was afraid of him. I had hideous nightmares about him.

Meanwhile, secretly—as if I were breaking one of the most sacred school rules, such as not walking on the withered grass plot beside the dreary Chapel—I began at the age of ten to write my first novel. I was encouraged in this venture by the enormous—almost disastrous—effect that my first synopsis of the story enjoyed, when I told it in a tense whisper after 'lights out' in the dormitory.

The novel was called *The Ioki of Egypt*. It was concerned with an Egyptian mummy in the vaults of a private art collector. Ioki, for such was the name of the embalmed princess, came to life one evening around midnight in 1925. And—so far as I can recollect—she was extremely annoyed at having been embalmed in the first place and then at having been purchased in mummified form and transported over to England. She was—needless to say—endowed with supernatural powers, and her ways of wreaking her vengeance on the art collector, and indeed upon anyone who did not believe in her divinity, were so terrible, and I managed to relate them with such realism that Egerton Major—normally a sturdy figure and fearless on the rugger field—was

reduced to a screaming fit, and the Matron had to be sent for to administer a sedative.

The completed novel was almost two thousand words long. I wrote
it clearly in long-hand and sewed the pages together so that they were
firmly bound. I did not send the novel to my family because each
senior member of it was convinced that I must not for an instant
consider writing as a profession; I must become a lawyer. After all, on
my father's side, my grandfather Robert Ormond Maugham had been
solicitor to the British Embassy in Paris, and my great-grandfather,
Robert Maugham, had been a founder of the Law Society; while on
my mother's side, my grandfather, Robert Romer, had been a Lord
Justice of Appeal and so had my uncle, Mark Romer; and his son, my
cousin, Charles Romer, was also to become a Lord Justice of Appeal.
I was born from two famous legal families, and I, in my turn, it was
decided, must become a lawyer. So it was useless to send my novel to
anyone in my family; and I sent it off to Edgar Wallace, for whom my
father had recently appeared in court. I waited in suspense for a week.
Then came a long serious letter, written in his own hand, praising my
work and expressing fascination in Princess Ioki's powers. Mr. Wallace
concluded with the hopes of a sequel. I wish I hadn't lost that
letter.

I immediately began a sequel. But there was to *be* no sequel—
because, after I had given a rough outline in the dormitory of volume
two, Ramsbottom Minor was seized with convulsions and rushed down
to the Matron screaming that the Ioki of Egypt was chasing him.
Thereafter *The Ioki* was banned—as alas, have been several of my books
in other lands. But if I was banned from writing, I could still read. I
visited the library whenever I was allowed, reading books indiscrimin-
ately, from Percy F. Westerman to Robert Louis Stevenson and Rud-
yard Kipling. Stevenson's *Ebb Tide* and Kipling's *Kim* are books I shall
never forget.

*   *   *

About that time I became aware of several mysteries about the life
around me at the school, which I could not understand.

Fist, there was the mystery of Mr. Merrick, one of the senior masters.
Mr. Merrick was slim and neat, with strange piercing eyes. It was
rumoured that he could hypnotise anyone he chose. What was certain
was that, before supper each evening, two or three boys would visit his
room on the first floor of the school building for what was called 'extra
tuition'. One of these pupils was a boy of twelve called Hewson,
whose parents lived in India because his father was an officer in the

Indian Army. Hewson was fair-haired, with large gentle eyes, a wide mouth and a snub nose. He was quiet and shy; he did not seem to have many friends. He slept in the bed next to mine, and I liked him, though I never thought we could be friends because he was two years senior to me. One evening, after he had attended an 'extra tuition' by Mr. Merrick, he came into the dormitory looking white and frightened. When we asked him what was wrong, he would not answer. After 'lights out' I heard him crying. In the faint moonlight I could see that his head was pressed into the pillow to stifle the sound. I leaned over towards him.

"What's wrong?" I whispered.

"Shut up," he whispered back. "Let me alone."

"Please tell me."

"You wouldn't understand," he whispered. "You couldn't understand . . . You're lucky . . . He says you're too young . . . So you're all right . . . Now leave me alone."

Hewson's occasional fits of sobbing occurred throughout that year. Each time it was after he had been given an 'extra tuition'.

Next was the mystery of Neal.

Neal became a friend of mine when I was eleven and he was twelve. I caught him stealing some toy bricks out of my play-box, and his smile of apology had been so endearing, the freckles on his impudent face were somehow so attractive, and the way he stood was so graceful, that I forgave him immediately. A term later we were in the same form which was taken by Mr. Rudge, who was thirty and had won a Blue at Cambridge for rugger.

Mr. Rudge was now stout, with heavy shoulders, and a red face with thick jowls. For some reason, he seemed to take a violent dislike to my friend Neal.

"Neal!" he would shout, "you're not paying attention again. You *ought* to be in a higher class. So you *would* be if you weren't thoroughly lazy . . . and if I find you staring out of the window once again, I'll have you sent to the Headmaster to be whipped."

Neal was obviously afraid of Mr. Rudge. Each time the master shouted at him he would turn white and the impudent expression would leave his face, yet he never looked down at his book as the rest of us did when Mr. Rudge shouted at us. His hazel-coloured eyes were fixed on Mr. Rudge's face in a look of fear to which was added an odd stare of entreaty.

*   *   *

41

Later that term I had a letter from my mother. She wrote that because Hamswell House was inconveniently far from London, and because my father wanted a country house he could visit more often, Hamswell had been sold; they had bought a house called Tye near Hartfield in Sussex. And now that I was at school and no longer needed a governess, Rose was leaving.

I can still recall the misery which that letter caused me. I can still remember hurrying to the lavatories at the back of the school building so that I could cry in peace. But when my mother drove down to visit me two Sundays later, I made little of my disappointment that Rose would not be there to welcome me on the first day of the holidays. My Tommy façade could now be put in place to suit the occasion. "Robin looking splendid", my mother wrote in her diary for that day.

I did not see Rose again for forty years, though we often wrote to each other. "I could not bear to meet you," she would write, "because I could not bear the pain it would cause me, knowing that I was no longer with you, but it was like heaven hearing your voice on the telephone."

Rose, my former love, now lives in a comfortable house in Wimbledon with her sister. Her hair is white, but there are few wrinkles on her face, and kindness—pure kindness—still glows from her faded blue eyes.

*　　　*　　　*

The fact that my dearest friend had been taken away from me drew me closer to Neal. I loved his sense of fun and I admired his hatred of authority. Mr. Rudge's bullying of Neal had now become savage and horrible. It was painful to see the tears sliding down Neal's freckled face, and by now the bullying had become physical. Mr. Rudge was the school's rugger instructor. When Neal was at the outside of a scrum, Mr. Rudge would hurl his sweating body forward so that his head would thud against Neal's thigh.

Then two events occurred to perplex me still more.

The first was that on a Sunday evening, instead of his usual sermon, the Headmaster told us that he had sad news to deliver to us all. Mr. Merrick had suffered a nervous breakdown. He had therefore been forced to leave the school suddenly; he regretted that he had been unable to say goodbye to us. He was unable to leave behind any address, for he was touring South Africa.

The next startling event was that, one evening at playtime, I saw Neal coming out of Mr. Rudge's room. He looked embarrassed when he saw I had noticed him.

42

"He made me write out an exercise I'd done wrong," Neal explained.

From that evening, Mr. Rudge's attitude to Neal changed. His voice was no longer gruff when he spoke to him, and soon Neal had definitely become the form favourite. Neal was due to pass the common-entrance exam the following term. He had asked me to stay at his mother's country house for a week during the holidays and, perhaps to console me for Rose's departure, my parents had consented.

"But where's his father?" my father asked.

"Dead," I replied truthfully.

*   *   *

"You know that Mr. Rudge will be there," Neal said to me casually a few days before the end of term.

"What?" I cried out in astonishment. "Mr. Rudge?"

"Yes," Neal said. "He's coming for the holidays as my tutor to help me get through common-entrance."

*   *   *

Neal's mother's house was near Rye. His mother was a vague, large-breasted woman with dyed hair, over-tight clothes, and protuberant eyes. Both her clothes and her eyes seemed to be trying to escape from their confines. The house was long and rambling; it had once been a rectory. Neal's bedroom was at the end of the east wing. Mr. Rudge slept across the corridor. I slept next door to Neal. I woke quite early; I was hungry, and I had forgotten to ask the time of breakfast. I knocked at Neal's door and walked in wearing my pyjamas. Neal was already awake and he waved to me cheerfully as I came in. He was naked.

"Did you sleep well?" he asked.

"Wonderfully. Did you?"

Neal gave a little smile. "On and off," he said.

I noticed that he was lying in a double bed, but both pillows seemed to have been rumpled. He beckoned to me to come over to his bed. When I came near he threw back the light coverlet and pointed to the space next to him. I got in and lay beside him. He put an arm round my neck. I felt pleased that he was really fond of me.

"How green are you?" he asked.

"I don't know all the facts of life—if that's what you mean?"

"But you know why Mr. Merrick had to leave all of a sudden?"

"No."

"You didn't guess?"

"No."

43

"Well, you remember he used to have two or three pupils in of an evening?"

"Of course."

"I wanted to be one of them. I thought it was some magic secret or something. But he wouldn't let me come. So one evening, I decided to find out for myself. So I crept round the balcony and looked in. There was a chink in the curtains. I could see what they were all doing. Well, I knew I wouldn't be believed, so I jumped down and ran to the Headmaster and told him to come and see for himself. Mr. Merrick left the following day."

"What were they doing?"

"Do you still not understand?"

Neal's right hand was still round my neck. He had begun to breathe heavily. He turned and kissed me. Then his left hand began to unbutton my pyjama jacket, and his hand slid across my stomach and began stroking me. I was excited yet I was very much frightened. The arm round my neck tightened. His gasps became more rapid. I looked at his face. It was scarlet, and his mouth was wide open. Suddenly fear overcame the pleasure his left hand was giving me. I wrenched myself away from him.

"Wait," he said. "Just sit on the end of the bed—if you're afraid of me. But just listen. This was what Mr. Merrick was doing with his special 'pupils'—only he went a lot further. And as soon as I saw what he was doing with the boys naked in his room I called the Headmaster because I hated Merrick, and I got him the sack. But what I'd seen taught me the facts of life—from that point of view. And then I suddenly realised why Mr. Rudge always pressed himself against me at rugger. So I made an excuse to visit him in his room, and he was quite different. He was very gentle, so I got to like it. Then when my mother suggested having a tutor these holidays, so I could be certain of passing my common-entrance exam, I suggested him. So if you're green and don't like it, please don't bother. I've got him across the corridor, and he'll come to my bed whenever I knock at his door."

I stared at Neal in amazement. Suddenly he threw off the bed-clothes so that I could see him naked. The hair was beginning to grow round his crotch. He flung out his arms so that the full beauty of his body was exposed. He smiled up at me slyly.

"So don't worry yourself," he said. "I've only got to knock at his door. But I'd like to do it with you all the same."

I thought of Mr. Rudge's coarse, smelling body pressed against that lean figure on the bed.

"Thanks," I said. "But give me time to think it all over."

44

"You've only got a week, remember," Neal said.

"I'll remember that," I said—and I left the room.

Each night I thought about entering Neal's room, and each night I could feel the warmth of his hands pressing against me. But then I remembered the stink of Mr. Rudge's body, and I thought of that hairy gross body pressing on top of Neal's slender limbs, and I never left my bed.

*　　*　　*

When I returned to Tye House I felt very lonely. The house, built in the Dutch style of some fifty years ago, was large, but not nearly as lovely as Hamswell. I missed Doreen and Kathleen. Above all, I missed Rose. I wandered about forlorn. My sister Diana had been sent to a finishing-school in Paris; my mother always seemed to be too busy to play with me.

"Why don't you make friends with that nice little girl whose people have taken that cottage at the end of the drive?" Mabel, the housemaid, suggested. "Ever so friendly they are. Hopper's the name. He runs a grocery business in Tunbridge Wells, but they've moved out here for her holidays because the doctor said the little girl needed real country air. She's only eleven. Just your age."

I was cross because Mabel would not play draughts with me.

"I'll think about it," I said.

Three days later I met the girl. She was swinging on the end of the front drive gate. My father had forbidden me to do this, explaining that, on the lever principle, weight at one end of a gate put undue strain on the hinges at the other. When the girl saw me approach she waved to me cheerfully and swung all the faster. She had dark curly hair and light blue eyes that seemed to shine with an almost defiant vitality. But her arms and legs were slender, and her lips were very pale. She was quite wiry but delicate. This reassured me.

"You'll break the hinges," I said.

"Why? Is it your gate?"

"No, it belongs to my father."

"Is he the old man with grey hair who always wears a suit and goes out with a walking-stick?"

My father was then over sixty.

"That's him," I said.

"My father's only thirty-five," she said.

I felt I must show some loyalty to my family. "My mother's not much more than that," I answered.

"My mother's only thirty."

45

I felt I was losing ground. "What kind of car have your people got?" I asked.

"No kind. We've got a motor-bike and sidecar. It fair goes whizzing along. I bet our motor bike could beat your mouldy old Rolls any day."

"I bet it couldn't."

"I bet it could."

"How much do you bet?"

"Sixpence."

"Have you got sixpence on you?"

"No. Have you?"

"Of course I have."

"Show me."

I fumbled in my pocket and produced the sixpenny bit my mother had let me take off her dressing-table that morning. I held it up for her to see. Suddenly she jumped down from the gate, snatched the coin from my hand and rushed down the drive. I ran furiously after her.

"Just try and catch me!" she called over her shoulder, and swerved into the wood which flanked the drive and sloped down into the valley. And I followed her, plunging into the undergrowth, tearing my bare legs on the brambles, forcing my way through thick bushes. Fronds whipped against my face and slashed my neck. I was close behind her and about to spring when I tripped and fell head downwards.

For an instant I was stunned. Then I felt a stabbing pain on the left side of my forehead. I put up my hand to touch the place, and it was wet. I looked with horror at the blood on my hand. I was afraid, and I wanted to cry, but I controlled myself because of the girl. There was a rustle in the bushes behind me and she appeared. She stared at me, then knelt quickly beside me.

"Got a hanky?" she asked. There was a slight tremor in her voice.

I fished in my trouser pocket and handed her a handkerchief with an acid-drop sticking to it. She popped the acid-drop into her mouth and dabbed my forehead with the clean side of the handkerchief before tying it round my head.

"You'll be all right," she said. "Mum can patch you up."

"I'd better go home."

"We live closer."

She bent down and took my hands and pulled me up.

"What's your name?" she asked.

"Robin. What's yours?"

"Patricia. But Mum and Dad call me Pat."

"I like Patricia."

"I like *you!*" she said, and leaned forward and kissed me.

46

She was still holding my hands. I turned my head away so that she would not see the tears in my eyes.

"You'll be all right," she repeated. "Come along."

She let go of my left hand and dragged me slowly up the hill towards their cottage.

*   *   *

When we came into their small living-room, Mrs. Hopper was sitting in an armchair darning socks. She was a small, plump woman with a broad, rather shiny face.

"Well, this is a surprise!" she said. "But whatever have you done to your forehead?"

"He fell down and cut it open on a tree-stump," Patricia said. "Mum, can you have a look at it?"

"Of course I can. Just be a good girl and fetch me the kettle from the kitchen. Lucky it's near on the boil. And then bring me a basin. Now, young lad, sit yourself down in this chair and make yourself comfortable. We won't be long."

While the two of them fussed around washing the little gash with a clean handkerchief dipped in warm water, tearing up an old shirt into strips to make a bandage, I lay back happily, even though my head was hurting. Their evident concern made me feel brave and important. For once I had had an adventure such as Tommy might have had.

Mrs. Hopper was neatly and gently bandaging my head when Mr. Hopper came in from the back yard. He was wearing a shirt without a collar and dirty old grey flannel trousers tucked into his socks. He was a tall, wiry man with sandy hair and a sharp-pointed face and red-rimmed eyes. As he stood watching us, his head cocked on one side, he reminded me of a bull-terrier.

"Hullo, now what's happened?" he said, a little annoyed. "Been to the wars?"

"If you was to get that oil off your hands," Mrs. Hopper said, grinning at him, "you might get a cup of tea."

"That's not a bad idea," he said.

"I expect our wounded hero could do with a cup as well," said Mrs. Hopper.

As we sat round the table drinking tea and talking, I watched them carefully. I was convinced that the proud way Mrs. Hopper spoke of Patricia's achievements at school and the affectionate glances she gave her and Patricia's seeming love for her mother were all part of some monstrous deceit. I could not believe that parents and child could really be friends with each other. But when Patricia begged for chocolate biscuits and Mrs. Hopper went to get some from her private store, and came back with a full tin which we finished between the four of us, I began to wonder. Surely deceit would not run to chocolate biscuits?

Patricia walked with me half the way down the drive.

"How do you feel?"

"Far better," I lied. In fact I felt slightly sick.

"Did you like Mum and Dad?"

"Yes, I did."

"They liked you too."

"How do you know?"

"The way they looked at you. I like Mum best."

"When can you and I meet again?"

"Tomorrow after dinner if you like."

"After dinner?"

"Yes. I'll meet you by the white gate at three."

"What if I'm not allowed out?"

"Why shouldn't you be?"

"I might be ill or something."

"Don't worry. I'll be by the gate every afternoon at three till you come."

"Thanks."

"By the way, there's something you forgot," she said, and held out the sixpence.

"You keep it."

"Honest? Can I really? Thanks no end."

I took her hand and kissed it.

"Good night, Patricia."

"You are silly!" she said, and ran off down the drive.

*　　　*　　　*

When I reached our house, it was past seven, and my mother was angry. She was angrier still when she found out who had bandaged my forehead.

"Why didn't you come straight home?"

"Their place was nearer."

"Nonsense. They had no business to keep you. And wherever did she find that ghastly bandage?"

"It was one of Mr. Hopper's old shirts. She tore it up into strips."

"A shirt! You don't mean to say she put that on an open cut?"

"It was perfectly clean."

"I suppose she used some disinfectant?"

"I don't think so."

48

"The woman must be criminally insane. Now, darling, we'll go straight up to my bedroom and I'll get out the medicine chest and bandage you up properly."

That evening for the first time I dreamed that I was Tommy. I was riding a fierce black horse when I saw the pirates advancing towards Patricia across the darkening plain. I clapped my bare legs against the sides of the horse and we galloped towards her. The pirates were only a few yards off when I leaned down and swung her up on to the saddle. As we charged away into the night I could feel her cheek pressing against mine.

The following morning I was feverish, so I was kept in bed all day. I did not see Patricia again until Monday afternoon at three o'clock.

*   *   *

It was a hot afternoon without a breath of wind. The sun beat down from a clear blue sky. The bandage round my head was damp with sweat.

I found her swinging on the end of the white gate which had now dropped at least six inches.

"You'll bust the hinges," I said.

She laughed. "Then I won't be able to swing any more, will I?"

"Daddy will think I did it."

"No, he won't. I shall say to him: 'I bust your gate, and you can't touch me, you silly old man.'"

"He'd tell your father."

"Dad might give me a belting."

"Surely he doesn't beat you?" I asked.

"Not half," Patricia said, "when I've been at all naughty."

Suddenly she pulled down the top of her dress. There were red marks on her back. I was horrified, yet at the same time I was excited.

"What shall we do this afternoon?" I asked after a pause.

"It's too hot in the sun. Let's go somewhere in the shade."

"Do you know the stream at the bottom of the wood?"

"A real stream?"

"Yes, I saw a frog there once. Come on, I'll show you."

It was far hotter inside the wood than out on the drive. We sat on a bank beside the stream and played a game of throwing stones on to a boulder on the far side. I found it difficult to talk. I would think of something bright to say, and for a while our conversation would flow easily; then it would splutter and stop. Patricia did not help me. She was awkward and moody.

"I don't believe there are any frogs down here," she said after a long silence.

"Would you like to go home?"

"Why not? If you like we could play at dressing-up. We've got masks and all kinds of things."

"All right."

"I know," she cried suddenly. "Why don't we play at dressing-up down here?"

"We've got no things."

"Yes, we have. I can dress up in your clothes and you can dress up in mine."

"That would just be daft."

"Very well. If you don't want to, let's go home."

"No, I don't mind. Let's try."

I walked behind one of the beech trees.

"I'll throw you across my clothes," I said. "And you can chuck me back yours."

"All right."

I peeled off my shirt and shorts and threw them down to her. A few seconds later her blue cotton dress landed at my feet, and I slipped it on and walked down to the bank. She had flattened her hair, pushing it back behind her ears. My shorts fitted her exactly. Tommy might have looked as she did when he was eleven.

"You're simply wonderful," I said.

"You look plain stupid." She laughed.

"I bet I do," I said, and made a pirouette and fell over backwards on purpose.

"Mind out or you'll spoil my frock. Now you pretend you're me and I'll pretend I'm you. Get it?"

But the game soon palled and silence pressed down on us again. "I've never known it so hot," I said after a pause.

"If only we could go swimming!"

"The nearest pool's on the road to Edenbridge."

"Why don't we just kneel down in the stream? We can splash water over each other. At least that would get us cool."

I hesitated. I did not want her to see me naked.

"Come on! I'm going to, anyhow," she said, and threw off my shirts and shorts, slipped off her knickers, and stepped naked into the shallow stream. I looked at the marks on her back, and once again I felt a strange glow of excitement. I hesitated.

"Coward!" she called out. "Aren't you coming down?"

Her frock had begun to embarrass me. I pulled it off, kicked off my

50

shoes, took off my pants and climbed down the bank. Even before I had reached the stream she began splashing me, scooping up the water in her hands, laughing when she saw me flinch as the ice-cold drops poured down me. I knelt down quickly and churned my arms round like a flail, showering water over her.

"Now who's the coward?" I called out, as she moved away, choking and laughing.

Suddenly, she sprang up the bank, seized her clothes and mine, and ran away with them.

"Now what will you do?" she cried.

I leaped up the bank and rushed after her. She could not run fast carrying a bundle of clothes, and I soon gained on her as she ran along the bank of the stream. When I was close behind her, she swerved towards a beech tree and flung herself down on a stretch of moss between the roots. I was so close to her that I could not stop, and fell down beside her. She tried to scramble up again, but I grabbed her arm.

"You beast! Let me go!"

"Then give me back my clothes," I said laughing.

"I won't."

"Oh, yes, you will," I said, and snatched hold of her other arm. But she twisted round in my grip and flung her leg over mine. For a while we wrestled fiercely. Then, at the very same moment, we both stopped struggling and lay without moving, our bodies locked together, her cheek against mine.

*   *   *

While the rooks cawed in the branches of the beech tree high above our heads, and the bees droned round the honeysuckle by the stream, we lay together motionless, without speaking. And gradually a peace such as I had never known crept over me. I must have felt as if I were a ship that had been lashed by fierce winds and foaming waves but now had passed through the entrance to the harbour and was gliding across flat, calm water towards security. The taut sails could be furled and the ropes loosened. Then at last I felt the bonds that had kept me caged up in myself melting away, and I was released from the constraint of shyness. Holding her in my arms, I poured out the fears and loneliness from my heart. I told her of my father who disliked me because I disappointed him, of my mother who loved me only when I did nothing to annoy her, of Mr. Grove, my form-master at Highfield, who loathed me. And as I spoke, Patricia's arms held me closer, as if the pressure of her body could drive my fears away.

51

The sun was slanting through the trees when we got up and dressed. With our hands linked we made our way towards the drive.

"Can we meet tomorrow at the same time?" I asked.

"What are you doing in the morning?"

"Got to go into Edenbridge to see the dentist."

"Right. Three o'clock, then."

"Where?"

"By the stream. But we'd better keep our place secret."

"I won't tell anyone."

She stopped and kissed me on the lips.

"Do you like me?"

"More than anyone," I said.

*   *   *

The following afternoon I found her waiting for me by the stream. The feeling of security had left me. I felt nervous and embarrassed. Once again I could think of little to say, and our conversation limped along awkwardly. Presently she took my hand and drew me towards the bed of moss between the roots of the tall beech and knelt down, her hands in her lap. I lay down beside her. For an instant she did not move. Then she raised her hands and began gently to unbutton my shirt.

During the next seven days of warm sunshine that followed we met every afternoon by the stream. In the morning we might play catch or touch-last on the lawn, or, if we had money, walk down to the village to buy sweets. But, at three, without a word being said, we would meet under the beech tree and strip off our clothes and lie down and clasp our arms round each other as if we were two halves of one single being and could only become complete when joined together. Our happiness was so intense that for the first few minutes we never spoke, but lay quietly together listening to the rooks flapping through the tall branches, inhaling the heady stench of the wild garlic that grew thickly around us. Later we would begin to talk, sharing our secrets, discussing our problems, planning excursions we should never be allowed to make.

Patricia enjoyed life. She was devoted to her mother and basked in her affection. She was amused by the school she went to near Edenbridge, and excited by making new friends. And as the days passed, she was able to communicate something of her happiness to me. I no longer felt lonely. I no longer lay awake yearning for Tommy. I had a friend at last, and I could hold her in my arms and feel her breath against my cheek.

*   *   *

The blow fell on Saturday morning at breakfast. I knew from the expression on my mother's face as she lifted her head to be kissed good morning that something was wrong. My father was slitting open his letters in silence with a fruit knife. I helped myself to porridge and cream and sat down between them.

"Darling, have you been playing with that gate at the end of the drive?" my mother asked.

"No."

My father put down his knife and turned toward me.

"You haven't been swinging on it?"

"No."

"At any time?"

"No."

"Then perhaps you can explain to us why, on returning from Hartfield yesterday evening, we should have discovered that the hinges were broken?"

I was silent. I was afraid I was in for a cross-examination. My father was famous for his cross-questioning as a barrister.

"I am asking you a question, Robin."

"I know."

"Then I suggest you should be good enough to answer it."

"I didn't know the hinges were broken."

"You have not answered my question. I am asking you if you can explain why they should have been broken."

"No, I can't," I mumbled.

"You can't or you won't?"

"Freddie . . ." my mother began.

"Kindly allow me to handle this matter as I think fit. You can't or you won't?"

"I can't."

"You haven't ever swung on the gate?"

"No."

"Is that true? Think carefully."

"Not since you told me not to."

"And you know of no one else who has been tampering with the gate?"

"No."

"That girl you play with lives in the cottage opposite, doesn't she?"

"Yes."

"You have never seen her swinging on the gate?"

"No."

"That is strange—because two of our servants have. And since you tell us that you have not damaged the gate, I can only presume that she is responsible. I shall therefore be forced to visit her father and demand compensation for the price of two new hinges and the cost of replacing them."

There was silence. My father took up his knife and began slitting open another envelope.

"I was wrong," I said. "I did swing on the gate."

"So you lied to us?"

"No, I just forgot."

"You just forgot?"

"I only did it once after you told me not to."

"And when was that?"

"Yesterday evening."

"So you did break the hinges?"

"Freddie, please . . ." my mother said quietly.

"I must insist on being allowed to deal with this myself. I'm afraid, my dear Nellie, that you fail to appreciate the seriousness of the matter. Property has been damaged. It is our duty to find out who damaged it. Now, Robin, did you break those hinges?"

"They weren't broken when I left."

"I suppose they snapped by chance a few minutes later?"

"I don't know," I mumbled.

My father saw that I was about to break down, and he had a fastidious dislike of scenes.

"Very well," he said. "You have lied to us and you admit disobeying me. You can go up to your room and remain there until suppertime."

"But Freddie, it's such a lovely day," my mother protested.

My father turned away from her impatiently.

"I presume you have a holiday task," he said.

"Yes."

"What is it?"

"*Pilgrim's Progress*."

"Have you started it?"

"Yes. Well, not really."

"What do you mean—'not really'?"

"I've looked through it."

"Well now, I suggest you should start to *read* through it. I shall examine you myself this evening. Now you may go."

As I stumbled from the room I heard him say to my mother: "My dear Nellie, merely because he's only a child there's no reason . . ."

Then the door closed and I walked wretchedly up the oak staircase to the top floor.

I paced nervously up and down my room until Mabel came in to console me. She had heard of my disgrace through the curious grapevine that seemed to run between the dining-room, the nursery and the servants' hall. Perhaps the parlourmaid had overheard from the pantry. I could not bear to think of Patricia waiting for me by the stream. When Mabel produced two pencils and a block of paper and suggested we play noughts and crosses, I knew what I must do. I took the pad and laboriously wrote out in my best script:

"I cannot be there today. See you tomorrow. Robin."

Mabel was afraid to deliver it. But after half an hour of cajoling she agreed to give it to the errand boy from the village who usually called about eleven o'clock. So I wrote out the full address on an envelope.

*   *   *

Every day of August—even when it rained—I met Patricia secretly under the beech by the stream, and gradually I grew stronger and happier, though I dreaded the moment when we should have to say goodbye. But Patricia promised that she would write every week and that she would persuade her parents to take the cottage again for the Christmas holidays, and I believed it as her hot tears fell on to my cheek our last afternoon together; for I believed that we were so close together, so much part of one single being, that neither time nor space could divide us. I shall never forget those periods when we were completely alone in ecstasy and innocence.

But she never answered my letters, and soon I gave up writing to her. And when I returned home at Christmas I learned that Mr. Hopper had bought a grocery business in the Midlands and all three of them had moved to Birmingham. I never saw her again.

*   *   *

At Highfield the oldest enemies I had had to deal with were aged thirteen. But at Eton College, which I entered when I was myself thirteen, there were boys of seventeen and eighteen. Of course I had known this before I arrived at Mr. Butterwick's House where I boarded. Mr. Butterwick had been one of my eldest sister Kate's admirers, and I had been put down for his House when I was three weeks old.

When I arrived at Eton, Mr. Butterwick seemed to me an ogre of a man with a fierce face and a growling voice. I was convinced he had taken an instant dislike to me. When I met him thirty years later I found to my surprise that he was an affable man of medium height.

Perhaps age had mellowed him; perhaps age had partly removed my own fears and fantasies.

'Houses' at Eton differ widely. Mr. Butterwick, when he had risen from being a master to the importance of being a housemaster, had taken over a House which was slack at games and lacked team spirit. It had a poor morale. And he decided to change this. He determined to make his House efficient at games and hearty in outlook. In this he certainly succeeded. But by the time I arrived there the atmosphere was alarming. Our sports coach was a big spotty-faced lout, almost nineteen, with the muscles of a wrestler. His narrow lips were set straight as a matchstick in his mouth. His expression was enthusiastic yet grim as he urged on the 'lower boys' of the House at football practice when he was coaching us in the Field Game. The night before the first Inter-House match he summoned our whole team to the 'library', which was a living-room for the senior boys of the House. There he stood, with his back to the fireplace, towering over us, gently switching the sides of his striped trousers with a long cane.

"If you don't win the match tomorrow," he said, "I shall whip every one of you."

This information did not improve our morale, but luckily we won the match.

*   *   *

For my first year at Eton I lived in a state of intermittent panic. One of my duties as a lower boy was to cook the sausages and eggs for my 'fag-master's' tea. I'd been warned not to burn them, because if I did I would be sent to the Captain of the House to be caned. I lived in a nightmare. From the first week I was unpopular. I was shocked by the dirty stories and swear words I now heard for the first time. This made the other lower boys consider me an opinionated prig. My slender build invited bullying. When I was frightened and revolted by their horseplay I was considered effeminate. I lost my way among the school buildings and arrived several times late for class. I was given a final warning. Even now, over forty years later, I can remember moments of horrible panic. I can remember one particular early winter morning in horrible detail. On the pavement I could hear the boys' feet scudding on their way to early school. I was late, and they had stolen my only tie. I rushed into the room next door and pulled open the drawers. The school clock was striking. There was no hope now. I would arrive late at my class again. And next time, the master had said—next time it would mean a beating. Frantically, I rushed into another room. As I remember this panic, I realise that nothing in the war ever frightened me quite so much. Life has never faced me since with such stark over-whelming terror—not even in the Agadir earthquake.

*   *   *

My memories of Eton are strangely acute. I can recall precisely—as if the whole film of it were running through my mind—the movements and dialogue which led to a turning-point in my life.

Each boy in our House had a small room of his own. It was a strict rule that no boy should enter another boy's room after lights out. M' Tutor, as we called our housemaster, would make a nightly round of the House to make certain this vital rule was kept. Along the corridor from me lived a boy of my age—fourteen. I will call him Drew. He had never joined in bullying me, and for this reason alone I was grateful to him. He was dark-haired and lithe, and there was an odd secretive look about his lean face and dark eyes. He was a fine athlete and a favourite of M' Tutor for that reason. At prayers in the dining-hall in the evening I would often look up and see him gazing at me.

One evening after M' Tutor had made his nightly round, the door of my little room opened and Drew came in and closed it softly behind him. By the glow of the fire which we were allowed twice a week I saw that he was wearing only a dressing-gown. He sat down on the chair by my small table which I used as a desk.

"I want to talk to you," he said quietly.

"Talk to me tomorrow," I whispered back. "There'll be the hell of a row if you're caught here."

"I won't get caught," Drew replied. "M' Tutor's done his rounds, and he won't come back because he's got a dinner-party tonight. I saw all the cars outside."

"What do you want to talk about?" I asked.

"You," he said.

"What about me?"

"You're just plain wet."

"Thanks for the compliment," I said.

"But you don't *need* to be so hopeless at everything. You could get on quite well if you tried."

"And do what?" I asked.

"Do you know what they call you behind your back?"

"No."

"The walking dictionary."

"Why?"

"Because you use such idiotic long words. The kind of words grown-up people use. And they think you're showing off."

57

"Well, I'm not," I answered. "At home I live with grown-ups most of the time, and I suppose I pick up the words they use."

"Then start picking up the kind of words *we* use."

"I'll try."

Drew got up from the chair and came and sat at the end of my bed. "You're still pretty green, aren't you?" he said.

"I suppose so," I answered.

"You play with yourself, of course. You toss yourself off."

I could feel myself blushing. "Yes," I said, "sometimes."

"Have you ever done it with anyone else?"

"No."

"But someone must have tried."

I thought of Neal with his freckled face. "Yes," I answered.

"Then why didn't you do it?"

"I'm not sure, really," I said.

"I bet I know why," Drew said. "It was because you were scared. You were scared of being found out."

"Perhaps."

"But what if you were dead certain you'd *never* be found out? Then what?"

"I'm not sure."

"Do you think it's wrong?"

"People think it is."

"Not all people don't. Some people who are really intelligent go in for it. Shall I tell you a secret? Promise you'll never tell any of the others?"

"Yes."

"Well, it's this. My last term at prep school the Headmaster himself caught me doing it with another boy one night in the gym. We weren't doing much. I mean, we'd still got pyjamas on. Well, he told us to go to his study.

"When we got there, he told us to stand five paces apart. Then he told us to take off our pyjamas, so we were naked. 'Now,' he said to us, 'is there anything wrong with that? Answer me.' So we said, 'No.' Then he put his arm round my shoulder and led me over to the other boy, and then he put his arm round our waists and drew us together so that our bodies were clasped together. 'Now,' he said, 'is there anything wrong with that?' I guessed what he wanted me to say, so I said, 'No', and after a pause, my friend said 'No' too. Then the man took hold of us and pressed us gently together, and after a while we came. 'There's nothing wrong with it,' he repeated. 'But you must keep it a secret because most people are so stupid they think it a crime, and you can get

58

put into prison for what you've just done.' So then he unlocked the door of his study and we left him. But he sent for me the following night, and he made me do it with him . . . I went with him several times before I left school."

I was silent. Drew's story had revolted me. I wondered if it was true.

"So you see," Drew said, "there's nothing wrong with it so long as you don't get found out. And if you swear to keep it a secret, and I swear I'll never tell a soul, then—if we did it—there isn't a chance we can ever be found out."

I was silent. I could feel my heart thudding against my chest, and I was afraid. I felt I was walking in darkness near to a precipice. I knew we would both be expelled if we were found out.

"I've been mad about you ever since I first saw you," Drew said. "Quite crushed on you."

I was certain that at least this was the truth, because I could remember that each time I looked at him in prayers, he had been staring at me. But I was still frightened.

"Wait till tomorrow night," I said hesitantly. "Give me time to think about it."

But even as I spoke I knew I wanted it now. And then I remembered the boy at the window in London when I was a child. I had been frightened so I had sent him away. I no longer believed in the boy who could fly. But this was real. The boy was sitting at the end of my bed. Suddenly he got up, and I was afraid he would go. But he didn't go. Very slowly he took off his dressing-gown and threw it on to the chair and stood before me naked. His shoulders were heavy, his skin was very smooth, his waist and thighs were so delicate that his genitals seemed almost obscenely large.

"Please," he said.

"I promise I'll let you know in the morning."

"No," he answered. "It's got to be now."

I was silent. A coal flashed in the grate, and I saw that his whole body was taut and trembling. I could feel the power of his desire surging through the little room.

"Please," he urged. "You've got to say 'Yes' now, otherwise I'll just stand here waiting all night."

I laughed because I was happy. I knew that at last something a part of me had longed for—or rather something Tommy had longed for— was going to happen.

"All right."

Slowly and quietly he slipped into my bed and put his arms round my neck. I pressed his lithe body against me. The skin of his waist was

59

very warm and smooth. I wanted to remain in that wonderful state of calm mixed with the most intense happiness I had ever known. But soon Drew's body began to move, and gently he turned away from me, so I could caress his lean back and heavy shoulders. Then he took my hand and guided it so that presently our bodies were joined together.

* * *

I had thought that my experience with Drew would change his attitude towards me in the House. But the following day he was as aloof and distant as ever, and he made no effort to help me when I was being bullied by the other boys. Yet, that night, after our housemaster had been round the rooms, Drew came to visit me again.

"Why didn't you do something to help me?" I asked Drew when we were clasped together.

Drew kissed my forehead. "Don't be so wet," he said. "If I suddenly started defending you and became your friend, they'd all guess at once that something was going on."

With that explanation I had to be content. I could have argued with him, but I was afraid of losing the happiness I now possessed. Meanwhile, each term—or 'half' as we called it—dragged by. Grey afternoons of trudging along the Slough road towards the distant playing fields were followed by long evenings as an oarsman rowing in the Lower House boat, being shouted at hectically by a coach. While I was still a lower boy, I made no friends except Drew. And Drew could visit me only in secret. Moreover, I was beginning to get suspicious of him.

Drew was waiting for me one day when I came into my room. He beckoned me over to him and told me to lock the door. This was dangerous because a strict House rule forbade one to lock one's door. It was possible to jam it shut with a scout's stave, but this was not allowed and could be punished by a caning.

"Don't be a fool," I said to Drew. "Anyone may come in."

"Don't worry," Drew said. "It's all right."

And he took my right hand and put it into his pocket. But he had cut the outer seam so that my hand slipped right in and touched the flesh between his thighs.

"You do the same with your trousers, and we can always pull back our hands at a second's notice."

I still kept the pathetic hope that one day Drew would become so fond of me that he would prove himself my friend publicly. I welcomed any chance of contact with him, so I obeyed him. But later that afternoon, when I was alone in my room again, I began to wonder if I were

60

the only person who had slipped his hand through the split seam. One evening, after three hours of rowing in a skiff on the river, and being shouted at by the zealous coach, I began to walk back towards the House. Then, suddenly, I began to run, for I was in a frantic eagerness to see Drew. I walked quickly into his room. Drew was standing behind the door. With him was an older boy called Tait, an upper boy—very popular because he was good at games and always seemed contented and full of vitality. Drew and Tait moved apart as I came in. Tait laughed. His pale hair had fallen over his forehead, and he was sweating. Drew was breathing heavily.

"So we've got a visitor," Tait said, pushing his hands down into his trousers. "Care to join us?"

For an instant I gazed at his fleshy nose and large blue eyes and wide smile. Then I turned round and left the room.

The following evening, during the period when we were supposed to prepare our work for the next day, Tait came into my room. I said nothing. For a while he walked round the room in silence. He carried an exercise book in his hand.

"You're supposed to be good at French," he said. "Can you help me with this translation?"

"I'll try," I replied.

I sat down at my desk. Tait opened his exercise book and showed me the page he had to translate into French. I took a piece of paper and began to write. As I spoke he slid his right hand down between my thighs. I got up from the chair. He put his arms round me and held me tight against him. I could feel that he was trembling.

"Don't be afraid," Tait whispered. "It's all right. I know you've done it with Drew. Just let me feel you. That's all I want."

His forehead was sweating again, and he was trying to smile.

"I'm sorry," I said. "But I can't."

His large hands were now thrust deep into his pockets. His blue eyes glared at me.

"I could help you," he said. "I could stand up for you. Please let me."

"I'm sorry," I repeated.

Tait strode to the door. "You're just a little runt," he said. The door slammed behind him.

That night when Drew came into my room, I let him get into my bed, but I lay without moving.

"What's wrong?" he asked.

"You know what's wrong," I said. "You've been doing it with Tait."

Drew was silent for a moment. His hand stroked my shoulder gently.

"Yes," he said after a pause. "I've been doing it with Tait. But do

61

you think I care tuppence for him? I do it with him because he could make life hell for me if I didn't."

I said nothing. By the light of the moon coming in through the half-open window I could see that Drew was gazing at me solemnly.

"Can't you see that it doesn't matter?" he asked. "We're together. That's all that counts."

"So you let him . . ." I began.

Suddenly Drew grasped me fiercely. "Yes. I let him," he said. "I've told you I let him. And if you weren't such a stupid little idiot, you'd let him too."

I was silent. I did not move. Presently Drew slipped out of my bed and left the room.

For three nights he did not visit me; and I lay in agony, thinking of him being grasped in Tait's sinewy arms. For the first time in my life I felt the misery of jealousy which springs from an intensely possessive love. Then, on the third night, my door opened quietly and Drew came in. Without a word he took off his dressing-gown and got into my bed. I kissed his shoulders and put my arms round him.

*   *   *

We never referred to Tait again. On several occasions Tait came into my room on some pretext or another, but in spite of his threats I would never let him touch me. Whenever it was possible I continued to have Drew—until two years later when he was expelled from school for being found in bed with a small boy.

*   *   *

Looking back at those years, I now believe—at the age of fifty-five— that if I had my chance again I would have behaved differently with Tait for the sake of gaining his friendship. For the sake of his protection I would have given in to him—to a certain degree. But I still am not sure that I would have been right to do so.

*   *   *

Meanwhile I continued to be bullied, and I was often unhappy— except during the moments I spent with Drew. My mother's diary for this period contains, at the end of the holidays, the perpetual entry: "Robin miserable at having to go back to school."

I *was* miserable, and my mother indeed knew it, but it never occurred to either of us that I could leave Eton. The school was a prison in which I was sentenced to live for a fixed number of years. My father regarded my evident unhappiness as yet another sign of the weakness of my character and of my hopeless ineptitude, as he would have called it, at games. My mother continued to hope that I would presently become a more robust person and that I would grow accustomed to the prison walls.

For my part, I knew that for three terms a year I inhabited a place of anguish. I was aware that outside the little confines of Eton there existed a vast world about which I was pathetically ignorant. But this world could in no way affect me because I was enclosed in the life of the universe of Eton as firmly as a toy figure in a glass ball. Outside the sun might shine, or the winds might scatter the waves. But inside the glass ball the snow still fell relentlessly. Stupid though I was in most of my personal relationships, I at least had the sense to discover that there were two escape routes from my cell; one immediate and one future. The immediate escape I discovered lay in music. The future means of escape lay in working so hard that I would pass at a young age into Cambridge and thus earn my release.

*   *   *

I had become Captain of the Lower Chapel Choir. I enjoyed choir practice, and it satisfied my sense of the theatrical to walk slowly into Chapel each morning in my long surplice carrying a large cross, with the whole choir following in pairs behind me. But as yet, music as such was something which I could admire only from outside—even though I might be performing myself. I was happy to be a member of a small group whom Dr. Henry Lee—Eton's Precentor of Music and perhaps the finest organist alive at the time—would invite to hear him play in company with Sir Walford Davies, on the organ in St. George's Chapel, Windsor, which had a double console. I recognised that to such people music was the reality; it was their day-to-day social life which was a vague dream. However, I was still an outsider.

Then, suddenly, there came a change. Mervyn Bruxner was appointed as Assistant Precentor. Previously my piano lessons had been dull and uninspiring. *Now*, with his fierce enthusiasm and keen sincerity to teach everyone in contact with him to understand and to love music, Mervyn Bruxner made each piano lesson he gave me an hour of enchantment. Within a year, music had become a world into which I could escape from all my petty little miseries. It has remained so ever since.

At the same time I concentrated on my long-range escape route. I was no more intelligent than anyone else in my class, but I worked for longer hours, so I was sometimes highly placed in the end-of-term exams. Now that I am a writer by profession, I find it strange that in those days music exerted a far stronger hold on me than did literature.

63

Robin Maugham in his Highfield days

Robin Maugham with his father

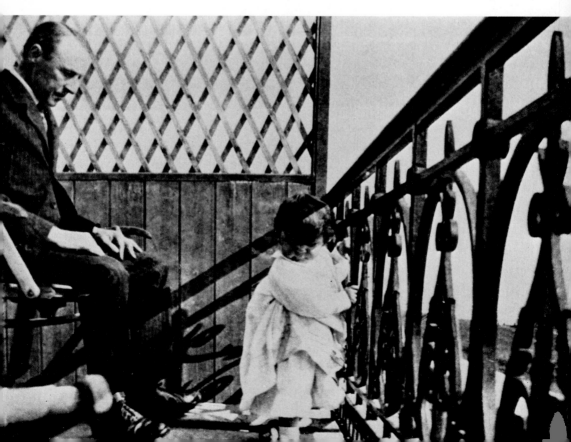

I pushed open the door of the shop. A little bell tinkled as the door opened, and I closed it behind me. The shop was empty. Then a man, presumably Mr. Morrison himself, came hurrying down the staircase at the back. He was about forty-five, I reckoned, with silver hair, a short nose, and rather full lips. He was neatly dressed and very clean. He was wearing a pair of steel-rimmed spectacles, which seemed to accentuate the oddly pious expression of his face and made him look more like a clergyman than a shopkeeper. He gazed at me for a moment, then smiled pleasantly.

"And what can I do for you?" he asked.

There was something unusual about his cockney accent. It was somehow unreal—like that of an inexperienced actor trying to play some dialect part. I asked him if I could see the four-ten gun in the window. He walked over to fetch it. He moved with light, precise steps. Carefully he laid down the gun on the counter. I looked at it, entranced. The barrels were oily and gleamed faintly in the afternoon light. The butt was well carved.

"How much is it?" I asked.

"Four pounds and twelve shillings," he said.

I must have sighed because the man smiled at me once again. "Haven't you got that amount?" he asked.

"No," I said. "I haven't."

At school, boys paid tailors' shops or bookshops on order forms which had to be signed by the House Dame—a rather grand type of housekeeper. I also had one shilling a day to spend at the school stores (two eggs on fried bread cost ninepence, and 'three of long'—chips and tomato sauce—cost threepence). In addition to this my parents gave me an allowance of six pounds a term, but half of this I had already spent.

The strange man smiled at me yet again. "Look at the gun," he said. "Feel it. Handle it. And you'll see it's worth every penny I'm asking."

As he spoke, I heard the shop bell ring. I turned as a boy of about fourteen walked in. He was very slender, with straw-coloured hair and violet eyes. The shopkeeper's attention switched off from me as if he had flicked a light switch.

"Ronnie," he said to the boy, "your tea's upstairs. Hurry along up or it'll spoil."

Ronnie gave me a cheerful grin, then turned back to the shopkeeper. "Right-o!" he said and sprung lightly up the stairs.

The shopkeeper turned back to me. "Four pounds twelve," he said. "But if you come back the next afternoon you've got some time off I'll see if we can't do something about reducing the amount."

He walked round the counter towards the door. "And now, if you'll forgive me, I'm closing the shop," he said. "I must get up to my boy. See you soon."

That night, images of the gun's dark, smooth barrels and of Ronnie, with his long, straw-coloured hair and graceful movements, flitted through my dreams.

Two weeks later I visited the shop again. I had managed to beg a pound note from my mother when she had come to see me. So I now had four pounds; I was full of hope. The shop window had changed. One section of it was now devoted to wireless sets, and a small card announced: 'Wireless Sets Sold and Repaired'. However, the four-ten gun was still there. From an open upstairs window came the sound of jazz distorted by a loud crackling noise. I walked into the shop. Mr. Morrison greeted me warmly.

"I was wondering if I'd ever see you again," he said.

"I've got four pounds," I announced.

"That's better than nothing," Mr. Morrison replied. "By the way, do they allow you to have guns at school?"

"No," I answered. "I'm going to ask you to have it packed and posted to my home, if you don't mind."

"That'll cost more."

"I know," I answered. "But I've got four whole pounds." And I held out the four pound notes for him to see. For a while there was silence. Mr. Morrison had stopped smiling. Behind the steel-rimmed spectacles his eyes were watching me carefully.

"How old are you?" he asked.

"Fifteen," I answered.

"So I expect you have plenty of larks with the other boys in your House?" Mr. Morrison said.

Somehow I had a feeling that if I said 'No' too definitely I'd never get the gun. "Sometimes," I replied cautiously.

Again there was silence. Suddenly he leant forward and touched my chin. "You've got very smooth skin," he said. "My boy, Ronnie, doesn't have to shave either. But in some ways he's old for his age. And he's very clever with his hands. That's why I'm setting him up in the wireless business."

I was still holding the four one-pound notes. With an abrupt laugh Mr. Morrison leaned forward and took the notes from my hand.

"All right," he said. "Gun's yours."

He pushed an account book and a pencil across the counter. "Write down your name and address," he said. Then he went to the window and took out the gun. "You've got a real bargain there," he said. "You're a very lucky young lad. And I don't mind telling you this, if

Ronnie hadn't taken a fancy to you I'd never have let the gun go so cheap."

I broke open the gun and looked down the barrels. They were immaculately clean with a light coating of oil.

"I'll be closing up shop quite soon," Mr. Morrison said. "So there'll be no interruptions. Why don't you go upstairs and have a chat with Ronnie? I'll join you presently."

I hesitated.

"Ronnie doesn't take a fancy to many people," Mr. Morrison said. "So you can count yourself lucky on that score too."

He put his arm around my shoulders and pushed me towards the stairs. At the top of the stairs, leading off a small landing, was a door. I knocked and opened it. The music still blared from the loudspeaker. Immediately facing me was a long kitchen table strewn with parts of wireless sets. At the far end of the room there was a double bed. Ronnie was lying on it, naked except for a pair of blue shorts. He looked up at me. "What are you doing up here?" he asked.

I stared at him in surprise. "Your father said you wanted to see me," I stammered.

The boy sprang from the bed and walked up to me. He stood very close to me so that I could hear his whisper above the noise from the loudspeaker. "*Father!*" Ronnie said. "Is that what he told you? That he's my *father*?"

"But isn't he?" I asked.

The boy shook his head in disgust. "I'll say he's not," he whispered. "He's just taken me on. Better him than a reform school . . . And you get used to almost anything in time."

I gaped at Ronnie. Then suddenly I understood. I looked at the alabaster-white skin of his shoulders and at his small waist. I began to feel sick. I could think of nothing to say.

"Can't you see what he wants?" Ronnie whispered. "He wants us to do it together, so he can join in with the two of us . . . Have you paid him for the gun?"

"Yes," I answered.

"Right-o!" Ronnie said. "I'll see that you get it safely. But if you know what's good for you, you'll leave now, and you'll leave quick."

Then he put his arm round my shoulder and kissed me on the mouth. "Perhaps one day we'll meet again. At any rate, I hope so," he said.

I put my arms round him. For an instant I held him tight. Then I walked quickly out of the room.

Mr. Morrison was moving, with a key in his hand, towards the door when I came down the stairs. He looked up at me in surprise. "You didn't stay long," he said.

"Sorry," I muttered, "but I remembered I'd promised to help a friend with his prep. When will you send off the gun?"

"Tomorrow," he said. "I'm scrupulously honest in my business matters."

* * *

Three days later, when I rang up our house in the country, my mother told me the gun had arrived. I was pleased. But I still couldn't forget the image of Ronnie lying on the bed. And in my imagination I could now see Mr. Morrison beside him.

"Better him than a reform school." Ronnie had said, and I felt sad that there was nothing I could do to help the boy. However, I was so haunted by the thought of him being under Mr. Morrison's influence that I decided to visit the shop once again, on the pretext of ordering cartridges.

Once more I walked down the side street. But when I reached the shop it was empty, and a 'TO LET' sign was stuck across the window.

I walked into the little sweet-shop next door and asked if they knew where Mr. Morrison and Ronnie were.

"Mr. Morrison's mother's died," I was told. "It seems she left him some money. So they packed up the shop and moved to some place where she'd lived."

So Ronnie was another person I never saw again.

* * *

As the days passed, I realised how much I had been shocked when I had discovered the truth about Mr. Morrison and Ronnie, for I had never believed that a man could lie in bed with a boy and love him in the ways that Drew and I did each other. I now saw Mr. Morrison as personifying the evil which I had sometimes sensed when I had seen one of the older boys in my House coming out of a small boy's room.

I longed for the end of term. At last the day came, and after an evening in London at my father's town house, 73 Cadogan Square, I went down to Tye House, near Hartfield. My mother greeted me with relief—as one might greet a convict coming out of prison.

That night I could hardly sleep, for I knew what I must do at dawn. As soon as I saw a faint glimmer of light in the mist covering the lawn I got up and dressed hurriedly. I wore old corduroy trousers, a worn turtle-necked sweater, and a shabby tweed jacket—which I felt was the appropriate gear for a hunter. Over my shoulder I slung a satchel con-

68

taining cartridges. Then I took up the four-ten gun which was lying on a small side-table so that I could constantly look at it. I moved quietly down the stairs. I closed the front door of the house. In the trees around the lawn the birds were already twittering. I crossed the garden and moved stealthily into the wood. Suddenly I stopped. About fifteen yards away from me there was a large rabbit sitting on its haunches. I crept closer to it. At that moment I felt that I had shed my hopeless, aesthetic self. I could almost feel Tommy taking over. In a second I had become a ruthless sportsman to whom killing animals was a daily pleasure. I lifted the gun up to my shoulder. Then I fired. The pellets from the first shot hit the rabbit's hind-quarters, and it began to crawl towards the undergrowth. I fired again. This time the pellets hit the rabbit's head. But it still wasn't dead. It was still twitching horribly. I knew that what I ought to do was to grasp hold of its hind legs and strike hard at the base of its neck. But I didn't dare to touch that quivering, bleeding, mangled creature. Instead I bludgeoned it to death with the butt of the gun. I left the corpse lying there. I walked back to the house. I cleaned out the gun and put it away in a chest-of-drawers, I never used the gun again.

*   *   *

But though my desire to shoot and kill was finished, Tommy still lived on, and he now began to force me into playing another role.

My parents had bought, as an investment, and as a protection to their privacy, an Elizabethan farmhouse whose grounds marched with ours. The bailiff had taken my mother to a local sale at which she had bought for me—at the price of fifteen pounds—a compactly built chestnut pony called Cracker. A neighbouring farmer gave me riding lessons. I took to Cracker, and eventually—after several falls—Cracker took to me. Soon, I was able to go out riding alone through the lovely fields and almost impenetrable woods which surrounded our house.

My riding master, however, wanted me to become one of his star young pupils. I was made to join the local Pony Club which met in a clearing beside a large field. There were jumps of different heights all round the field.

It was at a meeting of the Pony Club that I met Shirley. She was a slender girl of about fourteen with flaxen hair, a snub nose, a wide mouth and startlingly bright eyes. Her hair was cut short so that she looked rather like a Renaissance page-boy. I immediately fell in love with her. Shirley enjoyed both prestige and popularity as the champion show-jumper of the district. My father, who by now had been appointed a judge of the High Court, and my mother were away in London. I had been told that I could ask any friends I made at the Pony Club back for tea. But Shirley, whose father was a retired lawyer, presented a problem. Her elder brother of sixteen guarded her like a watchdog. Secondly, she seemed inseparable from her friends. So I asked the whole lot of them to tea—some as young as twelve—and they all accepted. Tea was a great success. The servants, who had had little to do for the past fortnight, were amused to see a group of children gathered round the long refectory table in the living-room, with its minstrels' gallery. Not only were there hot scones to be eaten with strawberry jam and cream from the farm, but—as a special treat—they had produced ice cream with hot chocolate sauce.

After tea, I suggested that we should play hide-and-seek, for Tommy and I had already made a plan. I did not even have to cheat because I knew by instinct that I would not be chosen to be the seeker by the old chant of 'Eena, meena, mina, mo'. I was delighted when Shirley's brother, George, was chosen. Obediently, but rather sulkily, he closed his eyes and began to count aloud up to one hundred. Meanwhile, we were all scampering away to discover a good hiding-place in the large, rambling house. I moved quickly, for I had carefully chosen my hiding-place. I took Shirley by the hand. I was sweating with excitement. Together we rushed along the minstrels' gallery and ran up a short flight of stairs which led to my bedroom. There I opened the door of an L-shaped cupboard which was built into the wall. My mouth was dry as I spoke.

"If we get right to the back of the cupboard," I told Shirley, "even if he looks in, he won't see us."

Shirley hesitated, then crept into the cupboard after me. There was only just enough space for the two of us to hide in the recess. It was very hot. Shirley was wearing a light cotton frock. I was dressed in white trousers and a short-sleeved, open-necked shirt. Our bodies were pressed side by side, close together. I put an arm around Shirley's neck and drew her closer to me. Then, in the darkness, I began to stroke her hair, and presently I began to kiss her forehead, then her cheeks, and then her mouth. I could feel her arms around my shoulders. I slipped my hand down the front of her dress and placed it over the small cup of her right breast.

"Don't. Please don't," she whispered.

But I could feel that she was quivering. I knew that she was as excited as I was. I unbuttoned my trousers and slid her hand along my thighs until it reached my groin. Then, with my other hand, I began to stroke her thighs, moving my hand gradually higher and higher, until it touched her knickers. Her soft hand was holding me. In the cupboard the air was stifling. We were now both sweating. Suddenly I felt an ecstasy more intense than I had known even with Drew. And I came in her hand. At that moment she gave a violent shudder and a little moan of pleasure. Then she leaned against me limply. Suddenly, the cupboard door was opened. Neither of us moved, for in the recess we thought we were safe. But George had heard her little moan of fulfilment. He had picked up the torch from my bedside table. He now bent his head and moved along the cupboard, past the coat-hangers, until he reached the recess. For an instant he shone the torch on our two sweating faces. Then he switched it off, for he had already seen all he needed to see. Perhaps shame for his sister made him dread to see more.

"Come out," he said. "Come out, both of you." Then he turned round and scrambled out of the cupboard.

As soon as Shirley and I reached the living-room where all my other guests were assembled, for their hiding-places had also been found. George announced that he and Shirley must bicycle home or they would be late to change for dinner.

By now, I was infatuated with Shirley. I needed desperately to see her again. So the next morning I looked up the general's name in the telephone directory and asked the Hartfield operator for their number. A male voice answered the telephone. I think it was George.

"Can I speak to Shirley, please?" I said.

"I'm afraid she's not here," the voice said. "She's gone to stay with some friends in Eastbourne."

A week later I rang again. A maid answered the telephone and told me that Miss Shirley was not coming back to the country that summer.

Tommy had been defeated. My other self took over.

*　　*　　*

At a tennis party I had met the vicar of a church in the neighbour-hood. We had discussed church music together, and I told him that I had started to have organ lessons. In his kindness the vicar had said that if I came to his little church I could play there as long as I liked—provided I had the money to pay the organ-blower.

The pedals were stiffer than at school. There were only two manuals and far fewer stops. But provided I could find Stan Lakin, who pumped the bellows for two shillings an hour, and so long as there wasn't a service or choir practice, I could play whenever I liked. Whereas at our own parish church, two miles nearer home, the vicar allowed me to play for only one hour—and then only under the supervision of his peevish organist.

71

At first I thought that my paying Stan Lakin, who was concealed behind a purple arras near the vestry, heaving like a Titan at the old-fashioned bellows, would worry me. After all, he was eighteen—only two years older than I was. Mr. Agnew, the vicar, reassured me. Stan's parents were perfectly well off, he said; but he was a bit weak in the head, and he didn't mind pumping the bellows because he liked the sound of an organ.

I slid my fingers into the concluding major chord of F and managed to press the correct pedal with my foot. I looked at my watch. I had been practising for one hour and fifty minutes. In ten minutes' time I must stop because I had only four shillings in my pocket. My parents could easily have afforded to give me a special allowance for my organ practice. But they disliked Mr. Agnew. My mother thought—quite wrongly—that he was High Church, merely because (probably from absent-mindedness) he had bowed rather frequently to the altar during the only service she had attended at St. John's. I closed the book of exercises, pulled out all the stops and let rip for three minutes with broad, imposing major chords and plaintive minor ones. Then, to give Stan a rest before the full-blast performance of Handel's *Largo*, with which I always ended, I played a little hymn tune which I had composed in the music-room at school that term. I used only a plain diapason, so as to consume less air. As I finished, a voice from the aisle of the church said: "What was that hymn?"

I turned and saw Mr. Agnew. I had not heard him come in. He must have been well over sixty, with thin white hair and a face that reminded me of the weather-worn stone saints outside the church. His features were blunt and indistinct. He was almost ugly, but there was a warm kindness I could feel whenever I met him.

"Good evening, Mr. Agnew," I said. "Well, as a matter of fact, I wrote it."

"Did you now? I thought I'd never heard it before. Do you mind playing it again?"

I was delighted to—even though it might mean sacrificing my *Largo*. I pulled out the tremolo stop for effect and played the tune again. When I had finished playing he said: "The tremolo doesn't improve it. But I like the tune very much—very much indeed. Could you attend choir practice tomorrow?"

"Yes, I think so, sir."

"If you've no objection, I'd like my choir to sing your tune as an anthem the Sunday after next. I know words that will fit perfectly. I shall play it through to them tomorrow evening to teach them the tune. But I want to make sure I get it right."

I was so excited I could only just speak.

"Thank you, sir," I managed to say.

"Seven o'clock then," he said, as he walked out. "Good night, Robin; good night, Stan."

In a daze I closed the shutter that rolled down over the manuals and thanked Stan and paid him—I think I may have shaken his hand, because I felt in a way that he was my collaborator—and I hurried out of the church. My parents made me change into a dinner-jacket for dinner; I did not want to annoy them by being late.

As I raced home on my bicycle, my heart was full of pride and happiness. I had always wanted to be a composer; I would persuade my parents to let me leave school at seventeen and study music in Vienna, where I had heard of a brilliant teacher. Wild visions swung into my mind as the lane curved and dipped its way through the hay-fields. The dappled keyboard glittered beneath my poised hands. The strings had enunciated the opening theme. I was watching the conductor's baton, and as the beat came my hands crashed out the first heavy chords of my concerto. The dressing-room was full of people; cameras flashed as my hands were clasped and shaken. Suddenly the crowd divided, and there stood Shirley in a shining white evening dress, her hands stretched out. The scene faded as a haycart rumbled towards me. I glanced at my watch. I was going to be late. I pedalled feverishly.

My parents had started eating by the time I reached the dining-room. "Good evening," I said, and sat down at my usual place between them.

My father took out his gold watch and flicked open the lid.

"You are five minutes late," he said.

"And darling, your tie's crooked," my mother added. "Did you have a bath?"

"No."

"Civilised people bathe before dinner," my father said. "Where have you been?"

"At St. John's."

"Why?"

"I practise the organ there. I told you."

"What a hideous little church!" my mother said.

"It's Norman."

"I know, darling."

"Hard as you may find it to believe," my father said, "your mother *does know* about church architecture."

"I only meant . . ."

"And had you wished to be accurate you should have said that the

73

church *was* Norman—before the Victorian vandals restored and ruined it," my father concluded, smiling at my mother across the four early Georgian candlesticks.

I decided I would keep my important news until the end of the meal. As Judkins, the parlourmaid, was handing round coffee, I spoke. "Can I have high-tea tomorrow and skip dinner?" I asked.

"Of course you can, darling," my mother said. "But why?"

"Well, actually Mr. Agnew wants me to be at choir practice to-morrow at seven."

"Choir practice? But your voice broke ages ago and you've sounded like a corncrake ever since."

"He doesn't want me to sing."

"Then what does he want?"

"Well, actually . . ."

"Robin," my father began.

"You see . . ."

"Will you kindly allow me to speak?" my father said.

"Sorry."

"I have told you time and again that it is the sign of a second-rate mind to sprinkle your every sentence with stock phrases such as 'well actually' or 'as a matter of fact'," my father told me. "Now then. Please tell us what you want to say directly, without meaningless verbiage."

I stared down at my empty coffee-cup. I reminded myself that I was sixteen; I was no longer a child; I could find a job as a waiter in a hotel or I could go to sea; I could look after myself. But I still felt the tears of anger and humiliation pricking my eyelids.

"It's nothing really," I muttered.

"Tell us what you were going to say and let us judge," said my father. "Why does Agnew want you to attend choir practice?"

"Because I've written a hymn."

"Indeed! Can you recite it to us?"

"Well . . . I mean, I haven't written the words, I've written the tune."

"Without any words?"

"Yes. Mr. Agnew says he can find words to fit."

"And he wants you to play your little tune to his choir?"

"No. I think he'll play it himself."

"Is there no organist?"

"Yes. But Miss Gaunt isn't as good as he is."

"Presumably you mean from the standpoint of technique," my mother said, laughing.

My father smiled at her faintly, then turned back to me.

"Why should Agnew trouble to play your tune to his choir?" he asked.

"Because he wants them to sing it as an anthem next Sunday week."

My mother clapped her hands together. "How distinguished!" she cried. "Congratulations, my little Mozart!"

Then she saw my father's face, and her smile faded.

"It think it an impertinence of Agnew to arrange this without even consulting me," he said. "Our name is involved, and this folly may make us the laughing stock of the entire village."

"But Freddie . . ."

"You realise that one of his motives is to get you back into his church?"

"Does that matter? I need only go once."

"To be ridiculed because of an old man's whim?"

"But the tune may be very good."

"My dear Nellie, what do you suppose Robin knows about composition?"

"His report last term was quite enthusiastic."

"For his piano playing, not his composition."

"But he's had lessons. Haven't you, Robin?"

"Yes."

My father sighed. "Nellie, just ask yourself how much a music master at a public school knows about the most complicated of all arts. Do you suppose that anyone able to write a symphony—one sonata even—would listen all day to a lot of young dolts hammering out mazurkas?"

"I've had an idea," my mother said. "Why doesn't Robin play us the tune so we can judge for ourselves?"

My father put down his coffee-cup.

"Let us hear it by all means." He rose from the table.

There was an upright piano in the living-room. I sat down nervously at the stained keyboard and began to play my hymn. But even as I played the first few chords I knew that I was lost. The jangling notes were out of tune; the hammers on middle C and F sharp were stiff; the dampers were faulty. The tune sounded very different from what I had played in the peace of the church. When I had finished there was silence.

"I think it's charming," my mother said. "But I can't quite see how it could be sung."

My father lit a cigar. "You play the chords most impressively," he said. "I had no idea that you had made such progress."

He paused, and for one delirious moment I thought that at last I had done something to please him. "But I'm afraid that I must agree with your mother," my father continued. "There is no tune at all."

"But there *is*," I insisted. "Only it's my fault for not bringing it out."

"You believe there is a tune a choir could sing unaccompanied?"

"Yes. I do."

"Could you sing the refrain yourself?"

"Yes."

"Unaccompanied by the imposing chords?"

"Yes."

"Then your audience awaits you."

"But I've got no words."

"When I was young we just sang 'Lah, lah-la, lah' like that," my mother hummed, with an encouraging smile.

"Very well."

"We're listening, darling."

While I sang the tune I tried to forget them both sitting there without moving; I tried to think of the choir in surplices and the congregation listening devoutly as the music rose to the vaulted roof. But it was useless. I had started off in too high a key, and I had to begin again in a lower one. I could hear my untrained, rather husky voice trembling from nervousness and cracking on the high notes. I broke off half way through.

"Please finish it, darling."

"I can't."

For a moment my father examined the end of his cigar.

"Are you aware of the reason *why* you can't finish it?" he asked.

"My voice isn't up to it."

My father watched the smoke he had exhaled spiralling up towards the gallery.

"I'm afraid that is not the only reason," he said in his quiet, reasonable voice. "The most important reason is still to be expressed. It is this. The tune—such as it is—does not lend itself to the human voice."

He turned to my mother, who had taken out a novel from the bookcase and was reading furtively.

"And I'm sure that you agree with me, Nellie," he said, with a slight frown at her.

My mother put down the book and turned to me with a sigh.

"Darling, you must admit the tune isn't precisely inspiring." Then, seeing my despondency, she tried to make a joke of it. "I mean, one can hardly imagine the early Christians chanting it as they strode across the forum towards the ravening lions."

"You haven't heard it properly," I said. "If only you'd let me play it to you in the church."

"But I'd love to hear you play it on the organ. You know I would."

"We'd both appreciate the chance of hearing your progress," my father said. "But so far as the hymn is concerned you must confess that we've given you every chance. And we are both of us agreed. You have assembled a series of pleasant chords, but you have not composed any tune at all. I am sorry, Robin. But in the morning I must ask you to inform that poor senile crock Agnew that his choir will not perform your hymn the Sunday after next or at any other time."

As they went out, my mother made a little grimace at me to indicate her disappointment and blew me a kiss.

*   *   *

The next morning I telephoned Mr. Agnew, but the deaf old house-keeper who looked after him bellowed that he had left for the church. It was a fine day; I had nothing better to do, so I bicycled across to St. John's.

The church door was open, and even as I reached the lychgate I could hear the soft notes of the organ playing my tune. I crept up the aisle. Mr. Agnew was sitting at the console, his head raised yet inclined to one side, listening to the quiet, reedy notes filling the little church. He was using the upper manual to pick out the melody, and he had made several improvements to the tune itself. Listening to it now, I knew that despite what my parents had said I had written a tune as good, if not better, than dozens of other hymn tunes that were droned out on Sundays. When he had come to the end Mr. Agnew turned and saw me and waved his hand cheerfully towards the pew where I was sitting.

"I've been all morning learning it," he said. "Stan has got quite impatient with me. But I think I've got it right, don't you?"

"Yes, sir."

"I hope you don't mind the small changes I've made?"

"I think they're fine."

"I wasn't expecting you until this evening, you know."

"Mr. Agnew . . ."

"But now you're here perhaps you'd like to listen to the chorale we're doing this next Sunday."

"The reason I came . . ."

But he did not hear me. He had already started playing a Bach

77

chorale. It was 'Jesu, joy of man's desiring'. And as the quietly lilting but steady notes struck and echoed from the whitewashed walls, I knew that Tommy was close to me; he had come once again to comfort me, and I waited for him to speak.

"There's no need to tell him," a voice seemed to say quietly in my head.

"I must."

"Why?"

"I said I would."

"What does that matter?"

"Besides, if the choir practised it, they'd find out."

"By then it might be too late to stop it."

"They'd never trust me again."

The chorale had finished. Mr. Agnew was walking down the aisle towards me. He looked worried.

"You look ill, my dear boy," he said. "Can I do anything to help?"

"It's nothing."

"Would you like a glass of water?"

"I'm all right, sir. But there's something I have to let you know," I said. Then I told him of my parents' decision.

*   *   *

I returned to Eton in a spirit of rebellion. I grew my hair long. I resigned from the Officer Training Corps. "This," M' Tutor growled, "of all the stupid things you've done, is the stupidest. Because a great war will come, and all your contemporaries will be officers, and you will be a common soldier." A war did come, and for a year I was a trooper and it was far more pleasant than being an officer.

I took up fencing which let me off having to play the boring Field Game. I spent more time than ever in the music-rooms and won a Harmsworth prize for music. But far more important—now that I was an upper boy I could visit other Houses. Through Michael Isaacs, whose family, the Readings and the Erleighs, had long been friends of my parents, I met at Mr. Crace's House a group I soon joined—Marcus Rueff, Patrick Gibson, Ben Astley, David Parsons, and Airey Neave. They talked about Suetonius and Mozart, Michael Arlen and Adler, and though they were all good at games they never discussed them. I am certain that if I had been in Mr. Crace's House I would not have been persecuted. On the contrary, I would have enjoyed each term and my outlook would have been wider.

In other Houses I met Michael Pitt-Rivers whose intelligence and charm attracted me—and do still—and John Gwyer, cool, poised and

78

civilised, with whom I started an Eton magazine called—because it sold for sixpence—*Sixpenny*. I had passed all the examinations necessary for me to get into Cambridge. I now began to write almost daily to my father and mother to let me leave school and study music for a year in Vienna before going up to Cambridge.

"I am afraid that it is perhaps my absurd mentality," I wrote to my mother, "that does not adapt itself like wax to the iron tracks which it must needs run along in this House. I find it difficult to mould my character perpetually. On occasions I can adapt myself brilliantly, but I can't keep it up."

During my last two terms, I felt less lonely because my sister Kate's son, David Bruce—four years younger than I was—had arrived from Highfield. He settled down very quickly at Eton and his happiness somehow infected me. He was a tougher, more resilient person than I was. He was popular, and he ended up his days at Eton in the glory of being Captain of the House and a member of the elite school group known as Pop who were allowed to wear coloured waistcoats and meet in a room of their own. They also dealt out quick justice with their canes on boys who they felt were a menace to the school.

During my last holidays I pleaded with my mother and with my father to let me leave school and go to Vienna. But my father firmly refused to allow such a thing. Perhaps he then hoped that there was still a chance that I would gain some form of distinction at athletics in school. I had already got my Colours for fencing, and this encouraged him to believe that I might get my Colours for some other sport.

Each week of my last two terms at Eton my letters asking to be released from prison became more frantic and hysterical. At last, my father relented and said I could leave. I was a member of the French Society and appeared in *Le Bourgeois Gentilhomme*. I played in an Inter-House Field Game and scored a goal—and as I walked off the muddy field I said: "Thank God, I needn't ever play this bloody game again." This remark lost me a form of House Colour called Shorts. I didn't care. Freedom was approaching. That evening I played Beethoven's *Moonlight Sonata* in the School Hall. A few days later I left Eton for good.

But for several years I would not go near the place. I could not even drive through Slough without feeling physically sick. Even now, scenes from those ghastly days disturb me.

PART

TWO

I WAS NOT YET EIGHTEEN WHEN I WENT TO STAY IN
Vienna. My darling sister Kate was to accompany me for the first
two weeks. Rooms had been booked for us in the Koenig von
Ungarn. I was then to enter a pension run by a fat and respectable
Austrian baroness. The most famous piano teacher in Austria had
agreed to give me an audience to determine whether I was worthwhile
as a pupil.

*   *   *

I was about to leave England when, one morning at breakfast in the
large, gloomy family house in Cadogan Square, I could see from the
violently trembling copy of *The Times* in my father's hands that something had gone wrong.

"Such a meeting would be highly unsuitable," my father was saying.
"The man's a drunkard and worse."

"Then Robin needn't meet him if you don't want him to," my
mother replied.

"But the man's staying *in the same hotel*," my father answered
reproachfully.

Gradually I found out what had occurred. My Uncle Willie had
calmly written a letter to my father saying he was delighted to hear I
was going to Vienna because his American secretary, Gerald Haxton,

was already there staying at the Koenig von Ungarn, and would be able to look after me.

"I will not *have him* stay in the same hotel," my father declared.

"You can hardly force Gerald Haxton to move out," said my mother.

"Then *Robin and Kate* must change their hotel," replied my father.

So cables were sent off, and Kate and I were dispatched to a different hotel in Vienna with severe instructions never to meet the infamous Gerald Haxton. But, of course, we did—quite by chance. We met him the first night we went to the opera, and I was extremely disappointed, for he didn't look wicked at all: he was a smart, dapper, lean man of forty with a small moustache, a cheerful laugh and an innocent smile. I felt I had been grossly deceived by all that I had heard about him, and I was almost reluctant to accept his invitation to show me round Vienna after Kate had left. But a week later, when Gerald got blind drunk in a *weinstube*, I began to appreciate that he wasn't quite as innocent as he seemed. However, by then I had been impressed by his sophisticated man-of-the-world pose. I was grateful for his flowing hospitality, and—let me confess it—I was flattered by his interest in me. So I found a taxi, managed to pull Gerald into the back, and dropped him at the Koenig von Ungarn—and I accepted his slurred invitation to lunch with him the following day.

Gerald was almost always full of charm and full of liquor during the ten years that followed. If Willie was invited to a party he made sure that Gerald was invited with him. But Gerald felt himself snubbed or ignored at some of the smart parties on the Riviera. One evening they had gone to an extremely large party given by a film star and his wife. Gerald disappeared to a bar at the far end of the garden. Presently he approached the group of people in which Willie was standing. Gerald was swaying slightly.

"I don't know about you, ducky," he said to Willie, "but I'm going down to the pool to have a swim."

At the word 'ducky' Willie stiffened. There was silence, then a titter. Willie did not move. Gerald lurched away. A few moments later the hostess came up to Willie.

"I'm sorry we can't swim tonight," she said, "but the pool's been emptied."

Willie stared at her for a second in silence, then moved swiftly away. When he was out of sight he began to run towards the pool which was in a part of the garden not floodlit that evening. At the bottom of the empty pool, Gerald was lying crumpled and motionless, naked except for his white briefs. Blood was seeping from his head. He was in hospital for several months.

But Willie always forgave Gerald's transgressions, for in many ways he was a wonderful companion for him. Willie was shy and reticient; he was frequently depressed and silent. Gerald, an excellent host unless drunk, was ebulliently, irrepressibly friendly. When the two men travelled around the world together, it was Gerald who made the contacts that Willie needed for his stories. Gerald helped him find the raw material he wanted for his work; his boisterous spirits could lift him from his occasional fits of gloom. Gerald's diligence saved Willie from all the minor irritations of travel, and his resourcefulness, at least on one occasion when they were out sailing, saved Willie's life; for had Gerald lost his head when—in Willie's words—the 'great mass of water . . . caught the boat and turned it over', my uncle would have been drowned.

*   *   *

I was wonderfully happy. The two weeks I had spent with my sister Kate in Vienna were full of laughter and of wonderment at the beauty of the churches, palaces, and museums. Moreover, Kate had managed to get two letters of introduction to an Austrian lady and an Austrian gentleman, both with distinguished-sounding titles.

When we were admitted to the lady's ante-room there were three very stout, middle-aged gentlemen sitting upright on little gilt chairs, each with a grey bowler hat covering his lap. Then a fourth, and even stouter gentleman emerged clasping his bowler hat in his left hand and buttoning his fly with the right. As he left the stout man nearest the door got up and hastened into the room.

"We're in a bordello," I said to Kate in a stage whisper.

"So we are," Kate answered placidly. "We shall have to visit her out of business hours."

Kate's second letter was to a squat baron of immense wealth. From the moment we entered his drawing-room his interest was focussed on me rather than on Kate.

"Ven your sister is gone," he said to me, "you shall come and stay a veek in my *schloss*. You shall meet many young boys to play vith. Ve shall all make you very 'appy." With which words he gave me a sharp pinch on the bottom.

When we met the baroness, whose pension I was to live in at fifteen shillings a day, she took Kate aside and led her into her sitting-room.

"I 'ear your brother 'as been invited to stay vith this varon in 'is *schloss* for a veek," she said. "It is 'ard for me to explain to you vat is wrong with this man."

"Try," said Kate, who was enjoying herself immensely.

"Vell, 'e is one of those men as 'ow ve call 'omosexual," said the baroness.

"Really?" said Kate. "Well I never! Then we must refuse his invitation. But, if I may say so, I shouldn't worry too much about Robin—he's capable of looking after himself."

After Kate had left me I went to see the famous music teacher. He lived in a large studio cluttered with furniture and two grand pianos. To my dismay I discovered that he spoke hardly a word of English, and I spoke only a few words of German. However, he sat me down at the piano and told me to play him something. I chose a Chopin waltz. The Maestro listened in silence. "*Gut*," he said when I had finished. "*Ganz gut*. You 'ave style but now I teach you to play proper."

He then placed a coin on the back of both my hands.

"Now," he said, "you play same valtz and do not let the coins to slip."

I tried to explain to him that I had been taught to play the piano in the Matthay Method where you could turn your wrist in a run. He was obviously going to try and teach me the Leschetizky Method, a method which insists that the backs of the hands remain unmoved and only the fingers move. I tried to play the waltz again but the coins kept slipping. As the Maestro grew more annoyed with me his English became less comprehensible and his German faster.

"*Es geht nicht*," he said, and showed me to the door.

I learned many things in Vienna at the age of seventeen; the piano was not among them.

Meanwhile Myles Hildyard had arrived to stay at the pension. I had not known him at school because he was nearly two years older than I was. I recognised him at the Vienna races when, holding his head high and with a look of great arrogance—which I was to discover concealed a fierce shyness and a profound sensitivity—he walked straight into the owners' paddock and examined each horse as if it belonged to him. We soon became great friends—and we have remained so ever since. Myles introduced me to his friend George Morton, whose stepfather and mother lived in a small castle at Klosterneuburg. The days that followed were glorious. After our German lessons Myles and I would take a train to Klosterneuburg and swim in the pool or in the Danube. In the evenings I would spend the money for my music lessons on going to the Vienna Opera House where I saw some of the greatest performances I have ever known. I even went to a fancy-dress ball in the Palace of

Schönbrunn which was attended by Dollfuss, the Austrian Chancellor. Each morning, I would awaken to a sense of freedom and joy.

During this period I received two or three letters a week from Gerald Haxton.

'Dear Darling Robin', he would begin, or 'Beloved one', or 'Sweetheart'. In my stupidity and innocence I thought he was being facetious, so I replied to him in a similar strain. Then he telephoned me from the Villa Mauresque, in the South of France. Willie had granted him a short holiday and Gerald wanted me to meet him in Venice. He would be sending me a ticket shortly. I must tell the baroness I was spending a few days at Klosterneuburg.

I did not know that the baroness listened to every telephone call on an extension in her bedroom. She now rang up Sir Walford Selby, the British Ambassador, and told him I was leaving for Venice with my middle-aged lover. From one of the ambassador's sons I later gathered that His Excellency had taken the view that it was no concern of his. The ticket arrived. It was third class. In high spirits I left for Venice. The train was packed. The wooden benches were hard but I didn't mind. I read *Death in Venice* and looked out at the wonderful scenery. It was a tiring journey. By the time Gerald met me in Venice, I was exhausted. It was late but he took me out to supper. He then took me to the Danieli Hotel, and we went up to his double room. The night was very hot; we both stripped to our briefs. It was not until that instant that I realised what I might have let myself in for. Then Gerald rolled over from his bed which was close beside mine and clasped me in his arms. At that moment I realised he had taken my facetious letters completely seriously and believed I was in love with him. As his hands began groping me, I made an involuntary movement of revulsion. I pushed him away. For an instant Gerald lay on his own bed glaring at me.

"Those letters," he began.

"Listen, Gerald," I said—and I tried to explain.

"I should have known," Gerald said and turned out the lights. Presently he was snoring.

We were both awakened by the telephone ringing. It was perched on a ledge above our beds. Gerald made a grab for the receiver.

"You are being called by the Villa Mauresque," the concierge said. "One moment."

There was a faint crackle. Then I heard my Uncle Willie's voice on the line.

"Good morning, my dear Gerald," he said.

The line was surprisingly clear.

"Good morning, Willie," Gerald replied.

There was a slight pause, and then Willie said, "And was the young man satisfactory in bed?"

"I'll telephone you later," Gerald said, and put down the receiver quickly.

To this day I do not know whether Willie had planned that Gerald should seduce me—perhaps because he loathed my father for reasons I shall reveal later. Or perhaps it amused him to think of his own lover having his own nephew. Or perhaps he hoped that once I had been seduced by Gerald I would be ready to accept his own proposals of love. In either case I felt shocked and disgusted.

During our remaining days together Gerald was very kind to me. He took me sightseeing around Venice. He was a superb companion. He never made any reference to what had happened. But when he was driving me back to Vienna in Willie's heavy Voisin Coupé, he picked up an Italian boy and took him into his bedroom in the small inn at which we were sleeping that night.

*   *   *

Myles Hildyard and I were staying by the lake at Klopeinersee when Dollfuss was assassinated. A Nazi putsch was expected at any moment. My mother's brother, General Sir Cecil Romer who was Deputy C.I.G.S.,[1] telephoned her to say there was a danger of war. My mother sent me a telegram asking me to return to England. But Myles and I decided to spend a few more days by the lake. We were sun-bathing, half-asleep on the shore when—to my amazement—I heard my uncle's voice.

"There's the young man," Willie's voice said. "And how beautifully brown he is."

"We've come to rescue you," Gerald Haxton announced. "We're taking you to Bad Gastein and then putting you on a plane for England." He turned to Myles and said: "Would you like to come too?"

"No thanks," said Myles who disliked Gerald intensely. "I'll find my own way back."

"Then go and pack," Willie said to me. "I want to be back in Bad Gastein in time for dinner."

That evening, after we had eaten blinis and blue trout, Gerald got up from the table and said he was going to the casino. I was left alone with Willie, Presently he leaned towards me and I could see that he intended to say something of import. I took a gulp of hock.

"I would like, if I mer-may, to give you a word of advice," Willie

[1] Chief of the Imperial General Staff.

88

stammered. "You are quite an attractive boy. Der-don't waste your assets. Your charm won't ler-last for long."

With those words he rose from the table.

* * *

"How much you've grown," my mother exclaimed as she embraced me on my return to Cadogan Square. "You're quite a stranger."

For the first time we began going to theatres and cinemas together. From that moment onwards I adored my mother even more—and I know now from her diaries that she loved me. A few weeks later we went down to Tye, and my sister Honor came to stay.

Honor immediately appreciated my passion for music. Almost every evening we would drive up to London to attend the Promenade Concerts conducted by Sir Henry Wood in the Queen's Hall. Although Honor was happily married and had a child she was restless at that period. She shared my passion for music and my interest in musicians. She had made friends with Bratza the violinist, who had once been an infant prodigy, and with his brother Doushka Yovanovitch, the pianist. For one splendid week we accompanied them on one of their tours of England. I would sit in the back seat of Honor's car holding Bratza's Stradivarius violin on my lap.

Those happy days, in retrospect, seem to have been filled with Honor's sensitivity and enthusiasm and with the peace of mind I experienced when I sat beside her watching her work on a pastel drawing. I now dreaded entering the realms of authority and discipline in Trinty Hall, Cambridge. Both my father and my uncle, Lord Justice Romer, had been in the college. I already knew that a portrait of my grandfather on my mother's side, another Lord Justice Romer, would stare down at me disapprovingly from the oak-panelled walls of the dining-hall.

* * *

On October 6th, 1934, I drove up to Cambridge with Humphrey Tyldesley-Jones whose parents were close friends of my family. I felt a little apprehensive. But as soon as I had moved into my little set of rooms in the college, I had an instinct that all was going to be well. I soon became convinced that I was very lucky to have been sent to Trinity Hall. Though the college contained a tough group of rowing hearties, Humphrey and I soon made friends with five or six freshmen with whom we always sat in Hall.

I had made a bargain with my parents that if I was allowed to take the English Tripos I would take the Law Tripos in my last year and go to a crammer in London for my Bar examinations. One of my closest friends at school had been Marcus Rueff. He was now at Trinity College and our friendship was happily renewed. Red-haired, elegant, witty and benign, well-read, with an astonishing knowledge of music, he was one of the most colourful men of my generation at Cambridge. He was killed fighting in the Western Desert.

Lionel Elvin, to whom Marcus and I went for tutorials in English Literature, was not only widely read but was an ardent humanist and Socialist. He treated us as if we were his equals in age; he never condescended; and he related English Literature to the everyday life of the people in the period we were studying.

But I was still suspicious of authority, and I stood in awe of the Senior Tutor, Dr. Owen Wansbrough-Jones—until my first serious encounter with him.

I had written a play called *Thirteen for Dinner* which Robin Duff, who was the President of the Cambridge Amateur Dramatics Club, decided to put on at the A.D.C. Theatre. The disadvantage of writing a thriller called *Thirteen for Dinner* was that one needed thirteen actors to be at the dinner-table in addition to servants and butlers, so I had a cast of nearly twenty.

There was a regulation that we were allowed to stay out of college after ten o'clock in the evening only twice a week. But since I had to attend rehearsals every night, this meant that for four or five nights of the week I had to climb into Trinity Hall in darkness and over a very high wall, the top of which was encrusted with broken glass. It was winter, and there was sometimes ice and snow to make my ascent more difficult. Throughout the rehearsals I used to dread the prospect of having to make the climb. Then I was summoned to see the Senior Tutor. I attended, as regulations laid down, in cap and gown.

"Now Maugham," Dr. Owen Wansbrough-Jones said in a very quiet, almost bored tone of voice. "It's not so much that I worry about you maiming yourself for life each night when you climb into college. But it disturbs my repose, because you happen to climb in opposite my bedroom window. So do you mind, if you need to rehearse your play each evening, being good enough to ask permission for a late pass, which will promptly be granted to you?"

Until that moment in my life, I had hated authority. From then on, I learned to respect it when wisely exercised.

A few days later I received a letter from Willie. "You are most unwise to attempt to write a full-length play, let alone to allow it to be produced," he told me. "Undergraduates are a notoriously dangerous audience. You must be prepared not only to be booed but also to see your set broken up and all the props destroyed."

Thirteen for Dinner opened at the A.D.C. Theatre on February 11th, 1935. The undergraduate audience cheered loudly. There were even shouts of 'Author!' The play ran to packed houses every night of its week's run, and it made me fifty pounds in royalties which I spent on giving presents to my unpaid, hardworking cast. I was now, I felt, a professional writer. Soon I was invited to write short stories for the Cambridge magazine *The Granta*, and I quickly became friends with its editor, Charles Fletcher-Cooke, who was also President of the Union.

Charles was over a year older than I was. He was bespectacled, brilliant and, in those days, highly neurotic. He suffered from what he would call his 'apprehensions'. On a bad 'apprehension' night, I would walk with him up and down King's Parade for hours on end until he felt himself strong enough to face returning to his digs. He shared my passion for theatre and each week we would dutifully attend the Festival Theatre to see one of Norman Marshall's excellent productions. I could hardly believe in the happiness which filled me each day. I was learning; and I was enjoying the process. Sex no longer disturbed me as violently as before. Only occasionally were my emotions stirred by some attractive young undergraduate. In Vienna I had made up my mind that I would forget about Drew and the passions that he had aroused in me. I was determined to be normal. This resolution was very much helped by the fact that in London I had met in G. B. Stern's room in Albany a girl a year younger than myself—Gillian Dearmer, the daughter of Dr. Percy Dearmer, a Canon of Westminster Abbey.

Peter—as G. B. Stern preferred to be called by her intimate friends— was at that period a best-selling novelist, and she lived in style. I had met her through my sister Kate, and had immediately been attracted by her wit and exuberance. Peter had been determined to arrange a meeting between her two favourite 'protégés', as she called us. Thus Gillian and I had met—each of us—as we confessed later— bristling with suspicion of the other. But the confrontation was a great success.

Peter put Gillian into at least two of her novels, and she was always described as 'having the charm of a young colt'. Indeed, with her slenderness and unconsciously endearing movements, Gillian did remind one of some beautiful young animal. She had a wonderful sense of humour and a pleasantly dry wit—and she still has. During the following Summer Term she would come down to Cambridge to visit me. We would dine at some country inn, and then walk through the soft misty fields hand-in-hand. I was very much in love with Gillian and I knew that she was in love with me. Already I felt that we were, in effect, engaged.

*   *   *

While I was at Trinity Hall I can remember only one unpleasant incident.

Marcus Rueff and I were producing an evening of short one-act plays at the A.D.C. Theatre. I was directing three of them, and I found it convenient to have preliminary readings in my rooms in college. Two of the actors were slim and very effeminate, and they sometimes— in their dotty way—used heavy make-up in the streets in day-time. One of the senior members of the Trinity Hall Boat Club who also rowed for Cambridge was called Whitelaw. He was very tough and already a great womaniser. Whitelaw was enraged by seeing my two young painted friends tripping gaily across the college quadrangle. He voiced his complaints to four or five other rowing hearties, and a message was sent to me telling me that I was sullying the good name of the college by inviting obvious perverts to visit my rooms. I was warned that if I continued to encourage such visitors my rooms would be broken up. Both the message and the threat enraged me. I made up my mind to confront Whitelaw directly. But it was obvious that if physical violence occurred, Whitelaw would knock me out easily.

Suddenly I found a solution.

I was walking down King's Parade with two college friends when the moment I'd been waiting for came. Advancing towards us along the pavement was Whitelaw in the centre of a group of his red-faced, loutish friends. I walked straight up to Whitelaw and slapped him with the back of my hand across the face. Before he could recover from his surprise, I spoke.

"I'm challenging you to a duel," I said. "Since I'm the one who's been insulted I shall have the choice of weapons. I choose sabres. My seconds will call on you in the morning to arrange a time and place."

While he still gaped at me, the three of us walked past Whitelaw and his group of friends and went to have a drink at a pub to discuss the best place for the duel. I had no intention of maiming the man. But I had been taught a particular fencing feint whereby I could make a slight cut at his right wrist and so disable him.

Whitelaw—I discovered later—was in a state of consternation, so he went to see Dr. Owen Wansbrough-Jones. Once again I was summoned to appear before the Senior Tutor. Once again I appeared punctually, suitably dressed in cap and gown.

"Now, Maugham," Wansbrough—as we called him—began, "I'm

not going to allow you to stroll around the college challenging my senior undergraduates to duels."

Suddenly he smiled and his stern creased face was transformed.

"It's just not on," he said. "So I have arranged for Whitelaw to make you an apology for any threat he may have used. And I am now asking you, when he comes to shake hands with you, to apologise to him for slapping his face. Is that clear?"

"Yes, sir," I answered.

"Right," Wansbrough said, moving towards a side-table. "And now shall we take a glass of sherry together?"

*   *   *

I got a second in the English Tripos—which disappointed my father who had hoped I would get a first. That vacation was now marred by the shadow not only of my father's disapproval of me but also my dread of having to study Law.

*   *   *

Even as a child I had disliked the atmosphere of Law. I suppose I must have been about seven when my mother first took me to the Law Courts in London to hear my father plead.

"One day, when you're grown up, you'll be a lawyer—like your father," she said. "And you'll never forget the day when as a child you first saw him in court."

I shall certainly never forget the day or what occurred. We walked along dank, gloomy corridors that smelled faintly of cabbage soup and stopped in front of some tall doors panelled with frosted glass. A policeman nodded his head when my mother gave her name, and we were ushered into a large courtroom and placed on a shiny wooden bench behind the witnesses. My father looked more of a stranger than ever in his grey wig. His voice sounded alarmingly hollow as he cross-examined a witness. He never raised his voice, but I could hear every word he said, though I could not understand what it was all about. His questions were put calmly and evenly, one after the other, and I could see that they were making the unhappy-looking, red-faced man in the witness box very angry.

"Why is Daddy making that poor man so cross?" I asked my mother.

"Quiet, darling."

The questions continued smoothly in my father's cool, dispassionate voice, and the red-faced man began to tremble and shake with rage.

"I think the poor man's going to be sick."

"Hush."

"But look! He's taking out his hanky."

"You must keep quiet," my mother whispered.

As she spoke, my father asked yet another question in his indifferent yet glacial voice, and the effect on the red-faced man was disastrous. His eyes bulged, his arms jerked about in the air like a clockwork toy, froth covered his mouth; and at the height of his fit I burst into loud tears and was led by my mother, sobbing, from the court.

*   *   *

The evening before I was due to return to Cambridge my father summoned me to his study.

"I have a few words to address to you," he announced. "I have allowed you two years to indulge your infatuation with writing. To-morrow you will be returning to study for the Law Tripos Part II. I want you to take your studies seriously. The notion I've heard that you should become editor of *The Granta* is the purest folly. You will stop writing for *The Granta* because it will distract you from your work. And you will stop your idiotic efforts for what you suppose to be the Socialist cause. That is all I have to tell you."

Clearly our meeting was at an end, so I turned and left the room. I was determined to work hard for the Law Tripos; I was equally determined that I would continue writing stories for *The Granta*. In retrospect, I find that a third of those stories were quite bright, but the rest were without merit.

I kept my writing secret from my father. However, one afternoon he arrived unexpectedly, with my mother, to visit me at Trinity Hall. As we wandered round the town I was horrified to see my name in vast letters: "New Story by R. Maugham", the posters proclaimed. So each time we approached a poster my mother, who knew the terrible truth, would engage my father in fervent conversation while I moved hastily between his line of view and the blatant poster.

*   *   *

I cannot explain why I had become such an ardent Socialist. Perhaps it was a reaction from the staunch Conservatism of my father. Perhaps it was caused by my disgust when for the first time I discovered the gross inequality that existed at that time in England.

I took my duties to the cause most seriously. In order to learn about the iniquities of capitalism I worked in my spare time in the Cambridge juvenile employment office. What I learned about juvenile employment strengthened me still further in my faith in Socialism. Children were monstrously exploited by the factory owners of the district. A factory which made wireless sets closed down. Hundreds of children, therefore, came to the office. They had been employed in cutting the metal bases for the sets. The law laid down that children working with metal-cutters must be provided with gloves. But the law did not state that the children should be compelled to wear the gloves. The factory owners paid the children by piece-rate. I could see the results of this system during that morning when the children came in one by one in the hopes of finding some new employment. A boy or a girl whose hands were unscarred would have been making only twelve shillings a week. The children whose hands were hideously scarred would have been making over twice that amount.

During the holidays I visited the East End of London to learn about living conditions. The slums were hideous and soul-destroying. A bucket in the back yard might serve as a latrine for a family of ten. Most of the roofs leaked on to soiled beds which might be shared by three or four children. The overcrowded, dark and badly ventilated rooms reeked of damp and unwashed linen. Mice abounded, rats were not uncommon. Any form of privacy was impossible. The rents of the hovels I visited were absurdly high, and payments were frequently weeks behind. The inhabitants all seemed to be in the hand of the tallyman, or of some form of loan society. I found it hard to understand why the inhabitants did not join together in a vast mob and surge to Mayfair and Belgravia to overthrow their oppressors.

*   *   *

Back at Cambridge, I dutifully attended the law lectures and worked as hard as I could. I continued to write—by then I was the editor of the Trinity Hall magazine—and I continued my labours for the Socialist cause. There now existed in me a conflict between the person who wanted to lead the life of an extremely left-wing writer and the person who was being forced into the life of a conformist lawyer, sweating over the textbooks on Real Property, learning daily more about the complex apparatus which kept the Establishment secure. I realise now that the character of Tommy, the Communist in my novel *The Man with Two Shadows*, must have sprung subconsciously from the extreme form of Socialism in which I believed at that period.

*   *   *

In the summer of 1936 I had a letter from Willie inviting me to stay at the Villa Mauresque. Since I was now grown up, my parents made no effort to stop me going, so I accepted gladly. I was now certain that I could cope with the wiles of Gerald Haxton.

Willie and Gerald greeted me warmly. They showed me around the villa—which Willie had bought in 1928. It was beautifully situated on the end of Cap Ferrat, the promontory that stretches into the Mediterranean between Monte Carlo and Villefranche. I was almost overwhelmed by the luxury and splendour of the place, with its vast, cool, high-ceilinged rooms beautifully furnished, its large garden with long glades of lawn between the pine trees, and its swimming-pool set on the hillside behind the house with a view over the whole of Villefranche bay. I was most impressed by the opulence surrounding me—by the sleek male servants who would keep my glass filled with pink champagne, by the rows of oils and essences and scents in the bathroom which led off from my bedroom. I was fascinated by the flow of guests who came to lunch or dinner—Michael Arlen, saturnine and dapper; Osbert Sitwell, majestic, venerable and witty; Harold Nicolson, twinkling and benign; Barbara Back, graceful and unceasingly entertaining; Peter Stern, happily effusive and loquacious; Noël Coward, as always brilliant and urbane; Robert Hichens, constrained in an old-fashioned and tight-fitting gaberdine suit; Max Beerbohm, an aged dandy, still wonderfully spritely, speaking in the accents of the eighteen-nineties and choosing each word as fastidiously as he chose each garment he wore, courtly but carrying only a vestige of his exquisite past. The household seemed to be effortlessly run. It took me some time to realise that it was Gerald Haxton who was largely responsible for the atmosphere of happiness and comfort in which I was now living.

Gerald's attitude towards me was perplexing. He made no further sexual approach yet I could sense that he was still attracted to me. It was a rule at the Mauresque that everyone should bathe naked in the swimming-pool, and as I would lie sun-bathing, if I suddenly looked up, I would find Gerald staring at me.

By now I knew more about Gerald than when we were in Vienna. Willie had met Gerald while he was serving in a Red Cross ambulance unit during the early months of the First World War. Willie was then forty; Gerald, a handsome American, in his early twenties. He was wayward, feckless, and brave, and Willie was immediately attracted to him. Shortly after the war Gerald had become Willie's secretary and companion on his travels, and was the cause of Willie's divorce. Gerald had little interest in literature; he was mainly interested in Willie's books and plays because they brought in money. From the days when he had been a schoolboy he had grown used to being admired. He was already spoilt. He had begun to drink heavily, and he became wild and violent in his cups. His reputation was notorious; his behaviour was reckless. In the winter of 1915, when Gerald was in London, he was arrested on a charge of gross indecency. The case came up before Mr. Justice Humphreys on December 7th, 1915, and he was acquitted by the jury. But the judge was convinced that Gerald was guilty of the offence and made no secret of it. A few years later Gerald was declared an undesirable alien. He was never allowed to return to England again. This was one of the factors that decided Willie to live abroad. Gerald always pretended that the reason he never accompanied Willie on his trips to London was because he loathed the place. But the cigarettes he smoked still came from Bond Street, his suits from his old tailor in Savile Row, and his shirts from Jermyn Street.

*   *   *

When I was alone with Willie and Gerald they were considerate and affectionate to me. But both of them took pleasure in trying to shock me, and they both derided my romantic love for my darling Gillian.

"You der-don't really love the girl," Willie told me one evening. "You just want to go to bed with her. You're a ver-vigorous young man. You need a romp. And after dinner tonight, Gerald has decided to drive you into Nice and to take you round a brothel or two. You'll soon find out what you want."

That very evening Jean, the chauffeur, drove Gerald and me along the Corniche to Nice. First Gerald took me to various louche bars which he often frequented. Then, when we were both slightly drunk, we began to tour the brothels. The routine was always the same. Gerald would greet the madame who ran the bordello and order a bottle of champagne. Presently, the girls would parade naked before us. And I was appalled. My Socialist conscience was revolted by the spectacle of such degradation. Yet I could not help noticing that the girls seemed perfectly happy and indifferent to whether they were chosen or not. It was this brazen indifference which, I found, reduced completely such ardour as might have arisen in me. I could not see myself having any of them and, soon after midnight, I begged Gerald to give up the quest. But Gerald was drunkenly determined to find a girl who would please me—and he did. In the next brothel we visited I saw that one of the girls looked shy and embarrassed. She was about my age, wonderfully slim and attractive. Without hesitation I chose her. She led me up a flight of rickety stairs to her bedroom. While I undressed she told me that she was a stenographer in Paris. But in order to pay for her holiday in Nice she worked in the brothel twice a week. I now found her wildly attractive. In bed she was affectionate and eager; I made love to her with passion.

As Gerald and I were driven home to the Mauresque that night I was more than ever convinced that I was now a perfectly normal man.

*   *   *

The following day, when Willie had finished his morning's work in his writing-room, perched high on the roof of the Villa Mauresque, with its large window blocked up so that he should not be distracted by the beautiful views of the sea, we drove down to Villefranche to lunch on the yacht which Willie had given Gerald. I was still pleased with myself because I had so thoroughly enjoyed making love to the girl in Nice the previous night.

That afternoon the weather was perfect. The sun shone down on us from a cloudless sky, and there was a light breeze. While the cabin boy was preparing the lunch, the three of us sat on the deck of the forty-ton sailing yacht drinking dry white wine. Gerald was in high spirits, for he adored the yacht. Willie was obviously delighted to see him so tranquil and content. Meanwhile, as the two of them gossiped about guests who had been to the Mauresque and others who were arriving, I found myself watching the sixteen-year-old cabin boy who was naked except for a bathing-slip. He was slender; his body had been turned to a golden-brown by the sun. His skin was very smooth. Suddenly—to my dismay—I realised that I was attracted to him. I wanted to take him forward. I wanted to unfasten the string that held his faded bathing-slip in position. I wanted to slide my hands along the length of his body. I wanted to make love to him.

I turned round on deck and lay on my stomach so that I could conceal the signs of my excitement. At that age I didn't know that many people are ambi-sexual in this way.

*   *   *

The following evening, after dinner, Gerald took me to the casino in Nice. He'd spilt red wine down the front of his evening dress shirt earlier at dinner. He was already drunk when we arrived. He sat down at the *chemin de fer* table. The fact that he played wildly did not worry the management—they knew that, as always, Willie would pay his debts; however, the fact that he insulted almost everyone round the table did disturb them. A French player he would address as 'frog-face'; any lady he would address, with a grin, as 'you silly old bitch'. Presently the casino manager came up to me and told me that unless I removed Gerald he would have to call the police. To my surprise, when I told Gerald that I was tired and begged him to drive me back to the Mauresque in the Voisin Coupé we had taken out, he staggered to his feet without any argument. I took him by the arm and helped him to

98

walk out of the casino and along the Promenade des Anglais to the car.

"I've got a surprise for you," Gerald kept saying. "I've got a wonderful surprise."

I tried to make him let me drive, but he was too drunk to listen to reason. We swerved along the coast road until we reached Villefranche where Gerald turned right and drove down towards the harbour.

"Just wait till you see what's waiting for you on the yacht," he kept saying.

I followed Gerald as he staggered over the gangplank. The aft saloon was in darkness. Gerald switched on the lights. Lying on the double bunk, naked except for a pair of shorts, was a blond boy of about seventeen. As he lay there, his hair tousled, his limbs sprawled out in sleep, his lips slightly parted, his skin glowing like bronze in the dim lights of the saloon, he looked so innocent and beautiful that I felt the same keen stab of pain in my heart that I had felt a dozen years before when I had seen the farmer's boy riding back from the hayfields.

As we came in, the boy awoke and stared at us drowsily. Then he sprang to his feet. He smiled as he greeted Gerald in French. As soon as he smiled, the look of innocence left him. His face was now transformed by a strange look of yearning—as if Gerald were the only person in the world who could grant the fulfilment of all his wishes. Gerald kissed him on the mouth, then glanced towards me.

"*Laurent*," he said, "*je veux t' introduire mon ami—Robin.*"

Then Gerald turned back to me. "Robin," he said, "this is my little friend Laurent. Have a good time with him. He's a very sweet boy. You've nothing to fear."

Gerald poured himself a glass of brandy from a bottle on the bar. Then he opened the door which led forward.

"Goodnight, ducks," he said. "See you both in the morning."

He lurched out of the door and closed it behind him. I was left alone with Laurent.

For a moment there was silence. Laurent was staring at me solemnly. I could feel my heart thudding. I believed that both of us had been put into an awkward predicament for, though I was only twenty, the boy might not want to share the bunk with me for the night.

"*Puis-je t'offrir quelque chose à boire?*" the boy asked.

"Please," I answered. "I'd love a glass of wine."

"Red or white?"

"Whichever you prefer."

"It's very sweet of you to say that," the boy said. "But then I can see right off that you're a very sweet person."

Quickly he moved to the bar and poured out two glasses of red wine. Then he crossed the little saloon and handed me my glass, and raised his own.

"*Santé*," he said. He took a gulp of wine from his glass and put it down on the bar. Then he turned round and faced me. He smiled, and once again the strange look of yearning transformed his face. He stretched out his arms and put them round my neck. Suddenly he leaned forward and kissed my lips.

"*N'aie pas peur*," he whispered. "Don't be afraid."

*   *   *

At dawn, he was still lying in my arms. His face was unlined, once again his lips were faintly parted. His teeth were small and very white. He looked like a child. Presently he awoke and stared up at me for a moment without recognition. Then he smiled.

"You're very sweet. Do you know that?" he said. "But I must go. I must go to work. I work in a carpenter's shop."

"When can we meet again?" I asked.

"When you like," he answered. "Any evening, or any time Sunday."

I was so attracted to him that I could hardly bear to think of being parted from him for a whole day.

"What about tonight?" I asked.

"That's all right," he replied. "I'll meet you here at ten o'clock."

*   *   *

"How did you like little Laurent?" Gerald asked when we met by the swimming-pool at the Mauresque later that morning.

"I think he's wonderful," I answered. "I think he's very sweet. If you've no objections we're meeting on your yacht this evening at ten."

Gerald laughed. "Well, you are a one," he said. "And what about your beautiful girl-friend in England? What about your noble resolutions to be a fine, normal lad?"

"I know," I said. "But I can't help it. I've quite fallen for Laurent."

Gerald put a hand on my shoulder and laughed again. "Well, for heaven's sake, don't feel guilty about it, ducky," he said. "Enjoy yourself while you can. You've still got plenty of time to become a respectable Lord of Appeal like your father."

*   *   *

That night there were guests for dinner. I had secretly arranged with Jean, the chauffeur, that he should drive me into Villefranche. At a quarter to ten I looked nervously at my watch. Willie noticed my glance.

"You must excuse my nephew Robin," he announced to his guests. "I must tell you that he has to leave us all now. He has got a der-date with a girl-friend in Villefranche."

I stared at Willie in surprise. His face was expressionless, but he gave me a slight wink.

* * *

Laurent was in the saloon drinking red wine when I arrived. He greeted me enthusiastically. The cabin boy was asleep forward, he told me. We had got the saloon to ourselves.

"*Prends-tu un verre?*" he asked me.

"No, thanks," I said. "I've drunk enough already."

Laurent smiled and began to stroke my cheek.

"I don't need another drink either," he said. "So we can start making love right away."

That night Laurent seemed to reach an ecstasy of passion. "*Je t'aime,*" he kept saying. "I love you."

As I held him in my arms I stroked his wonderfully blond hair. I knew then that I was madly in love with this soft and slender creature whose lips and tongue were gently exploring my face. At dawn we were both still awake. Suddenly I realised that it must be Sunday. I kissed the boy's forehead. "It's Sunday," I told him. "So you don't have to leave."

But Laurent shook his head. "I must go back home," he said, "or my parents will be worried."

"Can we meet somewhere this afternoon?" I asked him. "Would you like to go to a cinema with me?"

Laurent began to kiss my shoulder. "I can't," he murmured. "I've promised my parents I'd go out with them. I'll meet you here tonight at ten o'clock as usual."

* * *

After lunch that day at the Mauresque I went up to my bedroom for a siesta. I couldn't sleep. I kept thinking about Laurent. I was appalled to realise that I really was in love with him. I felt that I was being horribly unfaithful to Gillian. It was less than six months ago that I had gone to Berlin with Gillian and her brother and mother for a holiday. One night, alone with Gillian at a café in the Unter den Linden, I had told her I was in love with her. I had even bought her a ring which I had given her as a token of my love and which she had accepted. I was indeed in love with Gillian. I was *still* in love with Gillian—I was sure of it. Yet here I was, sweating on my bed in the

Mauresque, longing for the evening to come, so I could hold little Laurent in my arms and make love to him again. My room seemed to have become unbearably hot. I decided to go for a dip in the pool. I opened the door of my bedroom and stepped out on to the gallery which ran round the central patio of the house. At that moment I saw the door of Willie's bedroom opposite open softly. And I saw Laurent come out of the room. I took a step back into my own room so that the boy should not see me. I watched him look around to make sure there was no one about. Then he closed the door carefully behind him and moved round the gallery towards the back stairs.

*   *   *

I found Gerald lying naked by the pool. He looked up at me. I tried to smile but I felt sick. Gerald was watching my face.

"So you've just seen dear little Laurent?" he said.

I couldn't speak. I nodded my head.

"Well, ducky," Gerald said, "you must remember you're not the only queer around the place."

Again I nodded my head.

"Then why so miserable?" Gerald asked—and for once his voice was very gentle.

"Because I'm in love with Laurent," I answered. "I suppose you think I'm a complete fool?"

"Yes, ducky, I do."

Gerald collected his bathrobe and walked down the garden steps towards the house.

*   *   *

That evening before dinner, when I walked into the long drawing-room the walls of which, in those days, were hung with paintings by Zoffany, Willie was sitting alone playing patience at the card-table at the far end of the room. When he saw me come in, he swept up the cards and stacked them together.

"Help yourself to a drink," he said. "I want to talk to you."

He moved across to the sofa.

"Sit down beside me," he said. He watched me with his brown eyes, and waited for me to settle down before he spoke again.

"Gerald tells me that you've got a lech on Laurent," he said. "Is that true?"

I took a long breath. "I'm in love with him," I said.

"Balls!" Willie said. "You've just got a simple lech on him, that's all. You want his body and you enjoy having him. Be honest with yourself. Rid yourself of cant. What do you know of that boy's mind? What's attracted you to him—apart from the fact that he's a good performer in bed? Do you think for one single instant that he's in love with you?"

I looked down at my glass. "Last night Laurent told me that he loved me," I said.

"And you *believed* him?" Willie asked scornfully. "You per-poor idiot! Don't you realise that he says that to every one of his clients? The boy may well be attracted to you, but that's because you're ler-lucky enough to have an extremely well-formed body. However, that's not the reason he lets you fer-fuck him all night. He lets you have him because each time he goes with you, I pay him his standard tariff—which, in fact, is almost the equivalent of three pounds."

Willie put down his glass and clasped and unclasped his hands. "The boy's nothing more than an accomplished little prostitute," he said. "The fact that he has persuaded you to believe that he's in love with you has annoyed me quite considerably. I refuse to allow you to make a complete fool of yourself while you're staying under my roof."

I looked at Willie. He was shaking with anger. I turned away from him.

"I've sent Gerald down to the yacht to pay Laurent for tonight," he continued. "Gerald will make sure that you never see the boy again."

Willie was silent. He picked up his glass and began to drink. I glanced at him once more. To my amazement, he was smiling to himself as if he had just finished telling an amusing story. The change in his expression was extraordinary. Even in my dismay, I could not understand the reason for it.

Still smiling, Willie rose from the sofa, went back to the card-table and spread out seven cards face downwards, to begin a new game of patience.

*　　　*　　　*

That night, as I lay in bed, I tried to forget my own unhappiness by thinking about Willie. Why had he been so annoyed that I had fallen for Laurent? Why had he smiled with satisfaction when he had announced that he had arranged that I should never see Laurent again? I decided that I should never know.

Perhaps it was Willie's childhood which had made him such an odd character.

Willie's father, my grandfather, Robert Ormond Maugham, was the solicitor to the British Embassy in Paris. He and his wife, Edith, lived in style. In Paris they had a large apartment in the Avenue d'Antin, and, in the country, a large house overlooking the racecourse at Longchamps. Willie adored his mother. He was shy and he stammered. His three brothers, all older than he was, were at school in England. But his mother—"very small, with large brown eyes and hair of a rich reddish gold, exquisite features and lovely skin", as he described her— gave Willie the warm love the boy needed to protect him from the cold world of reality.

She died when he was eight. Within two years his father had died, and it was discovered that the solicitor's wealth had been an illusion. Each of his sons was left with exactly one hundred pounds a year. Ten-year-old Willie was sent to live with his uncle, who was the vicar of Whitstable. I believe that Willie's character was permanently warped by the bitter years he spent in his uncle's bleak vicarage.

Then—when a young man—Willie gave up his profession as a doctor in order to become an author. There followed five very lean years. Willie never forgot his experience of what he called 'the grinding agony of poverty'.

"I hated poverty," he said. "I hated having to scrape and save so as to make ends meet."

For a while he was tormented by the prospect of being forced to admit defeat and give up his career as a writer. No wonder he was so desperately nervous at the first nights of his plays. Each one was a threat of defeat.

"Went to the first night of Willie's play *Lady Frederick*," my mother wrote in her diary on October 26th, 1907. "Willie was very pale and silent. He sat at the back of the box. I believe the play will prove a success with the public."

My mother was right about the play's success. It was a smash hit. Within a year three more plays of Willie's were produced in London. And at last the money began to pour in. It flowed in copiously from that moment. The sad thing is that it did not bring him happiness.

"Money," Willie told me once, "is a sixth sense, without which you can't make the most of the other five."

Even after he became a millionaire his uncle's attitude towards money was tinged by the memories of his poverty.

It was in 1913, when Willie was thirty-nine years old, that he met Syrie, the daughter of the well-known philanthropist Dr. Thomas Barnardo, and still married to Henry (later Sir Henry) Wellcome, of the firm of Burroughs, Wellcome, the chemists. She was smart, pretty and vivacious. Willie married Syrie in 1916. But, quite apart from the obvious incompatibility of temperaments, the marriage was bound to have failed—because even before he married Syrie, Willie had met Gerald.

*   *   *

Willie was now dependent on Gerald, not only for the smooth running of his house and the typing of his books and for the gaiety which Gerald enthused into every party, but also—it was now obvious to me—he depended on Gerald to produce young boys who could creep into the Mauresque by the back door and sleep with him.

Gerald was Willie's pander; Willie was rich enough to keep him. The villain of the piece, I now decided, was the capitalist system. My present grief had arisen because I had accepted as being natural the fact that a boy could be produced for me—as it were—on a platter. But I was now less certain of my inclinations; and I decided that in all honesty I must warn Gillian—if I could manage to do so—with gentleness and tact, of the fact that my character was too unstable for marriage. The letter I wrote now seems pathetically naïve, but I quote part of it—with Gillian's permission—because it shows my outlook at that time.

> Life here [I wrote] is incredibly different to anything I've known. I am appalled by the blatant rich I see every day who complain about the income tax, and are entirely selfish, sour, and petty, but very amusing—I give them that. Socialism they regard as the idiot's ideal. The poor are always with us, they say, and they're a crashing bore. One has got to stop them starving but beyond that there's no need to worry so long as they don't get above themselves. That is their attitude. An income of two thousand pounds a year is regarded as ridiculously small and impossible to live on. My God! Is it possible?

> I've come to the conclusion, darling, that I must never marry—but it's all right because by the time we're thirty it will be considered *comme il faut* to live in sin. So—if you are willing—when we're raddled creatures of thirty we'll live in ROARING sin!!!

Over thirty years later, Gillian told me that it was this letter which convinced her that our relationship could not last.

I returned to England, and as soon as I saw Gillian I realised that I had made a mistake in having an affair with Laurent. I still loved her. I went back to Cambridge determined once again to be normal and to work hard. I found I could interest myself in the Law of Tort and the Law of Contract, but I found difficulties in remembering Roman Law and Equity and Real Property because they bored me so much. However, I managed to enjoy myself. I was sad to leave Cambridge in June 1937.

*   *   *

I now lived in my room on the fifth floor of my parents' house in Cadogan Square. Each morning I would get up at seven thirty and take the underground from Sloane Square to the Temple and walk to the Law crammers where I spent the day. I felt it a mistake that I was leading such a sad existence, for a world war seemed to be approaching in which my friends and I would probably be killed. Only occasionally did I get a glimpse of the kind of life I wanted. For instance, Willie gave a dinner at the Garrick Club to which he invited me. Round the table were Osbert Sitwell, E. M. Forster, and Christopher Isherwood. Because I was so excited I sparkled and told amusing stories about Cambridge: I still have the postcard that Christopher Isherwood sent me saying, "Seldom have I laughed so much." On another occasion I was invited to dine with Osbert Sitwell. Unfortunately Rex Whistler, who was as Tory as I was Socialist, began an argument about the slums which grew quite bitter. In the drawing-room afterwards Osbert took my arm and led me apart to a small chair and made me sit down beside him.

"All you say is correct," he said quietly. "But I'm afraid you have ruined my dinner-party."

A few years later when Harold Nicolson introduced me to Guy Burgess I told him this story. Guy Burgess snorted with scorn. "You were right," he said. "You were completely right. But *now* you're sorry that you spoiled the party, aren't you? And I'll tell you why. It's because the Mandarins of the Establishment have got hold of you and poisoned your mind."

*   *   *

My parents now arranged for me to leave London as a judge's marshal to Mr. Justice Macnaghten. A judge's marshal—a relic of the past—is an official accompanying a judge on circuit, with secretarial duties. I got paid two guineas a day. My parents made a bargain with me. They said that I could spend all that I made on a journey abroad before I settled down as a lawyer.

Mr. Justice Macnaghten was a kind, bluff, honest man, liked by everyone who knew him. He was past middle age, and he had the disconcerting habit of falling asleep while he himself was addressing the court. On one occasion there was a case involving the insurance of a car, which had dragged on for three days. It was warm in court. I could see that my judge in his summing-up was growing sleepy. As marshal, I sat on the raised dais a few paces away from him. I prepared myself to move quickly.

"And there was the defendant in the car," Macnaghten continued drowsily, "with the father, the son, and the Hol . . ."—and at that moment I tapped him gently on the arm—"with the whole of the rest of the family," he concluded triumphantly.

Though kind, his sentences were sometimes severe. So on the pretext that I had never been inside a prison, I arranged for us to visit a local jail. The grimness of the cells and the pervading atmosphere of misery made a deep impression on him. On each occasion that I persuaded him to visit a prison, his sentences would be far lighter the following day.

As judge's marshal I could read the depositions before a case came on; I could therefore foresee the arguments which the police would put forward in prosecution. There were many cases—such as a boy of sixteen being prosecuted because he had had a girl of fourteen—in which my sympathy lay completely with the accused in the dock. On these occasions, I developed a technique for dealing with the detective who was going to give evidence against the accused. I had to administer the oath. Grimly, dressed in my dark tail-suit, I would advance towards the smug-looking detective. Grimly, I would point to the Bible lying in front of him in the witness-box.

"Take the book in your right hand," I would begin. "And repeat after me . . . *Right* hand," I would say before the detective had moved—and with any luck he would take it in his left. When he had got his hands arranged, he would then gabble the oath. "And repeat *after me*," I would say softly. I would then begin, "I swear to tell the truth, the whole truth *and nothing but the truth*." I would then nod my head significantly towards the jury. They would get the message and disbelieve the detective. With this ploy the accused would often be acquitted.

*   *   *

The money I had made as a judge's marshal was increased by a present from my mother. I decided to take a cargo boat to Mexico.

This is not a book of travel, so I will not write about my journey to Mexico and thence to San Francisco and Los Angeles. But the months I spent abroad gave me my first taste of complete freedom, and I rejoiced in it. I dreaded coming home.

By the time I returned, my father had been made Lord Chancellor of England, and war with Germany had come closer. When my father echoed the words of the Prime Minister, Neville Chamberlain, 'Peace in our time', I realised that there was no hope. War, I now felt convinced, was inevitable—because my father, though a brilliant lawyer, had been wrong in every political prognostication he had ever made. Moreover, Jane Forbes, who was one of the closest of my sisters' friends and who'd been my friend ever since she'd washed me in the bath at the age of six, had information which made her so certain that war was imminent that she had already made plans for women to serve in the A. T. S. and the W.A.A.F.—the Auxiliary Territorial Service and the Women's Auxiliary Air Force.

One evening after my Law classes I went to Lincoln's Inn to join up in the ranks of the Inns of Court Regiment. I was already late for a cocktail party, and I was dismayed when I saw a long queue of people waiting. "Perhaps," I thought to myself, "there may be some other queue round the corner." Sure enough there was. And round that corner there was an even shorter queue of three or four people who entered the building as I approached. I followed them. I was told to take off all my clothes. I took an eyesight-test stark naked; I was then briskly examined. Then I signed some document, was given a shilling, and went out.

As I emerged, a friend came up to me. "I never knew that you were interested in tanks," he said.

"I'm not," I replied.

"Well, you've joined up in the tank section of our regiment," he answered.

So there it was.

Meanwhile I continued with my visits to the East End, and I plodded on with my Law studies.

The Tories in those days represented to my mind the devil undisguised, and Neville Chamberlain was Lucifer incarnate. When Lucifer came to lunch with my family at Cadogan Square shortly after my father had taken his seat in the House of Lords, I glowered in resentful silence over the Dover sole and lamb cutlets, and bided my time. My opportunity came over the *crème brûlée*. Poor Mr. Chamberlain, noticing my concentrated silence, put some polite and trivial question to me about students and politics. I looked at my father, the newly made peer of the realm, straight in the face.

"Speaking as a member of the middle class," I began with slow deliberation. But before I got any further, my father had popped his monocle into his eye.

"Speak for yourself," he said firmly.

*   *   *

Through my sister Kate, who lived with her wonderfully hospitable husband Robert Bruce at 79 Cadogan Square, I had met various literary figures. One evening, I remember, Gillian and I were sitting on the carpet by the sofa while Hugh Walpole was discoursing. Suddenly he looked towards us both. "Nothing," he said, "nothing in life is more beautiful and touching than to see a young man and a young girl who are in love with each other."

"Nonsense, Hugh," said H. G. Wells in his high-pitched squeaky voice. "Every properly constituted young man wants to hop into bed with every properly constituted young girl—and that's the end of it."

Through Kate I had also made friends over the years with Humbert Wolfe and his friend Pamela Frankau. Humbert was one of the cleverest men I've ever met. While staying with us at Tye he would take up *The Times* and complete the crossword puzzle within five minutes and I didn't believe those who said he could accomplish this feat only because he set the puzzles himself. He was also splendidly witty. I will give only one example. Leon M. Lion, the impresario, was leaving Kate's house after a cocktail party. Leon was extremely courtly in a pompous, old-fashioned way; he was also very fond of drink. At the door, he inclined himself in a dignified manner and kissed Kate's hand.

"Gracious lady," he mumbled, "never have I enjoyed a cocktail so much."

"What you mean," said Humbert who was standing by, "*is* that you have never enjoyed a cocktail so *often*."

Humbert and Pamela were indeed a wonderful couple and I basked in the light of their friendship.

In April 1939 Humbert, who led a dual existence as a poet and as Permanent Under-Secretary at the Ministry of Labour, suggested that I should become private secretary to Sir Herbert Morgan who had just been appointed Director of the National Service Campaign. I was delighted by the idea. My parents had no objections. I began to work in the Ministry of Labour building with Sir Herbert Morgan of whom I became very fond. Red-faced, imaginative, convivial, and over-addicted to kümmel, his vision and vitality soon made an impact on the country. But his ruthless energy made him enemies. He was finally asked to resign after he had unfortunately mispronounced the word 'Aldershot' several times in a public speech.

But National Service, I soon realised, was being stifled by the incompetence of the top office and slowed down by the red tape in the various ministries concerned with it. After a few months I wrote a memorandum on the subject.[2] My memorandum had a success. Soon

[2] For the full text of my National Service Memorandum see Appendix II.

it was suggested that the full inside story of the incompetence in Whitehall should be told to a politician who could be guaranteed not to make it a party issue and who could be relied upon to appreciate the seriousness of our poor recruiting figures. The man chosen was Mr. Winston Churchill, then being, as he was to term it later, 'in the wilderness', suspected by many, admired in those days by only a few.

Shortly before I was to drive over to Chartwell for my first meeting with Mr. Churchill, my father, speaking as Lord Chancellor, made a violent attack on Churchill in a speech at the Constitutional Club. Politicians such as Churchill, my father said, who advocated war against Germany without considering the probable results 'ought to be either shot or hanged'. As I drove down to our country house, I read Churchill's reply in the evening papers. "The Lord Chancellor," said Churchill, had used "language which savours of lynch law and mob law abhorrent equally to the British character and Constitution."

I realised that my father was not going to be at all pleased if he learned that on Sunday I was going to have tea with his adversary who said his language savoured of 'lynch law and mob law', so I decided to say nothing about it.

"I intend to play golf this afternoon," my father said to me at lunch on Sunday. "Are you coming?"

I dreaded games of golf with my father—and so probably did he. I became so nervous when he tried to teach me how to swing my club that at each hole I would slice the ball into dense gorse and lose it, and such extravagances annoyed my father.

"I'm afraid I can't play golf this afternoon," I said.

"And why not?"

"I'm going out for tea."

"Are you?" said my mother in surprise. "You never told me."

"No, I didn't," I mumbled.

"And may we enquire with whom you're going to tea?" my father asked.

"I don't see why not," I muttered stupidly.

"What was that? I fear I didn't quite catch what you said."

"Yes, you may enquire," I answered, rigid with embarrassment.

"Then with whom are you having tea?" my father demanded.

"With Mr. Winston Churchill," I said.

Slowly my father fumbled for his monocle and put it up to his eye. He gazed at me sadly.

"Well," he said, after a long pause, "there is no accounting for tastes."

The monocle fell from his eye and he relapsed into silence.

I arrived punctually at Chartwell at half past three, and I was shown into Churchill's study where he sat smoking a cigar with a soda siphon on one side of him and a bottle of whisky on the other.

"Have some whisky," he suggested. "We'll have tea later."

I gave him a copy of my memorandum, sipped my drink cautiously and told him the secret problems of the National Service Campaign. He listened intently.

"You need have no worries," he said when I had finished. "Within a few months now, this country will be at war, and every man who can lift a rifle will be in the fighting services, and every woman who can lift a weight will be in the munition factories. However, when you have matters of interest—as, indeed, you had today—to convey to me, please do not hesitate. Come to see me immediately . . . And now I shall help myself to another drink . . . and then we may see about tea."

Little did I know then how important his invitation was to become in my life.

It was on that afternoon that I met Mary Churchill for the first time. Though she was only a girl, her quality of charm and vitality was as contagious as that of her father, and she was extremely attractive.

As I drove away from Chartwell, suddenly Mr. Churchill appeared at an upper window of the house. He seemed to be declaiming some speech. I had already said goodbye and the car had begun to drive away, so that his words may well have become inaudible—or perhaps as a result of my later head injury I have forgotten them. But in my mind I see him clearly, his hand uplifted at the window. Now in my memory, which I know must be at fault, I can only recollect that splendid voice, booming out from above the window-sill:

. . . we shall not flag or fail. We shall go on to the end . . . whatever the cost may be. We shall fight on the beaches . . . we shall fight in the fields and in the streets; we shall fight in the hills; we shall never surrender; and even if, which I do not for a moment believe, this Island or a large part of it were subjugated and starving, then our Empire beyond the seas, armed and guarded by the British Fleet, would carry on the struggle, until, in God's good time, the New World, with all its power and might, steps forth to the rescue and liberation of the Old.

PART

THREE

WAR WAS DECLARED ON SEPTEMBER 3rd, 1939. MY FATHER resigned as Lord Chancellor and was made a viscount. The Inns of Court Regiment moved to Sandhurst and was affiliated with the officer-cadets. My mother drove with me to Waterloo Station. Our chauffeur, King, helped to hoist my enormous kit-bag on to my shoulders. I kissed my mother goodbye.

As a trooper in the Inns of Court Regiment I wore a tight tunic with shining brass buttons and a gleaming leather bandolier. After my responsibilities as Sir Herbert Morgan's private secretary I found that being a soldier was tough, but delightfully carefree—especially during those early months when the war seemed so far away. Gillian had joined the A.T.S.; we could meet only occasionally. Meanwhile I was making friends not only with the men in my regiment—mostly young lawyers—but with Sandhurst cadets who were as young and attractive as Drew when he was at Eton and as Laurent on the yacht at Villefranche.

Meanwhile the so-called 'Phoney War' had begun.

As troopers, we were sternly drilled on the parade ground of Sandhurst. We were taught to fire a rifle, and we drove out in lorries for Tactical Exercises Without Troops, known as T.E.W.T.s, in which we were explained 'on the ground' the basic principles of tank warfare.

From these exercises we drove back happily, singing bawdy songs that I've never forgotten. In December the troop I was in, consisting partly of members of the Inns of Court Regiment and partly of cadets, was sent to Bovington for training in tanks. The winter was bitterly cold, and we lived in huts which had been condemned as unfit for human habitation in 1910. Many of the instructors had been in the Tank Corps for twenty years or more. One of the sergeant-instructors, in a pub one night, took me to an upstairs room which, he told me, he 'rented occasionally'. He produced half a bottle of rum from his pocket and we drank it. He drew his chair closer to mine and became more confidential. He now told me a story which at the time I disbelieved but which has since been partially confirmed. When Colonel T. E. Lawrence was at Bovington under the pseudonym of Shaw, he had made friends with the instructor—who was then a lance-corporal. T. E. Lawrence had rented the very room in which we now sat. One evening he had invited the lance-corporal to drink with him. He had then persuaded the lance-corporal to whip him and then to penetrate him. As he gave me the unpleasant details of the evening he had spent with Lawrence, the sergeant-instructor became visibly excited. Soon he was stroking my thigh. It was difficult to get out of the room without offending him.

A homosexual atmosphere seemed to hang as heavily over Bovington as the low rain-clouds in the sky. The damp and the cold were our mutual enemies. The hospital was full of men with pneumonia. Occasionally we would get a weekend leave, and I would drive with my friends to a small hotel in Bournemouth. For a while we could forget the discomfort we had endured.

*   *   *

Though I found it a frightening experience to drive a tank over the obstacle course, I passed with high marks out of Bovington. This pleased me because we all knew that we were being trained to become officers, but I was secretly afraid of my own incompetence to lead a troop of tanks into action.

After we had finished a course of tank gunnery at Lulworth, we returned to Sandhurst which seemed a haven of comfort after the hardships we had known.

*   *   *

On February 29th, 1940, I was invited by Mary Churchill to her 'coming-out' dinner dance at the Queen Charlotte Ball. I turned up at the portals of a famous hotel in London with a twenty-four-hour leave pass.

Half way across the foyer I was stopped by a tall man in a livery. "Are you a trooper?" he asked.

"Yes," I replied proudly.

He pointed to a large printed notice which proclaimed that the hotel was out of bounds to 'other ranks'.

"Can you read?" he asked.

"Yes," I answered pleasantly. "Can you?"

"Then cut out the funny business and clear out, or I'll call the Military Police," he said.

Up to that moment I was still moving across the foyer. I now stopped and faced the tall man.

"I wish to speak to the hotel manager," I said. "Here and now."

"If you want trouble, you're asking for it," the tall man assured me.

"For the moment I'm only asking for the hotel manager," I pointed out.

At that instant we were joined by a heavily jowled, shiny-faced, stout man who looked so unmistakably, so indelibly, a hotel manager that one felt he must have worn a tail-coat at his own christening.

"Now then," he began smoothly, "what's all the trouble about?"

Quickly and tersely I told him—adding my views about the monstrousness of reserving hotels only for officers in a war for democracy. Meanwhile I edged closer to the ballroom.

"We'll have to see about this," the heavily-built manager announced, with a flick of his eyes towards his minion.

"You will," I said. At that moment I brushed him aside and flung open the doors of the ballroom. A dance had just finished, and I marched across the floor to the Churchills' table. As I advanced, Mr. Winston Churchill, then First Lord of the Admiralty, moved forward to greet me. A few minutes later I was dancing with Mrs. Churchill. As we passed by the manager, I hoped he would at least have the courage to glower. But he gave me a rather uncertain smile.

*　　*　　*

Colonels of various distinguished regiments began to come down to Sandhurst to interview us with regard to our future commissions as officers. One of them to appear at Sandhurst was General Courage, Colonel of the 15th/19th Hussars—a regiment which we were advised to join. I arrived for the interview with my buttons shining like the sun and my bandolier glowing like burnished gold. I gave him a splendid salute and stood rigidly to attention. He was a pleasant, red-faced man, whose chest was covered with medal-ribbons.

"Now stand at ease, and stand easy," he said in a benevolent voice.

"I've got a few questions to ask you, and I can promise you they'll all be treated as entirely confidential."

As he spoke, I could not help looking down at the sheet of paper lying on his desk in front of him. On the top of it was written, 'Mark out of ten'.

"Now then," said the general, "the first question is: 'What's your handicap at polo?'"

"I don't play polo, sir," I answered.

Covertly the general wrote down a large *nought*.

"What games did you play for your school?" he now asked.

"I didn't play any, sir," I replied.

Again the general's hand traced the outline of a *nought*.

"What *was* your school?" he asked.

"Eton, sir," I replied.

The general's face brightened and he wrote down firmly, *ten*.

"What's your income?" he enquired.

By this time I felt the 15th/19th Hussars was not the regiment for me.

"A hundred pounds, sir," I answered.

"A week?" he asked.

"No, sir," I replied. "A year."

The general lowered his head in embarrassment and again wrote down a *nought*.

"What's your father doing at this moment?" he asked.

"He's a Lord of Appeal," I said.

Swiftly the general wrote down *ten*—and that was the end of the interview.

Later I heard that I'd been accepted for the 15th/19th Hussars, but two of my closest friends at Sandhurst hadn't. So I declined my commission in that regiment and joined the 4th County of London Yeomanry —the Sharpshooters—who were then stationed in the Midlands at Worksop.

*   *   *

There followed an intense period of training. I was very conscious of my incompetence as an officer. I was sad to have left my young friends at Sandhurst. I was cheered only by the Corps demonstrations which took place once a fortnight at some carefully chosen spot on the map, and at which one was certain to meet old friends.

The first demonstration was to prove the fording capacity of the new Crusader Mark Five tanks. We all stood on the banks of a very small river—almost a stream. When the brigadier dropped his handkerchief as a signal, the tank chosen for the demonstration surged forward promptly, towards the river, snorting and belching smoke, reached the river's bank, toppled forward and then disappeared completely from view. Bubbles arose from the murky water—and so presently did the four bedraggled members of the crew.

"Now *that*," said our brigadier—a man of determination—"that, if I may say so, was a demonstration of exactly how *not* to cross a river. *Far* more speed is required. Mr. Jenkins will now show you exactly how it should be done."

We all turned and looked at the subaltern in charge of the second tank. His face was ashen with fear. Once again the brigadier dropped his handkerchief. This time the tank rushed forward like a wild rhinoceros. It reached the bank of the river at high speed, plunged into it, nose downward, and was at once lost to view. The four members of the crew were rescued; the demonstration was cancelled for the day.

The second demonstration was to show us how to use a mobile bridge. This exercise was even less successful than the previous one because the mobile bridge got stuck in a lane twenty miles away from our meeting place. So once again our instruction was cancelled. However, at the third demonstration, the mobile bridge, which had been towed there several days previously, was already in position. Once again, the brigadier dropped his handkerchief. Immediately the huge machine gave a groan and a roar, and began to shudder. Slowly from out of it appeared two thick rails which rose trembling into the air. Higher and higher these two rails ascended, quivering each moment more alarmingly, until finally—instead of falling forward across the narrow river—they fell backwards on to the spectators. There were no further demonstrations.

By now France had been invaded, and my fellow subalterns and I were convinced that the British Army was so hopelessly inefficient that we were almost certain to lose the war. It became a patriotic duty to drink as much vintage port as we could swallow in order to prevent it falling down enemy gullets.

In the darkness of night, the regiment was now moved south. We drove our tanks on to flat railway wagons. We were stationed at Rudgwick in Sussex and allotted a long strip of coastline to defend against possible invasion.

At the height of the invasion scare in July 1940, I was asked to lunch at Chequers. (Churchill had become Prime Minister in May 1940.) Throughout the war, Churchill was always more interested in talking to junior officers than the top brass—partly from pure kindness, partly from his knowledge that it was from the men in the field that he could discover what was really going on. So half way through lunch he turned to me.

"Tell me about your regiment," he said. "Is your morale high?"

"Very high," I answered, thinking of the vintage port.

"And could you advance in your tanks from your positions on the Sussex Downs and repel Herr Hitler's forces on whatever beach they might land?"

"No," I replied.

Churchill stared at me with angry, glaucous eyes. "You couldn't?" he said. "Why not?"

"Because if Hitler invaded this afternoon, not one of our tanks could move," I answered.

For a moment there was a complete silence. Then Churchill thumped the table. "Why couldn't they move?" he demanded.

Opposite me, Professor Lindemann, Churchill's scientific adviser, was wagging his finger at me in secret warning, his face grim with disapproval. But I didn't care. I only wanted Churchill to know the truth.

"You practically invented tanks," I said to Churchill, "so you are aware, sir, that the trackplates are held together by trackpins."

"I know that, indeed," Churchill said, nodding his head.

"Those pins are kept from slipping out of position by small springs at the end of them."

"Yes, indeed."

"Those small springs can only cost a penny to produce—if that."

"You may well be right. I would say a farthing. But pray continue."

"Well, sir," I said, leaning back in my chair, "cost they a penny or cost they a farthing, we haven't got a single one of them in our regiment. So our tanks can't move."

The explosion came from Churchill with a low roar of anger. The table shook. Private secretaries were sent scurrying to telephones. The lunch-party was ruined. Lindemann glared at me with loathing. But by nightfall my regiment had got the springs for our trackpins.

*   *   *

In August 1940 the whole of the 22nd Armoured Brigade, of which we formed a part, was sent to the Middle East.

Most of the other ranks in the Sharpshooters were volunteers from banks, restaurants, shops, solicitors' firms: they were town people used to the comfort of their homes. If they had travelled to Egypt before the war, they would have gone as tourists. Now, in this ship, in the convoy, six hundred of them were sweating in their hammocks deep down below. They were not allowed above during the hours of black-out in the danger zone, for fear they would shine torches or strike matches. Their hammocks were slung close together; the ship was not built for tropical cruises, and there were few ventilators. As you climbed perilously down the hatchway, a hot blast of smelly air rose up to meet you. You were engulfed in a great nausea of sweat and vomit and oil and heat. Apart from the periods when they were allowed up on deck, the men lived and ate and slept and sweated in the hold, which had contained German and Italian prisoners of war on the recent trip to England. And we all knew now that we were in for a long voyage, because the convoy was heading south down the west coast of Africa. The odds were two to one on Suez for our port of disembarkation.

*　　*　　*

During the train journey from Suez to Ameriya we stared out of the window at the land of Egypt: first at the great stretches of desert now broken by long escarpments moulded into strange shapes by eternal winds, now running flat until the desert was lost in the horizon; then at the dramatic green of the delta. When the train stopped, hoards of clamouring boys rushed forward to sell bananas, oranges, fountain-pens, chocolate or dirty postcards. Diseased beggars whined for money ; blind, naked children were pushed aside into the dust, where they lay wailing piteously. Aggressive men waved their wares in the carriage window and shouted. It is sad that soldiers always saw the dregs of the Middle East, and seldom met the best; the bedouin, the fellahin of Upper Egypt, the Arab chiefs, the educated students. Our men were amazed.
"Like a lot of monkeys."
"Fuck off, you nasty old man."
"If this is Egypt, give me Brighton any day."
"Look what that boy's doing."
"Put it away, you dirty brute."
At Ameriya, lorries met the train to take us out to the camp we had been allotted. We had imagined canteens and a Naafi and huts to sleep in; or at worst, tents. In the blinding glare of the afternoon, we were driven out in the desert by a guide from brigade until we reached a barren stretch of sand where he stopped.
"Where's the camp?"
"Here."
"Where are the tents?"
"In bundles by that cairn. You put them up yourselves."
At that moment a wind stirred up the sand which, surging over the desert, swept across the camp in a blinding storm. We rallied the men

and struggled towards the cairn to collect the tents. I stumbled over something hard. I found it was part of a heap of officers' luggage. For a moment I watched the sand swirling round the trunk I had last seen lying on the carpet at home in London. Then I stumbled on towards the cairn. Sand stung our faces and hands and knees. Sand crept into our nostrils and into our mouths, grinding between our teeth. The sandstorm was our baptism to the desert. From now onward we were to live with sand. It would spread a gritty powder over food and drink, it would matt our hair, it would line our clothes and stick to the warmest parts of our bodies.

*   *   *

We thought that our tanks would for ever be our home and refuge, so we equipped them above the standard laid down with such extras as outside lockers, steps for mounting, inside containers for thermos flasks, straps and general additional fixtures. We were given good opportunity to get into Alex to purchase tinned foodstuffs, torches, cigarettes, stores, lamps, flea-bags and so on. For such purposes my troop started a fund which was subscribed to at my request 'from each according to his means'. Every item, military and private, was carefully checked and rechecked on each tank.

A few days later we packed up all our heavy kit, which was collected by lorries and taken into Alex. Officers were allowed to keep one small suitcase to be stowed on the mess truck. From then onwards the regiment was operational, and we slept by our tanks.

A driver, a gunner, a wireless-operator and a tank commander formed the complement of a Crusader. Three tanks made a troop. Six spare men travelled on the regiment's main supply lorries which were known as B echelon; the small group of lorries moving between B echelon and the tanks was called A echelon. The troop leader had three tanks and seventeen men under his command. He was directly responsible to his squadron leader for his men's welfare and efficiency. His men belonged to him and to no one else. He was at once their father, their commander and their friend.

Arranging tank crews is a tricky business. They are confined close together all day in the tank, and very close all night in their 'bivvy'. Sometimes a couple shares the same flea-bag. It is essential they should all be fond of each other, or at least be good-humouredly tolerant of each other. During a campaign your life is spent entirely with your tank crew. You eat, sleep and fight with them. You've never lived in such close proximity with three other men before. If there is no harmony, no affection, small quarrels and grievances begin; and these

122

become grossly magnified in the confined existence. Animal instincts are sharpened by such conditions; like animals some crews will never shake down well together. The ordinary man is not governed by reason; his feelings are not controlled by his mind, but by strange instincts he cannot understand. Some men will never like each other. Sensual affection, a sense of humour and a warm sentimentality provide the balm which soothes the irritations and smarts of everyday contact.

* * *

On November 18th we advanced to close with the Axis armour. A great wave of tanks surged forward, leaving long clouds of sand streaming in their wake. The following afternoon, in the distance, we could see a long line of transport stretching for perhaps three miles. We were ordered to advance. The moment I had been looking forward to, and yet dreading terribly for two years, had come at last. We were going into action.

"This is it, ahead of us now," I told my crew down the Tannoy mike. We drew nearer. Suddenly the quiet stretch of sand became a torment of shells, bullets, smoke and dust. Simultaneously tanks appeared from behind the transport and opened up on us. Then I realised that behind those harmless-looking lorries lay concealed big guns; and the Italian tanks were crawling out towards us.

That moment has seared itself into my memory so that sometimes in a dream I live again each instant of it. I can smell the smoke and feel the fat grip of the Tannoy between my hands. My mouth feels dry as I press the button to speak.

"Driver, halt. Two-pounder, six hundred. Traverse right, traverse right. Steady. On. Iti tank. Fire."

The gun recoils with a deafening crack, followed by a click as the empty round falls into the deflector bag. I watch the tracer soar across the desert.

"Right, and plus. Same target. Fire. Got it. Got it. Jolly good. Driver, advance left. O.K. Two-pounder, traverse right, traverse right. Steady . . ."

As the battle rages over the stretch of sand round Bir Gubi, this is what is happening inside our Crusader tank. Down in the front of the tank the driver is hunched up in his narrow compartment. Headphones are clamped tight to his ears so that he can hear my commands down the Tannoy above the roar of the engine. Between his legs are two thick levers. When he pulls the right lever a stream of compressed air pushes out a clutch between the engine and the right track so that the left track churns round faster, and the tank crawls to the right. The driver is peering through a slit in front of him in the steel wall which surrounds him. The slit is filled with a glass block four inches thick, and through it he can see dimly a narrow strip of sand ahead of him. He is blind on the left side because of the auxiliary turret. Now and then a shell smashes against the armour-plating in front of his body with such force that fittings inside his compartment crash in on him. He sincerely hopes that if anyone is hit, it won't be himself, because he reckons that so long as the tank can move there is always hope; but if he is done for, it would be some time before they could get the tank moving again.

In the turret three men are pressed close together. I stand in the centre with my head half out of the turret so that I can see what is going on all around me. If I crouch down into the turret I can look through the commander's periscope but my vision is limited, and I must be able to see all round so that I can conform with the rest of the squadron. Binoculars, the Tannoy and the wireless mike hang down from straps round my neck. I must be careful where I put my hands because the two-pounder in front of me recoils to within six inches of my stomach; I must keep my hands away from the recoil cage. If the gun's run-out has not been properly maintained it will recoil through my belly. Every man in a tank crew trusts the others with his life.

The wireless-operator, crouched close to my right thigh, is loading the two-pounder for all he is worth. He flicks in the shell expertly with his right hand so that the rim of the shell presses back two springs which let the breech-block fly back into position. When the gun is loaded he taps the gunner by crooking his left hand under the recoil cage. All the time he must be listening to the wireless and keeping it tuned. He cannot see anything that is going on outside the tank; he can only guess what is happening outside by listening to the wireless and to fire orders. But he knows when they have got our range by the rocking of the tank and the blast as a shell strikes the plating outside. He stoops to pluck up three two-pounder rounds at a time from the base of the turret, which he can hardly see for fumes of cordite. He flicks one into the breech, taps the gunner, and balances the other two on his knees. When these two rounds have been pushed in turn into the gun, he stoops down again.

The gunner's forehead is pressed tight against a padded bracket, placed so that his eye can look steadily through the telescope at the small circle of desert to which it is focussed. A leather-bound grip is clamped tightly round his left shoulder and under his armpit, and by moving his shoulder up or down he can elevate or depress the gun. His left hand grips the power-traverse lever; by turning his wrist he can move the turret left or right. His right hand grips the trigger handles. A tap on his right elbow tells him that the guns are loaded. He hears my fire orders on the Tannoy through his head-phones: "Two-pounder." His hand shifts from the Besa to the two-pounder trigger.

"Six hundred." He sets the range on his telescope.

"Traverse right." His wrist turns over to the right, and with a hiss of air the turret begins to turn round.

"Traverse right." His wrist turns over more to the right, and the turret screams round faster.

"Steady." His wrist turns back a little, and the turret moves very slowly. His eye is seeking out for the target in the small circle of desert it can see through the telescope.

"On." He can see a black tank with its gun pointed towards him.

"Iti tank." Yes, this is the target. He aligns the cross-wires of his telescope on the target, aiming off according to range, direction and speed of the tank and the wind.

"Fire." His right-hand fingers squeeze the trigger. Our tank is shaken with a great spasm. The smell of cordite fills the turret. The tracer soars into his vision and flies up as it strikes the Italian tank.

All four of us are slaves to the gun, shut up in the steel box on tracks which carries the weapon towards the enemy.

Those square boxes six hundred yards away are Italian tanks. I can see the flash as they fire at us, and then I hear the explosion.

"Traverse left. Traverse left. Steady on."

Got him. But he's still firing. Give it him again.

"Same target. Fire."

He's burning. He's burning. We got him.

"Driver, right. Move right."

God, that one nearly got us. Too busy looking at the target. I didn't spot them.

"Traverse left. Quick. Traverse left. Steady on . . ."

There are too many of them. At any moment we're going to be fucked. I'm not frightened. My voice sounds all right. I wish this smoke would clear away so that one could see more that is going on. C Squadron were in reserve, weren't they? That must be them charging in from the east. They're moving flat out. Good luck to them.

"Traverse left. Steady. On. Tank. Fire."

The blast from the two-pounder when your head is half in and half out is deafening. Put your head down next time just before you say fire. Shells are bursting all around us. How long do we have to stay in this

125

noise? It's those big guns behind the lorries. You can hear the shell whining towards you, and then as it lands the desert erupts into a towering cloud of sand and smoke.

*   *   *

The whole of our brigade had advanced under conditions of the greatest secrecy. Our tanks had been disguised as lorries. And then we had driven straight into the one prepared booby-trap in the Western Desert. In that battle we lost a third of our strength. We reformed; we were supplied with more tanks. We now advanced again. The fight between the Axis and the Allied troops in North Africa resembled two men fencing in a courtyard with their left hands bound to elastic bands attached to opposite sides of the courtyard. One man could drive his opponent three-quarters of the way across the courtyard, but he could advance no farther because the elastic band was stretched to the limit. Then his enemy leapt forward in turn until the band attached to his left arm could stretch no farther. The vital supply lines in the desert conditioned the speed of an advance and the time an advance could be sustained.

*   *   *

I hated the discomfort and danger of warfare in the Western Desert, but at least for a while I was rid of the two shadows of my father and Willie.

*   *   *

Imperceptibly mind and body change to endure life in the desert. Clerkly boys from snug homes in English towns were learning to live in burning heat, and with sand and sores in the desert where man in all things lived candidly with man. Twenty years hence those survivors would have learned again to depend on the cinema round the corner, television, water-closets, pop music and refrigerators, and to be careless of the welfare of the man next door. But now in bivouacs dotted round the desert, lean, sunburned men were drinking their evening brew and preparing to sleep. For instance, in one bivouac a commercial traveller, a bank clerk, a miner, a mechanic and a shop assistant might have settled down for a chat before turning in. The bivouac was made from a tank tarpaulin stretched out to form the sides and top of a low tent about three feet high. The sides were supported by wireless poles and a disused lorry hoop was placed over a dug-out two or three feet deep, so that they slept below ground level which kept out cold and sand. By day one side was left open. They got in at night by crawling under the tarpaulin to avoid showing a light outside, and slept stretched out

126

in one long row. The bivvy was lit by an oil lamp. There was very little room to move.

In one such bivouac, after a riotous leave in Cairo, when we were on our way back to the front which was known as the 'sharp-end', I was lying close to Nobby, the driver of the scout-car I used now that I had been appointed the regiment's Intelligence Officer. Nobby was slim and fair-haired. He reminded me of Laurent. Presently Nobby moved. He knelt in the sand behind me and lowered my head on to his lap. With the back of my head, I suddenly felt that he had a stiff erection.

"It's all right, sir," he whispered.

*　　*　　*

During the first campaign, I had been convinced that I would neither be killed nor wounded. For this reason I had managed to remain fairly calm and controlled. I could look forward to the future and therefore I could resist the temptations that sometimes came when I was sharing a two-man bivouac with a boy in my crew. But now—during this second campaign—I had a strange presentiment that I would be killed or very badly wounded. So I was prepared to spend the night with Nobby.

I was at brigade H.Q. when the shell landed that killed Nobby as he lay sprawled asleep in the sand.

*　　*　　*

On May 26th, 1942, the disastrous tank battle started which led to the Eighth Army's retreat to the El Alamein position. On the second day began what was known as the Battle of Knightsbridge. It took place near a disused well marked by a mound of stones which had been christened Knightsbridge. By noon the heat was so strong we could scarcely breathe. Light cotton shirts and shorts were black with sweat and clung to the body like a thin, wet bathing-dress. Sweat streamed down chest and back, to form a sticky ring round the waist where the shirt met the belt of the shorts. Gusts of desire excited our bodies, and then were forgotten in the dominant craving for water. Rigid self-control was required to stop a man putting his lips to his water-bottle. At noon, if we had no chance to brew up tea, which made a pint of water take far longer to drink, we would allow ourselves a few longed-for sips; but it was only to discover once more that the stale, chlorinated water from our bottles was hot and nauseating. Heat and thirst tortured us like a constant pain, which might only be forgotten by a determined act of will, or by the piercing agony of fear. And as I waited in my scout-car I could think only of my fear; for I was afraid now almost all the time because I was certain that something was waiting for me, though I could not tell its shape. Yet I would not resign myself to this horror, and I moved the scout-car from one piece of sand to another when I felt danger in the ground. Once a shell landed on the spot I had just left.

I stood by the side of the scout-car watching the enemy position through my binoculars. The enemy replied to our registration; shells began to fall heavily. Each shell seemed to whine towards us for a long time before it fell, and the earth vomited clouds of smoky sand. The attack would go in now at any moment. Suddenly a great crash burst in my ears. Something hit me in the chest and knocked me down. I stood up and got into the scout-car. Blood was pouring from my chest. I thought a piece must have gone in. For a moment I was stunned. I felt the scout-car moving along and gathering speed. Gradually I recovered. I looked down at my chest. It was rather a mess, but the bleeding had stopped. I wiped it with my handkerchief. Then I saw from the livid mark round the gore that I had been hit by a flat piece of shrapnel which had knocked me down but not penetrated. However, I was ordered back to A echelon to get properly bandaged and have a rest.

I lay peacefully by my fifteen-hundredweight truck, looking idly at the other vehicles well spread out in the leaguer. Air sentries were posted to give warning of attack by enemy planes, but a small leaguer, well dispersed, was unlikely to attract attention. The M.O. thought one of my ribs was broken, so I was tightly strapped with plaster.

Three miles to the north, the Guards' Brigade men, stern and unmoved, were holding the Knightsbridge box. I saw tiny specks in the air. I reached for my glasses. They were Stukas, and suddenly they wheeled and dived. I saw the eggs falling. Then a great black curtain rose from the ground by the box, and the earth shook from the huge explosions. I stood up. The Guards' box was covered with darkness, and I could still hear more bombs exploding. Surely nothing could live inside that area? Slowly the black smoke cleared away and disclosed four fires burning steadily.

Presently I went to sleep. I was awakened by a deafening roar coming near. I sprang to my feet as the roar was pierced by staccato cracks of cannon fire. Something hit my head, and I stumbled against the side of the truck. The roar disappeared. In a great silence I heard the patter of liquid falling on to sand, and then horrible moaning noises. I moved round the truck. Something was staggering slowly towards me. The head had been split open and half the face hung down, flopping with blood. Then I realised it was one of the men in my troop.

At that moment I had my first 'black-out'.

I can hardly remember anything more, though vaguely I can recall

Robin Maugham as a student at Eton

Highfield School

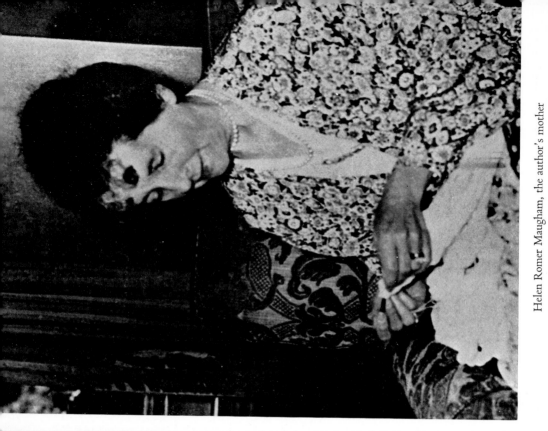

Helen Romer Maugham, the author's mother

Frederic Herbert Maugham, the author's father

putting my hand to my forehead and seeing it come away red, and stumbling off to get an ambulance. Dimly, I became aware of the close presence of Tommy who had not entered my consciousness since that morning in the church near Hartfield. Then I was lying in a bivouac, and somebody was saying: "You'll be quite all right. It won't hurt. I've given you morphine."

Presently I was lifted into a crowded ambulance. By now I realised that I had also been wounded in the left arm.

In the bunk opposite was a young Guardsman. He was in terrible pain; sweat was trickling down his forehead. He was groaning softly.

"Were you hit inside the Knightsbridge box?" I asked him to distract him from his anguish.

He stared at me. He tried to speak, but for a moment he couldn't because he was trembling so much. Suddenly he turned his face away from me. "I was not hit, sir," he said. "I had an accident, sir. I was cleaning my rifle when it went off and hit my foot, sir."

He turned away again. His shoulders were shaking. I managed to pass him a cigarette and struck a match for him. He began to cry. Through the haze of the morphine I'd been given my thoughts went out to him.

If we were alone I could tell you that I understand, I thought. Day after day the Germans stormed the Knightsbridge box, and when they could not overwhelm it, they tried to blast out your defences with shells and bombs. Day after day you have been shut up in hell, and you have known that tomorrow there would be more bombs and shells and death and blood. And the next day and the next and the next— unless you were wounded, and then you would be carried out of hell into a haven of peace and quiet and rest. Unless. Unless. Gradually you knew you could not endure the roar of the dive-bomber and the screaming shells. How long did you think over your plan? Did you reckon the pain of it? Yes. Because you could see the agony of wounded men all around you. But you could bear the torment no longer, and, like an animal caught in a trap, you must escape at the price of mutilating yourself. So you waited until no one was watching and then you pointed your rifle at your foot and held it steady. Then you pulled the trigger . . . I expect you are the bravest man here. So please do not cry.

Yet back home, stolid fools carry their wounds and medals like a carnation in their button-holes, and modestly say that fighting was quite good fun on the whole. And people listen because that is what they want to believe, because a man they love is fighting too. Perhaps he will come back and tell them the same thing, for nature cheats our memory to forget the pain of an illness, but to remember the flowers.

And so people do not hate war strongly enough. One day in each year they stood silent, thinking of those who died in the first Great War; they remembered the dead for forty minutes in twenty years, while the seeds of this war were being sown. But they did not hate war strongly enough to keep alert and vigilant and make constant sacrifice to prevent war coming again. And so this boy, born during the aftermath of the first Great War, must struggle to live for twenty years, to be tortured in the second war.

The doors of the ambulance were opened. It was night outside.

"Where are we?"

"Dressing station, Tobruk."

Stretcher-bearers carried us into a large hall like a huge barrack-room with a high, vaulted ceiling. The floor was covered with slabs, on which the stretchers were being put down. The two men stopped to look round for an empty slab, but all the slabs were covered with wounded men. The air reeked with the sickly sweet odour of pus and the stench of unwashed bodies. They put me down on the ground. I held my bandaged head with my hands because I was afraid someone would stumble against me. I tried not to listen to the groans and the screaming. More wounded were being carried into the turmoil. Orderlies moved quickly from one slab to another. Sometimes they looked at a man, pulled his blanket over his face, and carried him away. Sometimes they stuck a hypodermic into a man's arm and carried him to the operating-room next door. This hall was the ante-room of life or death.

My turn was coming. An orderly bent over me with a large syringe.

"I've had morphine already."

"This ain't morphia. It's anti-tetanus. Here, give us your arm."

He plunged the needle into my left arm, and I was carried away to have my head dressed.

The next morning we were driven down to the harbour and carried on to tenders, which chugged out towards the hospital ship lying graceful and cool and white against the blue sea. Here was the last ferry to peace. From now onwards I would not struggle against fate. I was just one tiny unit among thousands to be dispersed into hospitals in Egypt. My life no longer depended upon my conscious effort. I could lose consciousness now, and ships and tenders, stretchers and trains and ambulances would still carry me to hospital. If the ship was sunk there was nothing I could do about it. So I tried to relax and watch my body put into the cradle of a crane and swung aboard the crowded ship.

I can remember one moment in the hospital train: I was worried because I wanted to be sick; there was not a basin by my bunk, and I could not move to reach the lavatory. Above me a man was moaning softly. The sickly odour of pus crept like a poison into the lungs and made one retch. My clothes were caked stiff with blood.

*   *   *

The hospital between Cairo and Suez was composed of long rows of huts, sprawling in the desert. The sister carefully washed my chest and legs. I wished she had left me the soap and flannel so that I could have washed the parts she had not touched. Hot poultices were clamped round my arm, which was horribly swollen.

By day I lived in hospital. By night my mind returned to the Western Desert. My fever rose as darkness fell. I longed for a sleep that could bring oblivion. But soon after the sleeping-draught I felt the waves of pain washing over me, and soon the bed began slipping away, changing slowly into my scout-car.

Great crashes of sound were bursting in my ears, and the earth vomited clouds of smoky sand as the scout-car rushed forward clattering over ridges and dunes. For a moment the dust settled and I saw the colonel standing upright and fearless. I heard the shell screaming towards us. Then all the earth erupted in one blinding explosion. And I knew he was dead. I awoke with tears streaming down my cheeks. Indeed, our colonel died that day.

At the hospital the doctors dealt brilliantly with my arm. They inserted drain tubes and filled me with antibiotics but they were totally uninterested in my head, for it was a hospital for arm and leg injuries only.

"Are you sure there's nothing wrong with your knee?" they would ask when I complained of the shrapnel which was giving me violent headaches.

*   *   *

My days as a trooper in the Inns of Court Regiment and as an officer fighting in the Western Desert had convinced me that the hope of civilisation did not lie so much in Socialism as in what—for want of a better word—I must call Comradeship between men of every rank and class. Those days had also cleared my opinion of my own character. I had realised the measure of my cowardice and courage and of my powers of endurance; I had learned that I was capable of being accepted as a personality without any reference to my famous father or to my famous uncle. Gillian, by then, had married Richard Addis, an intelligent and charming lieutenant in the R.N.V.R. and a musician. But she remained —and still remains—one of my closest friends. I had also come to accept that my nature was predominantly homosexual.

131

I gave up worrying about the shrapnel in my head. After all, my regiment was still fighting, with heavy casualties. I was 'down-graded' medically, and given a month's sick leave. But while wandering around Shepheard's Hotel in Cairo I met Lady Spears—an old friend of my sister Kate—who invited me to convalesce at the residence above Beirut at Aley which General Spears occupied during the summer months. And thus it was that I became drawn into the Middle East Intelligence Centre.

While in Syria I worked out a plan for small units of Arabs, led by British officers, to stay behind in hiding if the Germans should invade North Africa in strength, which was generally expected at that moment. I argued that if this German invasion did not take place, the plan could easily be converted to peacetime use. And, indeed, out of my plan grew the Middle East Centre of Arab Studies.

The first person to support my plan was Major Altounyan, who I knew was one of the most important secret agents we had in the Middle East. Half Armenian and half Irish he was a doctor by profession and a poet by inclination. T. E. Lawrence in one of his last letters wrote: "An Armenian called Altounyan is one of three I most care for."

Altounyan decided that the most important person to whom I could explain my plan was Glubb, the Commander-in-Chief of the Arab Legion, so he drove me to Amman to see him. The car turned and twisted rapidly as it climbed the serpentine road up the side of the mountain between Jericho and Amman.

"Of the two, Lawrence and Glubb, I mean," I said, "which do you think the greater?" Even as I spoke the last word I felt it was stupid.

Altounyan was quiet for so long that I began to think he would not answer. Then he said:

"This one."

*   *   *

Outside the little house in Amman, three soldiers from the Arab Legion stood talking in a shelter from the wind. They sprang to attention. Glubb Pasha was expecting us, they said. We climbed up a flight of wooden stairs. His wife and small son greeted us at the door. Altounyan introduced me, and presently Glubb led me to his study.

"Sit down. I think you'll find that chair the most comfortable. Now. What can I do for you?" He sat down in a chair opposite me and produced a string of amber beads, and began playing with them, holding the string in his left hand so that the beads slipped one by one through the fingers of his right hand.

I handed him a copy of the plan. While he slowly read it, I observed him carefully. I could not help feeling disappointed. The stories I had heard from officers and Arabs, during the last three months, of this Englishman who commanded the Arab Legion, had woven a glorious tapestry in my mind. I knew that he had fought in the 1914 war and had won a Military Cross. Part of his jaw had been shot away, therefore the Arabs called him '*Abu Hunaik*' or 'Father of a Jaw'. As a young official in the Colonial Office he had come out to Iraq soon after the Armistice, and there the legend began. He dived fully clothed into the Tigris to rescue two Arabs. He settled disputes between warring tribes; he lived many years among the bedouin who now loved him. Succeeding Peake as Commander-in-Chief of the forces of the Emir Abdullah, he persuaded the feckless and independent bedouin youths to leave their tribes and join the Desert Brigade of the Legion which he welded into a tough, reliable force. This brigade was the leading reconnaissance force in the British advance to relieve Baghdad in 1941. Glubb was given a D.S.O. The Arab Legion was now recognised as an essential element for desert control. But if Glubb was admired by the British in the Levant, he was adored by the Arabs. I had heard stories of his kindness and generosity and courage. And this man, whom the Arabs worshipped, sat before me.

He was middle-aged and small of stature, with thin, white-grey hair, pale blue eyes and a bushy, iron-grey moustache. About his face there was an expression of gentleness and sensitivity. His manner was shy and diffident. His appearance gave no hint of the resolute leader I had imagined. He finished the notes, and put the folder on his desk.

"May I keep this?"

"Yes, sir."

"Well. What can I do for you?"

"I need your advice, sir, and your help."

While I explained, he leaned back, and I felt that he was studying me.

When I had finished, he paused for a while. Then he began to speak in a slow, even voice, quietly and without emphasis. And it was as if a dynamo had been suddenly switched on. The great wheel turned silently on its axis, and its quietness made the power it generated the more impressive. I was conscious of an intense force radiating from him, which kept me taut and on edge, so that I was exhausted from the effort of concentration when I left his room two hours later.

Though I have notes to guide my memory, I am surprised how vividly I remember what he said that afternoon.

"Your scheme is good so far as it goes," he said, "but how are you going to find and train the officers you need? It's not only a question of

133

teaching them Arabic, though that's going to be difficult enough in the time available. First of all, you've got to find the right men. Selection of the right people is much more important than the definition of their duties. You must remember that Arabs are by no means inferior to us in intelligence. They're as efficient as the ordinary Englishman in ordinary life. Their main failing is that they lack public spirit. But every Arab will immediately see through an inefficient or unpleasant officer. Arabs are very quick to size up the people they're dealing with. They can *sense* if an officer really sympathises with them and loves their people. They react most strongly to other people's emotions because they are temperamental themselves. That's why it's more important to choose the right individuals than the right policy.

"A knowledge of the language is obviously essential, but the officers you need have also got to know the people and the country. Even if they're young and the right stuff, it will take some time for them to learn. By the time they've learned, the need for them may have vanished."

"Their training wouldn't have been wasted," I said. "They would be useful after the war as officials out here."

"I agree," he said, "and we need them. If you can get the right men—officers and N.C.O.s who are fond of the people and want to stay in the Middle East after the war—and train them for work with these Arab bands, they could form the nucleus of a training centre for British officials after the war. If the Germans invade North Africa, I believe your idea will be valuable. I will certainly do anything I can to help. I could take some of the officers and N.C.O.s you select and send them out on attachment with the Legion. But concentrate on the training side of your scheme, and you will create something of permanent value. The Middle East, above all, wants leaders and has none."

*   *   *

Soon I had obtained the support not only of General Glubb but of General Spears in Syria and Sir Kinahan Cornwallis, our Ambassador in Baghdad, and of General 'Jumbo' Wilson. I now needed only political blessing from on high.

When I reached Cairo, feeling iller than usual, I went to meet a friend at Shepheard's bar. He grinned with amusement when he saw me.

"What's the joke?" I asked.

"Look at your face in the mirror," he answered.

I looked. My face was bright yellow. I had jaundice. By then I had learned to treat hospitals rather as one might hotels.

"What's the best hospital in Cairo?" I asked my friend.

"The Fifteenth General, without a doubt," he answered. "And if you dine with me, I promise to decant you there before midnight."

I woke with the worst hangover I have ever had to find a hatchet-faced matron glaring down at me. "Captain Maugham," she was saying, "you have no right to be in the Fifteenth General. This is a hospital for head injuries."

"Wonderful," I said. "Please X-ray my head."

At first they thought I was raving. But then they X-rayed me.

"Have you been going around with that shrapnel in your head for all these months?" they asked.

I nodded my head.

"But you must have felt very ill indeed."

"I did," I answered.

Then I was given the verdict. The shrapnel was lodged in the brain. I was a sick man and would be invalided back to England quite shortly. But first I was determined to implement my plan.

Visitors were not allowed until afternoon, so when one morning my friend John Adam Watson, the second secretary at the Embassy, stole like a fugitive into my room in the officers' ward, I knew this meant some development in my plan, which he had helped me to draft.

"Churchill is back from the Adana Conference," he said. "He wants to see you at four o'clock this afternoon."

"I'll get out somehow," I told him.

But Dr. Michael Kremer, who was looking after me, was away for the day, so my only hope was to approach the stern-faced sister in charge of the ward.

"Can I possibly go out for an hour this afternoon?"

"Certainly not."

"It's awfully important."

"I'm sorry, Captain Maugham. But that's quite impossible."

I glanced at her heavily creased face and at the rows of medals on her breast. She was obviously reliable.

"At the moment it's top security, but if I tell you why, do you promise to keep it to yourself? It's important."

"Yes."

"Churchill's at the Embassy. I've got an appointment with him at four o'clock."

She looked at me for a moment. Then she said, "All right. So long as you're only out an hour."

I felt sick and feeble as I got out of my taxi and walked into the Embassy. The ante-room was so full of generals that I recoiled and would have tried to escape if I had not been rescued and led into another office where the Prime Minister's staff sat about in attitudes of exhaustion.

The double doors at the end of the room swung open and disclosed Churchill in a boiler suit. He was radiant with vitality. "Whiskies and soda for all," he said, and disappeared within.

Suffragis sprang up from nowhere with drinks, and I was offered one—which I accepted, feeling that at least it could not make me feel any iller. It did not: it went to my head so that I felt almost capable of conversation with Churchill. The doors swung open again, and I was brought up to him.

"How are you? Come into the next room."

He beckoned me into a large armchair and offered me another drink and a cigar.

"Well," he said, "this is a far cry from Chartwell." Then he leaned back and looked at me with a smile. "And how is your father?" he chuckled. "Does he still love the Germans as much as he did in the days of Munich?"

"No," I replied truthfully.

"How is he?" Churchill asked.

"The last thing I heard about him," I said, "was that he had decided to join some Advisory Tank Board. And in his spare time—at the age of seventy-seven—he drives tanks himself furiously about the factory grounds."

Churchill laughed. "Well," he said, "it's taken a long time, but he's come round to us at last . . . Now tell me about your plan."

An hour later I had gained his blessing to my scheme. No red tape would now defeat me. As I walked happily back along the corridor which led to my room in the hospital I met the bemedalled sister.

"Well, at least you kept your word," she said.

"Of course I did."

"But next time, Captain Maugham, next time you want to spend an afternoon with your girl-friend," she said, "just tell me outright, and don't tell fibs to make an excuse. Do you understand?"

"Yes, Sister," I said.

*   *   *

In the summer of 1943 I was invalided back to England. The final implementation of my plan—even with Churchill's blessing—had been far harder than I imagined. I had much to fight against. But my enemy was not of flesh, rather he was an influence, seldom visible, creeping like a poisonous vapour into the courses of my plan. Sometimes I could see the shine of his trail: a movement order would be abruptly refused, a friend would be translated to another command without reason, a letter would fail to reach its destination, or the voice in my ear would grow faint as the line was tapped. Sometimes I saw him face to face in his various guises.

He was frequently a major, holding a cushy job in the Base Sub Area Office, conscious of his rank and safety, strictly punctilious, effusive to the senior officers, vicious with his subalterns and clerks. The pencil twisted in his pale, mean hands as he enforced the last letter of each regulation and ignored its intention. And once, my enemy was in the guise of a civil servant, sent, all cool, from Whitehall. "I don't know what the Treasury will think," he would say. "Of course the Minister of State should have been consulted before you saw Churchill. That was irregular. Most irregular."

I can almost grin now when I think how inevitable it was that the question of my flying back to England should have been referred to the civil servant. All day I waited in suspense. That evening I was told what he had said.

"I do not want Maugham to fly back to England. On no account is this to occur. The voyage round the Cape will do him good. It will cool him down a bit."

*   *   *

My mother had invited all the family and various old friends, such as A. A. Milne, for dinner to celebrate my homecoming. My sister Honor and her husband Sebastian Earl, had arrived late. They appeared in the drawing-room in Cadogan Square just as we were about to go down to dinner. Instinctively, I poured out a glass of sherry for each of them. Suddenly my father turned on me.

"How dare *you* pour out *my* sherry in my house to *my* guests?" he demanded. He was white and quivering. "How dare you?"

I was surprised and horrified by his attack. I said nothing. But I was furious that he should blame me for pouring out a glass of sherry for my sister and my brother-in-law. I was so enraged that he should upbraid me on the very first night of my return home from the war, that I refused to go down to dinner—until my mother asked me to come down just for her sake.

My mother had been as shocked as I was. "It distressed me so much," she wrote in her diary, "that I thought never again would I have a family dinner and risk such a scene."

*   *   *

In England I had discovered that a dangerous gulf lay between civilian life and the Fighting Services. I decided to start a magazine in order to try to bridge this gulf by showing to the Services the hardships that civilians suffered and to explain to civilians the roles of the Fighting Services. With the aid of Jane Forbes, who was now the Director of the W.A.A.F., and of William Collins, the publisher, I started a paper called *Convoy*.[1] It was a success; the first edition sold fifty thousand copies.

Although I was shortly to be invalided out of the Army because of my head injuries, I now became attached to A.B.C.A.—the Army Bureau of Current Affairs. Its Director, W. E. Williams, was a man of vision and force. He approved of the general idea of *Convoy*. He also believed it was important to explain one branch of the Fighting Services to the other. In order to do this I volunteered for a series of missions. Thus I flew in a Sunderland for sixteen hours on a submarine patrol over the Atlantic. The only two people I kept informed of these activities were my sister Diana and her husband, Kim Marr-Johnson. As my strength declined and the effort of my work for *Convoy* and A.B.C.A. increased and led to meetings with such characters as A. V. Alexander, the First Lord of the Admiralty, who was apt to stay at Diana's house singing songs at the piano until two or three in the morning, and with General Sir Bernard Paget, the Commander-in-Chief of our Home Forces, I began to drink more and more in order to get through the long days and nights.

Early in July, I was invited by Mary Churchill to stay a weekend at Chequers. Winston Churchill examined me closely about what had occurred in the Middle East since we had last met.

"On the occasions," said Churchill, "when I consider the obstructions of bureaucracy, I sometimes stand amazed that ever a single fighting man reaches the front with a rifle and ammunition at the right time and place."

On Sunday, Noël Coward came down to lunch at Chequers and sang his extremely funny song *Don't Let's be Beastly to the Germans*. The song pleased Churchill so much that Noël was almost hoarse by dinnertime.

I still had not realised the extent of my physical weakness. That evening—to my intense embarrassment—I collapsed. I'd been asked to stay until Monday morning, but after I'd had dinner in bed, Noël drove me back in his car to Cadogan Square.

However, I was still determined to continue my work. After a fortnight spent in the North Walbottle Colliery working as a miner so

[1] The complete text of my first *Convoy* editorial is given in Appendix III.

that I could explain to the Fighting Services what it was like down in the pits, I returned to London and tried to be allowed to fly in a bomber in a raid over Berlin.

My head wound was causing me fits of vomiting and severe headaches. It was at this stage that my sister Diana intervened. "You're too ill to make a bomber flight," she said. "At this moment of time—for various reasons—your death instinct is very strong. For instance, the reason you drink so much is that you have an obvious desire for oblivion."

A few days later I collapsed again and was taken to the Hospital for Head Injuries in Oxford where, to my joy, I discovered that Dr. Michael Kremer, who had looked after me in the hospital in Cairo, was now working. I was now suffering so badly from complete amnesia, or 'black-outs', that at times I discovered complete gaps in my memory. Often, however, one piece of the jigsaw brought back the whole pattern of events. During the second act of a play, for instance, the scene appeared uncannily familiar. Then I felt a curious stirring in my head, and a rapid excitement as my memory cut into the present, and I remembered the night when I had seen the play before and the weeks encircling that night which had previously been a blank.

*   *   *

My consciousness was also uncertain. I would be talking with a friend before dinner when a curtain would come down over my mind like a shutter, and I would remember nothing until it lifted, perhaps as I was saying goodbye, perhaps when I awoke in bed the next morning. The friend would have noticed nothing unusual. Only my conscious memory of what happened was suspended during the period. These black-outs worried me, and for a time I was afraid I was going mad, so I carried in my breast pocket an envelope with 'Please Open' marked on it. This contained instructions that if I lost consciousness I should be taken to Michael Kremer at the Hospital for Head Injuries at Oxford.

I was invalided out of the Army with a pension 'based on fifty per cent disability', and ordered to rest. Michael always promised me that I would not go mad. However, I only half believed him.

"If things get too bad," he said, "I can put you out completely for a month, and you'll awake rosy and relaxed at the end of it."

Meanwhile my plan was adopted, and the Middle East Centre of Arab Studies was started, in a small way, exactly two years too late.

*   *   *

The war had parted Willie and Gerald. When Willie returned to

139

England, in July 1940, to search in vain for a war job, Gerald stayed on in France for a while to rescue some of the more valuable pictures from the Villa Mauresque. Then he flew to Lisbon and eventually to New York, where he met Willie again and they travelled together to Hollywood. But in December 1941, Willie moved to South Carolina where Nelson Doubleday, his American publisher, had built him an eight-room comfortable house, called Parker's Ferry, on his plantation, twelve miles from Yemassee, in desolate yet oddly beautiful country. Willie enjoyed the peace and simplicity of his life there; he liked the placid routine. But the place was far too quiet for Gerald, who soon became restive. He was only just fifty; he was bright and virile, and he felt the war was a challenge to him to prove himself in his own right. He had grown tired of being tolerated by Willie's friends as a useful adjunct to Willie's existence. He wanted to succeed—personally and publicly—on his own, so he took a clerical war job. During the next two years in Washington, divorced from Willie's care and sobering influence, Gerald literally worked and drank himself to death.

On June 26th, 1944, Willie wrote to me to say that Gerald was very ill. He had had an attack of pleurisy in Washington and had then developed tuberculosis of the lungs. He looked pitifully wasted. Willie was taking him to a sanatorium in the Adirondacks, where the fine air might save him. Gerald, Willie wrote, had been very good, patient and cheerful, but he had not been told how dangerously ill he was. Gerald would be an invalid for the rest of his life. There was only a small chance of saving him.

In November 1944, Gerald died in the Doctor's Hospital in New York. Willie, stricken with grief, travelled down to South Carolina, buried himself in his remote little house in the wilds of Yemassee, and went—I can think of no other phrase to describe his condition—into a decline. He refused to leave Parker's Ferry and he refused to meet anyone—even his closest friends. It was then that Ellen and Nelson Doubleday suggested that I should come out to stay with him.

I was ill and jittery. The calm of Yemassee might restore my nerves; my presence might help to drag Willie from his decline. I was keen to go. And thanks to the kindness of Brendan Bracken in the Ministry of Information and of Victor Weybright, his American opposite number in London, I managed to get a passage on a ship to Halifax. I found Willie overwhelmed with misery.

"With the pills they've given me, I sometimes manage to sleep or doze for as much as six hours a night," he told me. "But I think of Gerald every single minute that I'm awake. I try to forget him all the eighteen hours of the day. You can't imagine what it was like—hour after hour—listening to that terrible cough that seemed to tear him to pieces."

Suddenly Willie lowered himself on to the sofa and buried his face in his hands. He began to cry with long racking sobs.

"You'll never know how great a grief this has been to me," he said when he had controlled himself and could speak again. "The best years of my life—those we spent wandering about the world—are inextricably connected with him. And in one way or another—however indirectly—all I've written during the last twenty years has something to do with him, if only that he typed my manuscripts for me."

Willie seemed inconsolable. But at least my arrival forced him to make a slight effort to recover. He took me to dine with Ellen and Nelson Doubleday and their family in what we both called 'the big house', and their friendliness and splendid if erratic hospitality did much to restore both of us. As the sunlit days passed by, Willie began to look less forlorn, and soon he began to manage a shaky smile. But it was not until New Year's Eve that I realised that Willie had managed to steer himself round the corner towards recovery.

There was a large party up at the big house on New Year's Eve. Willie and I were invited. A minute or so before midnight someone gaily suggested that we should all sing *Auld Lang Syne*. Immediately Willie's face froze with dismay—not because he was afraid that the hackneyed tune would remind him of Gerald: by now he could cope with that misery. I could see from his hectic glances to right and to left that the reason for his consternation was more superficial and immediate. From childhood Willie had had a morbid dread of physical contact with strangers, and he was now suddenly confronted with the prospect of his hands being crossed and then clasped in the sticky palms of two un-known females who had come in late and who were now standing on either side of him. Into his eyes came the look of a frantic hunted animal. I was wondering how Willie would get out of his predicament, when he spoke:

"When on New Year's Eve," Willie said, "I hear people singing that song in which they ask themselves the question 'should old acquaintance be forgot', I can only ter-tell you that my own answer is in the affirmative."

That did the trick. Hands that had been crossed and outstretched to clasp Willie's fell down in limp despondency. Mouths that had been open to chant merrily closed with a snap. And Willie had saved himself. At that instant he caught me looking at him and gave me a broad wink, and I knew that for a while at least he was back to his old form again.

But I wasn't. I was very nervous and I couldn't rid myself of the stammer that had begun after my head wound. At times I felt suicidally depressed as I thought of the friends in my regiment, officers and men, who had been killed or maimed in the desert. I thought of my nephew David, who had been severely wounded three times, and of his brother John, who had been killed in Germany.

In the wilds of Yemassee I came to the conclusion that I was close to going mad. One day I asked Willie if he thought that a psychiatrist could help my condition.

"No," said Willie firmly. "Certainly not."

"Why not?"

"Because he could do you no good. Your injury has exaggerated your defects, that's all. And you can't change your essential nature. All you can do is to try to make the best of your limitations."

Willie looked at my doubtful face. "I can ser-see you don't believe a word I'm saying. I can see that you think I'm being wilfully obtuse," he said. "So I'll tell you a story to show my point."

Willie wandered over to the side-table and began to mix a dry Martini. "Years ago," he said, "long before the First World War, I was quite fer-famous because I'd had four plays running in London at the same time, and I came to New York for the rehearsals of one of them. I was staying at the Ritz-Carlton, I remember. And one afternoon they rang up from the desk to say that there was a Mr. Maugham waiting downstairs to see me.

"'There's a mistake,' I told them. 'I'm Mr. Maugham.'

"'We know,' the desk clerk replied. 'But there's still a Mr. Maugham waiting here to see you.'

"'Then please send him up,' I said."

Willie finished stirring the Martini, poured out two glasses, and lit himself a cigarette. "Presently a young man was shown into the room," Willie continued. "And this was Mr. Maugham. He had dark curly hair and brown eyes and a sallow complexion. He was obviously sensitive, rather Bohemian and very highly strung. There was a striking family likeness."

Willie paused for dramatic effect—as he always did when telling a story. "But the oddest thing of all about it," he said, "was that the young man spoke with a pronounced stammer."

Willie handed me my glass. "And he told me that the Maughams came over to America a century ago," Willie continued. "But the essential characteristics had obviously still persisted in the young man."

Willie took a sip of his drink.

"We're the product of our genes and chromosomes," he concluded. "And there's nothing whatever we can do about it. And that's the reason why I tell you that a psychiatrist couldn't help you. No one can. Because we can't change the essential natures we're born with. We can't alter the essential product that we are. All we can do is to try to supplement our own deficiencies. Meeting that young man in the Ritz-Carlton made me certain of it. There's no point in trying to change. One hasn't a hope."

*   *   *

During my stay at Yemassee I explained to Willie that the doctors had said that my head wound and fits of amnesia made it impossible for me to practise as a lawyer. While I had been in various hospitals for head injuries, Michael Kremer had suggested that I should write the story of my existence in tanks in the Western Desert as a form of occupational therapy. I had followed his advice; my work had been published in book form—as *Come to Dust*—by Chapman and Hall. Richard Dimbleby, then B.B.C. book critic, had said it was "As good a piece of war reporting of the intimate kind as I've ever read". The book had sold out within a few days; a large paperback edition was about to be produced. I had decided, I told Willie, that my 'essential nature' lay in writing.

"Ner-nonsense," Willie replied. "You'll never make more than three hundred pounds a year as a writer. What I advise you to do is to marry a rich woman, ger-go into politics and you'll end up as Governor-General of some remote island—which must be a very per-pleasant existence. Emerald Cunard and I will help you to find an heiress—and the rest is easy."

But I didn't want an heiress; I didn't want to go into politics; and I didn't want to marry. I wanted to be a writer, and I wanted to travel. And I wanted, as Willie would put it, to have a romp—when I got the chance.

*   *   *

I returned to England, and I edited three more numbers of *Convoy*, which could appear only at irregular intervals because of wartime restrictions. The authorities would not allow me enough paper to print the large number of copies needed to make the paper financially viable. After seven numbers it expired.

*   *   *

My experiences in the war had made me believe that the mass of the troops were discontented with the old regime of the Tory party. But my personal loyalty to Churchill, and my admiration for him, had persuaded me to hope that he would be elected for another term of office.

After dinner on the evening of July 25th, 1945, I had been invited round to the annexe of No. 10 Downing Street. Next day we would know the results of the first General Election to take place since the war had begun. Though his son Randolph was frankly pessimistic, Churchill was still optimistic about the result of the election—so much so that Mary Churchill asked me to come in for a drink after dinner the following evening and to take her out to the Orchid Room later to celebrate.

By noon on the following day it was clear that the Labour Party had won. Churchill had been heavily defeated. I rang Mary up to ask if she still wanted me to come round. Yes, Mary said, she did. So I put on a dinner-jacket and went round after dinner, bringing an old friend, Michael Parrish, with me.

A few people were sadly gathered in the living-room of the annexe when we arrived—Diana and Duncan Sandys, Mary Churchill, Brendan Bracken and Jack Churchill, Winston's brother.

Suddenly the door opened and Winston Churchill appeared. Silence fell over the room as he walked in. He was dressed in his open-necked boiler suit and embroidered slippers. He looked stricken. No one said a word. We were all like a lot of actors who had dried up on their cues. He turned towards me. I was the newcomer. So I walked across to him.

"Good evening, sir," I said. "I'm so very sorry about what has happened."

For some reason this trite remark pleased him.

"Oh!" he said, smiling at me. "So you are sorry! And your father? And how is he? Is he sorry?"

"Yes, sir," I said. "He is sorry too."

"The only thing that matters is England," Churchill muttered.

He then sat down, beckoning me to a chair beside him. At that moment Anthony Eden came in, looking very fit and bronzed. He stayed only a few minutes.

"I expect I shall see you one of these days," Churchill said as Eden was leaving, accentuating each word ponderously.

"I don't think it's as bad as all that," Eden replied.

"The Labour Party have inherited a tough proposition," Churchill said, after Eden had gone. "We cannot stop these strikes. They will be better at it than we were . . . But hardly had I put down the reins of office, when the horse was taken from me—only to be ridden into a quarry."

144

Gillian Dearmer

Robin Maugham's sisters:
(*left to right*) Diana, Kate and
Honor

A portrait of Robin Maugham by David Rolt, 1938. (Now in the possession of Winifred Durnford.)

Robin Maugham as a subaltern in the Sharpshooters in 1940

Robin Maugham as a major in the Arab Legion
in 1947

I had the impression that Churchill was anxious to be fair to the victors, but he could not resist the suspicion that his defeat was the result of a secret Socialist conspiracy against him. And he gave instances of some of the more malignant behaviour of various members of the Labour Party. The future was grim, he told us. England had been through two great wars and had incurred large debts. America could be counted out on the grounds of Lease-Lend. But India and the Middle East countries were important and would have to be paid.

"We must be fair to the Labour Party," he said, turning to Brendan Bracken. "They have inherited terrible difficulties. We must lay off them for a few months and give them a fair chance. But if they start to tamper with the constitution then we must go out into the streets and protest ... That wretched man Morrison is the most dangerous man of them all, mark my words. He delighted and revelled in the power of 18B.[2] He was determined to oust me. An election was bound to come after this tedious war, and the Labour Party was determined to get rid of me."

"The Tories would have been nothing without you," Bracken replied. "If you hadn't been their leader they wouldn't have polled more than fifteen votes."

Suddenly Churchill swung round towards me as if I had just spoken. "So this little *contretemps* has surprised you?" he asked.

"Yes, sir," I replied.

"Did you speak in the election?"

"Yes," I said. "On two occasions, and both were for Harold Nicolson."

"He is out, too," said Churchill, "and I am sorry for it."

"Thousands of men who've been through this war will always look to you for leadership," I said. "I believe, sir, that you've been over-thrown by a mass of discontented people who will presently try to overthrow the Labour Party in its turn."

"I have only a few years to live," Churchill replied. "I am finished. It is up to people like you to carry on. I will never return to power. I have left my name in history, and I have no regrets."

"Will you lead the Opposition?"

"I am not quite certain that the Tories want me," Churchill answered. "But I can tell you this. The leaders of the Labour Party will try to go slowly. But they will find the tail of their party will lash them into precipitous acts. The people in front will be shoved on by the men behind. There will be more difficulties when the Japanese war ends,

[2] Clause 18B comes under the Defence of the Realm Act, by which arrest and detainment could be made without any prosecution being brought.

which will be soon. *We* have made arrangements on that score. But the Socialists will claim the credit for it. However, the main difficulties are internal. England has been bled white by the strain of these two great wars."

As he spoke, I felt that it seemed as if sometimes he would forget for a moment that he was no longer Prime Minister; but then, like a nerve starting up in a tooth, back would come the memory of his defeat, and almost in the middle of a sentence he would refer once again to his own position.

"Throughout the last six years I have grown accustomed to rise early and start work at eight and to go on working until four in the morning," he said. "Indeed I suppose I shall find it strange to have no labour on my hands. It seems incredible that tomorrow I have nothing to do." Then, as if trying to convince himself, he added, "But it will seem odd on the morrow when all the great affairs of State are no longer brought to me. Now it is up to you young ones. I have a short time to live. But I feel that history will give me a fair reading."

At that stage Diana and Duncan Sandys said good-night and left. Presently, Jack Churchill got up to go. Winston went on talking. But the flashes of his usual good humour died quickly. And now he shook his head wearily.

"For five long years the reins of office have been in my hands," he said.

He fell silent again, and Michael Parrish spoke for the first time. "Well, at least, sir, you won us the race," Michael said.

This cheered him up, and for a moment he was back on his old form.

"I won you the race," Churchill said. "But now you've warned me off the turf!"

Once more he fell silent. He was obviously exhausted. Mary decided it was time for her father to go to bed. But he would not listen to her. He still lingered. There were now only four of us left in the room— Mary, Brendan Bracken, Michael Parrish and I. Churchill looked desperately old and sad.

"I cannot go back to Potsdam," he said. "But unless Attlee and Bevin go back immediately, the conference will crash itself into nothing before reaching maturity and decision. Attlee came and asked Eden to help him out. But Eden was rather severe, perhaps too severe, and said, 'Let me have it in writing, and I will put it through the usual channels.'"

Churchill looked vaguely around the room.

"I expect my leisure will worry me at first," he said. "But at least I shall be able to devote proper time to my painting."

Suddenly he turned to Mary. "Bring me my sketch of the Black Prince's house," he said.

Mary fetched his picture of Marrakesh and stood it on the floor, leaning against the sideboard. Brendan Bracken stood up to look at it.

"You're standing too close," said Churchill.

So Bracken moved back.

"And now you're standing in my light," said Churchill. Patiently Bracken moved aside once more.

For a while we stood in silence looking at the gaily-coloured painting. Churchill was motionless. He was far away in his own imaginings. When, presently, he began to speak it was clear that his thoughts now flickered to and fro between the painting and the memory of his defeat.

"Another few days and I shall be proud of it," he said, staring at the picture. "And I shall be able to spend quite a time in painting during these last few years which are left to me . . . Yes. It needs a little mauving in . . . But the term of my mandate has been withdrawn by the people . . . Yes. It does need touching up a bit . . . And certainly leisure will be pleasing. And I am grateful for having been given the chance to rest during the few years left to me . . . But it will be strange on the morrow when the affairs of State are no longer in my hands."

Then with an effort he raised his head from the picture and moved slowly towards the door. Each step that he took seemed heavy with pain. At the door he paused.

"But I have no regrets," he said.

For an instant he hesitated. His eyes were bleary with tears. Slowly his gaze wandered round the four of us. But he didn't notice us. His mind was far away, ranging perhaps over lobbies and battlefields, assemblies and oceans, palaces and the broken slums of London.

"I have no regrets," he repeated. "I leave my name to history."

And he walked out of the room.

*   *   *

Suddenly, I was given the very chance to travel that I longed for.

After the war General Paget became Commander-in-Chief of the Middle East, and, as I have said, for some reason he had taken to me and I had done some work for him in England. Looking back on it now, I suppose the reason he liked me was because he knew for certain that I would tell him the truth about Service problems—however much the truth might displease him. I now received a secret message from him suggesting I should fly out to Cairo, with all expenses paid, and work for him as a completely unofficial and secret intelligence agent. My 'cover' would be that I was working as a journalist.

I was no longer officially employed by the Middle East Intelligence Centre. But I had maintained my friendship with its head—Brigadier Clayton—and I had the advantage of being one of the few Englishmen who had managed to become close friends with Glubb Pasha.

I accepted the offer gladly.

PART

FOUR

———

SOON AFTER MY ARRIVAL AT SHEPHEARD'S HOTEL I WAS telephoned by my friend Patrick Gibbs, one of Paget's aides. "We'll send a staff-car for you at eight o'clock," he told me. "Put on a dinner-jacket. I must warn you that you'll be the only civilian present."

I allowed myself plenty of time to change. I dressed slowly, savouring the joy of being back in Cairo. Outside I could hear the familiar blare of horns above the dull roar of traffic. The room reserved for me was in the front of Shepheard's, which I had heard was the oldest section of the hotel. The floor quivered slightly when a heavy truck passed along the road beyond the terrace. But the thick yellow brocade curtains, the massive wardrobe and the large empire desk looked impressively solid and enduring. I finished the whisky and soda I had ordered from the bar, locked the door of my room, walked down the broad staircase into the hall, handed my key to the porter and walked out on to the terrace. Presently the staff-car arrived. I opened the windows when I could smell the acrid tang of Cairo while the staff-car hooted its way through the crowded, dusty streets. At that moment I was excited, but my nerves were under control, and I had only had one drink all day.

As the staff-car approached the general's house, the lights outside the portico were switched on so that the gravel drive was floodlit. An orderly appeared in the doorway and saluted. He led me through the hall into a long white drawing-room. Standing at the far end of the room by a drinks tray were two officers. One of them was Patrick Gibbs and the other was my old friend Michael Ling.

"Good news," they said. "The boss is winging his way back from seeing Ibn Saud in Riyadh. They've just phoned through to say his plane was delayed. So we've got plenty of time to finish a jug of daiquiris."

We must have been gossiping for about twenty minutes when the double doors at the end of the room opened and two brigadiers came in. They were both stout and florid. The larger one moved in a curiously constricted manner, as if he wore corsets.

"The general will be here in a minute," the stouter one announced. "He's washing his hands."

When Patrick introduced me, I realised from what he had said that they must be the two assistants whom people called Tweedledum and Tweedledee. I was trying to make polite conversation when an orderly flung open the double doors, and General Paget appeared. He took six paces into the room and then stopped still for an instant, as if examining the group we made round the drinks table. Red-faced and stern, he was an impressive figure. Suddenly he threw back his head and smiled.

"Good evening, gentlemen," he said. His voice was crisp. Then he crossed the room and shook my hand.

"How are you, Robin? I'm glad you made it. You look perfectly fit. I believe that shrapnel did you good. Gave you a rest for a while. Have my aides been looking after you properly?"

"Yes. Thank you, sir."

"Patrick, where's my whisky and soda? Thank you. I told them we wouldn't eat for a few more minutes. His Majesty gave me far too much to eat and nothing whatever to drink. The old rascal can produce whisky when he feels like it, but he's as tricky as they're made. And nothing disconcerts him. There was a scuffling noise behind the curtains at one end of the conference tent, and I looked up to see a slave hurrying off a young girl who had obviously crept in to have a look-see. The King stared me straight in the face and then spoke to the interpreter, who translated the King's words thus: 'His Majesty says he spent his youth in wars depopulating his country, so that it is only right he should spend his old age repopulating it.'"

The two brigadiers laughed loudly.

* * *

After dinner, Paget drew me to one side. He waved to me to sit down beside him on a sofa at the far end of the room. He leaned towards me.

"Now tell me, Robin," he said, "what do your Arab friends in London think of this Arab League business?"

I can recall that while I paused before replying I looked at his hands, which were lying motionless on his knees. The tips of his fingers were broad and the nails well manicured. Then, as I stared down at his hands, what I can only describe as a curtain descended over my mind, and I remembered—and still can remember—nothing more until I woke up the following morning.

*   *   *

At first I did not know where I was. Then I saw the light filtering through the faded yellow curtains, and I realised I was in my bed in Shepheard's. But what had happened? Then with a sickening lurch I remembered arriving at the general's house, feeling tired and nervous, drinking several cocktails, sitting down on the sofa, listening to his question. And then . . . What then? I could recollect nothing beyond that moment. But I could guess what had happened. If only I had fainted—'passed clean out', as Patrick would have put it—the harm could be mended. But what I was almost certain had happened was something more shaming and alarming. I had had a recurrence of the black-outs which had kept me in the Hospital for Head Injuries at Oxford for nearly a year.

In the Hospital for Head Injuries I had been told that these black-outs—a loathsome expression, but no worse than 'fugues' or 'bouts of retrogressive amnesia', as the doctors sometimes called them—were the result of my head wound and would gradually grow less frequent and in time stop altogether. When I accepted Paget's offer I had not had an attack for over six months. And now, my very first night in Cairo, the wretched thing had happened again. My mouth felt dry. I drank a glass of water. At that moment I saw my clothes. They were lying in an untidy heap on the Recamier sofa—an old tweed suit I had brought out to wear in the desert and had left at the bottom of my suitcase, a flannel shirt, a brown tie. I got out of bed and opened the wardrobe. My dinner-jacket was neatly on a clothes-hanger. I lay down again in bed and tried to think. Obviously, I had come back to the hotel and changed out of my dinner-jacket into the tweed suit. Why? To go out in the town? Probably. My dinner-jacket would have been very conspicuous. But why had I gone out again? To meet an Arab who could give me information? Perhaps. To wander round the brothel quarter? Possibly—but unlikely. On leave from the Western Desert I had once

153

or twice been round the more famous brothels, but though drunk and elated, I had been depressed by the sight of the young prostitutes and disgusted by the older ones.

After my previous black-outs I had sometimes found a note or an address scribbled on a slip of paper which had given me a clue where I had been or what I had done. I looked in my engagement book. I turned to the date, December 17th. And there I found written clearly and firmly in my own handwriting: "Take Brigadier Clayton to see C-in-C at 11 a.m."

Clayton was head of the Middle East Intelligence Centre. C-in-C must be General Paget. Why should I ever have supposed I should take Clayton to see the Commander-in-Chief?

The telephone by my bed had started ringing. I lifted the receiver. It was Patrick.

"How are *you* this morning?" he asked.

I was determined not to confess my weakness unless I was forced to, so I hedged.

"Exhausted," I said.

"I'm not surprised."

I decided to bluff. "How do you think things went?" I asked.

He paused. Then he said: "Well, you were very outspoken. At one moment I thought that my great white chief was going to turf you out. But to the amazement of all he took it like a lamb. Though I warn you—don't try it on twice, and don't forget you're supposed to be turning up at the office at eleven pronto with Brigadier Clayton."

"So that's still on?" I said.

"Why shouldn't it be? It was your bright idea, wasn't it? Incidentally, would you like to lunch with me afterwards?"

"I'd love to."

"Fine. Let's meet at John's bar in Shepheard's at about one thirty. But I'll be there to welcome you at the office. Eleven pronto. Don't be late."

I looked at my watch. It was ten o'clock. While I shaved I tried to see the funny side of it. Here I was—committed to bringing two important British officers together—and I hadn't a notion for what reason. But though I managed to smile, my hands were still trembling. If I was forced to confess about my black-outs I knew my mission would be cancelled, and I was desperately anxious to be given the chance. First, I believed that I would find out more than the usual type of intelligence officer who spent his time sitting behind a desk devouring reports from unreliable agents. Secondly, General Paget had promised to provide transport and pay for my expenses. I could never have afforded the journey otherwise. My head wound had made me forget what little law I knew. What I made from writing articles and a few short stories wasn't enough to pay for the kind of travelling I wanted to do. At the age of thirty I was starting in a new profession. I could never earn enough money to pay for the tour that General Paget wanted me to make, and no newspaper would be prepared to send out an inexperienced reporter. Lastly, my long-range plan was to make myself an expert in Middle East affairs so that eventually I could get the job of correspondent on the staff of one of the few responsible newspapers. For these three reasons I dared not let anyone know about my black-out the previous evening.

*　　　*　　　*

I took a taxi to G.H.Q.; I appeared in Brigadier Clayton's office at ten fifty. He greeted me warmly.

"I was told you'd be coming round to report to me," he said. "We've an appointment with General Paget at eleven. Do you mind telling me just what it's all about?"

I did not hesitate. I had been expecting that question.

"If you don't mind, I'd rather wait until we meet the general," I said smugly.

At that stage I could only play for time and hope that something would happen to recall to me what had been in my mind when I suggested the meeting. At the worst I was determined to invent a reason.

Brigadier Clayton frowned, then got up stiffly. "In that case I suppose we might as well push along," he said, and opened the door for me. Together we passed through his ante-room and walked out into the corridor. As we crossed over to the block occupied by General Paget and his staff I could feel the sweat, cold beneath my arms.

Patrick Gibbs received us cheerfully in the outer office. His desk was half covered with telephones. The only paper on it was *The Times*. Glancing down I saw that he had almost finished the crossword puzzle. Paget had probably chosen him for his imperturbable good humour. Unlike me, he never panicked.

"The general's expecting you both," he said. "Come right in."

He opened the door leading to the general's room, ushered us in, and withdrew smartly. Paget was sitting on the edge of his desk, looking up at a vast map of the Middle East which filled the whole wall behind. For an instant he did not move. Once again I was amazed that a man could be so motionless and yet so alert. His stillness was like that of a leopard before it springs. Then he turned and smiled at us.

"Good morning, gentlemen," he said, and pushed a heavy silver cigarette-box towards us. "By the way, Clayton," Paget said, "have you by any chance got a signed photograph of Monty?"

Clayton was surprised, but long training made him disguise the fact. "I don't think so," he said cautiously.

"I've got to find one. You see, the last time he was out here, Monty gave me a signed photograph—cabinet size or whatever it's called—and after he'd gone I put it away in some drawer, and now we just can't find it. And the man's coming to dine with me on Thursday. You do see the fix I'm in."

"Perhaps the Embassy could help," Clayton suggested.

"Well, I suppose we'd better stop coffee-housing and get down to business," Paget said. "Supposing you kick off, Robin?"

The moment I had been dreading had come. I longed for a cigarette, but I knew my hands would shake as I lit it. Both men were looking at me. I said the only thing I could think of.

"I'd rather you started the ball rolling, sir," I said.

The cliché softened my refusal to begin.

"But it's your proposal, not mine. And you're here to sell us the idea."

"I know, sir. But I'd rather you started, just the same."

For an instant I thought Paget would be angry. Then he put his hands down on to his desk and rested them on a long white ruler and turned to Clayton.

"Very well," he said. "Now this is the form."

He got up, holding the ruler, and walked briskly towards the map.

"Of the countries we can consider as forming the fertile crescent," he began—and the tip of his ruler described an arc embracing the Lebanon, Syria, Jordan and Iraq—"we know perfectly well there is only one country that is unreliable."

At that moment it came back to me. I still could remember nothing of what had happened after Paget's question the previous night. But I could guess—almost certainly—the plan I must have put forward that evening. It had been at the back of my mind for the last six months.

"Over to you, Robin," Paget was saying.

"It may not work," I said. "But at the worst it could do no harm. My idea is that if I went first to Damascus . . ."

I looked up at Paget's face, and I knew that I had guessed right. I was saved.

*   *   *

At the end of a happy lunch with Patrick, I felt sufficiently strong to put the question I had been longing to ask.

"Did you think I was very outspoken last night?"

"Well, you did lay down the law a bit."

"When did you first notice I was getting a bit above myself?"

He looked at me sharply. "Don't tell me you can't remember?"

"Of course I can remember. I just wondered how it struck you, that's all."

"We were both fairly high, but I didn't realise how far gone you were till you sat down with my boss."

"I was drunk. Why not say it?"

"No. That's the odd part of it. You weren't drunk. If you don't mind me saying so, you made more sense than you usually do. But you were over-confident—you used a lot of slang words you'd never have dared use normally—and you were pretty indiscreet, though not half as indiscreet as my boss was later on when he got going." Patrick paused. "In a way," he said, "you seemed to have become a different person."

At that moment, with a shudder of disgust, I realised the truth which, for a long time, I had been afraid to admit to myself. I knew from the doctors that the first black-out at the moment I was wounded had been caused by the shock of seeing the soldier's head flopping with blood. I also knew that my subsequent black-outs were a form of escape from a situation or memory that my subconscious found unbearable. It was as easy as that. But from my actions during my black-outs I had discovered—from cautious enquiries to people who had been with me at the time—that a slight change of personality did take place during my periods of amnesia. It seems that I became a tougher and coarser person—far more confident and resolute—and a person who was only attracted to girls. By now I had discovered the explanation for it all. During the periods of my attacks of amnesia, which sometimes lasted for twenty-four hours, it was the other half of my nature, the half which I had called Tommy, who took over. From books on psychology I had discovered that this condition was known as 'disassociation of personality'.[1] Two different characters now inhabited my body:

[1] Roy Dixon-Smith in *New Light on Survival* (Rider, London, 1952) says:

The strange disorder of the mind known as 'multiple alternating personalities' may in some cases be connected with reincarnation. Here is a brief outline of this abnormality.

(a) *The normal waking personality.* Shock can split personality into two or more separate group-systems or sub-personalities each with its own separate consciousness, experiences and memory, and sometimes very distinctive character. If they remain above the psychological threshold that divides the conscious from the unconscious, they will be unaware of each other's existence; but if the level of this threshold changes, as it sometimes seems to do, those below it are co-conscious with those above it, but not vice versa. At whatever level these sub-personalities may be, the rule that the lower knows the higher and the

perhaps both of them had always been there. For I knew that I had no influence over Tommy when he took control. Tommy might have committed murder that previous night, and I might never know—or if I did know, it would be because the crime had been discovered, and I would be held responsible. Desperately, I tried to comfort myself. So long as I didn't have a black-out, I was safe, because it was only during such periods that Tommy could take over. I must therefore avoid the two conditions which seemed to make my black-outs possible—exhaustion and too much drink. I must not despair. Meanwhile I must conceal my disability as best I could: I was afraid of losing the opportunity of travel and intelligence work which General Paget in his kindness had provided for me. Had Michael Kremer been out in the Middle East I might have consulted him because I trusted him. But I did not dare to visit a new doctor in case I was sent back to hospital once again.

*　　*　　*

I will say little about my work at that time—if only because my efforts were largely futile.

One of my pathetic political illusions was that since Arabs and Jews were both equally semitic, there was a hope that a partition of Palestine might achieve a lasting peace between them. I knew that wiser Arabs, such as King Abdullah of Jordan, and the more moderate Zionists were secretly prepared to accept the partition. So there was at least a hope of avoiding a war between them. For this agreement I secretly struggled. And the position of confidence I enjoyed with General Paget helped me enormously. But when Paget retired as Commander-in-Chief, the whole position changed. I was told in Cairo that if I returned to Palestine I would be treated as an ordinary journalist—which meant, during those days of terror, that I would be allowed to see only precisely what the British High Commissioner intended me to see. This wasn't

---

higher does not know the lower applies. When one knows the other it may hate and criticise it. The disrupted personality may be reintegrated by psychotherapy.

(b) *The normal personality immediately below the natural threshold level.* This is the one that it first contacted by hypnotism and that functions in sleep and all states of physical unconsciousness. It shares all the experiences and memories of the normal consciousness and also has a separate consciousness, memory and activity of its own plus the super-normal faculties already referred to. It is one's *whole present personality,* whereas the waking one is only that duplicate portion of it which functions above the threshold. It is the personality which, as I have suggested, becomes the post-mortem primary one, and its greater powers and wider experiences must make us then superior to our present normal selves.

good enough. So I took a plane direct to Amman and went to stay with Glubb Pasha.

"What are you doing tomorrow?" Glubb asked me the first night at dinner.

"Whatever you're doing, sir," I replied.

"I'm visiting my Arab Legion position in Jerusalem. Why don't you come with me?"

I explained the reason why I was no longer allowed to travel freely around Palestine.

"We can easily solve that problem," Glubb said. "We'll make you a major in the Arab Legion."

The time was nine p.m. At dawn the following morning I left Amman with Glubb; and I was a major in his Legion. I even had an Arab identity card. With my identity card I could go wherever I wanted, and so I did. By then I spoke a little Arabic. I was very sunburned. So far as the British were concerned, I could pass as an Arab without difficulty. It was fascinating to observe the British in action through alien eyes.

One spring morning in 1947 I woke up in Arab Jaffa. The previous day I had bought a camera in Jewish Tel Aviv but I wasn't pleased with it. As a journalist, photographs were essential to me. So I wanted to change it for a better one. That morning the British had decided to impose martial law with the pathetic hope that it would 'freeze' the Jewish terrorists by preventing all movement in the Jewish areas of Palestine. But I wanted to get into Tel Aviv to change my camera, so I walked from Jaffa until I reached a barrier which was manned by a troop of the Brigade of Guards with Bren carriers and armoured cars. I was determined to get past. I used the oldest security trick in the world. As I saw the sergeant-in-charge looking towards me I came smartly up to the salute. He saw I was a major so he saluted back. I gave him a broad smile and walked straight into the middle of Tel Aviv.

The town was deserted. It was as if a great wind had swept the dust and rubbish and cars and pedestrians away from the streets. The avenues were very clean and empty. The roads were absolutely quiet. The faces of the concrete houses seemed to be dead, but one was uncomfortably aware of life within. A curtain would twitch, a hand would appear, or one could see in a darkened room the figure of a man watching, immobile. The town was in suspense. The Jewish photographer peered out of an upper window of his house in terrible alarm when he saw an Arab major approaching. I held up my camera and waved at him in a friendly way, and at last he let me in. I changed my camera. I stayed chatting for a while with the photographer and his pleasant wife from Vienna. Then I walked out into the street again.

Suddenly a British armoured car appeared. It was commanded by a burly major in the Guards Brigade whose scarlet face was dominated by a vast moustache. He glared down at me in contempt and fury.

"What the devil do you think you're doing here?" he asked superciliously.

His arrogance irritated me, so I remained silent.

"Can't you even speak English?" he asked, his moustache trembling with rage.

"I thought wogs of the rank of major could at least speak English," he declared indignantly to his men, who had begun to clamber down from their vehicle in curiosity.

I still remained dumb.

"Can't you understand a word I'm saying?" the major shouted angrily. By this time I had got his troop all round me.

"Yes, I can," I said suddenly. "And you can get fucked."

For a moment the major's men stared at me in blank astonishment. Then they burst out laughing. I waved to the major gaily and walked off. But the episode made me realise the full extent of the ordinary British officer's contempt for the Arabs—which the Arabs resented and still do resent bitterly.

*   *   *

"You're only meeting educated Arabs and the Effendi class," Glubb said to me when I returned to Amman. "I want you to meet and understand the bedouin and their way of life. What's more, you look as if some fresh air would do you good."

So I drove with Glubb to the Arab Legion fort at Jafer in Trans-Jordan, as it was then called.

Glubb inspected the parade drawn up outside the fort. The bedouin soldiers looked very smart with their skirted uniforms and their hair neatly plaited on either side of their necks. On the command 'Dismiss' they slapped the butts of their rifles, turned sharply to their right and rushed up to Glubb to kiss his hand. Later Glubb went to the fort's office to go through the books. He made notes slowly in his own note-book, writing laboriously in a round English hand. Then he wrote in Arabic in the Visiting Officers' Book, and his pen moved quickly.

As he sat at his desk writing, I examined him covertly. I decided that his personality was difficult to define. Even his appearance was hard to describe. He was wearing the horn-rimmed spectacles he used for reading. With his grey hair and moustache, he looked like a schoolmaster correcting his pupils' work. But then one caught a glimpse of the arresting blue eyes beneath thick bushy grey brows, and wondered at the quizzical expression on his face. It was an amused expression, and above all it was kindly. One felt that if one tripped up he would have a good laugh, but would not hesitate to take one to his home to recover. His fingers were blunt and capable; his hands were sensitive. His trim, compact figure and his bearing told that he was a soldier; five rows of medals showed his experience. At that moment he rose and walked outside the fortress, where the camel saddles with their brightly coloured trappings were laid out for inspection.

"You would think," he said, "that camels were easy to equip. But in fact they have more spare parts than a tank."

I wondered what accounted for the influence which Glubb had over the Arabs. First, I think it was his patience. I never saw him exasperated or angry; I never heard him raise his voice. Next, perhaps, it was his honesty and selflessness. He did not react personally. Most of us react according to our reception, but he seemed to be able to detach himself completely. Then he had a great sense of humour; he could make Arabs laugh. There was his deep affection for them which they knew. But, of course, the catalogue cannot be completed. For there is that undefinable compound of qualities we loosely call personality, which makes one of us weak and another strong.

It was now decided that I should make a journey by camel. The guide chosen for me was called Sudan.

Sudan was a young bedouin, full of vigour and impudence. He was finely built and carried himself proudly. He was so beautifully poised that it was not until he stood beside me that I realised how small he was—perhaps an inch or two less than five foot high. His face was dusky, oval in shape and perfectly smooth with soft down on his cheeks. Dark, sparkling eyes peered inquisitively through thin slanting slits beneath his delicate brows, which were set well apart. A great shock of thick black hair, dry and wavy, fell about his head and neck when he removed his kafiyah at the first halt. His feet and hands and waist were tiny. His brown skin seemed to glow with health and happiness.

That evening, as I wandered over the soft sand around the fort, I turned a corner and suddenly saw the fiercely-bearded sergeant-major passionately embracing a young Arab soldier. Later that evening we met for coffee around the fire.

"Next week I have leave," the sergeant-major told me in Arabic. "At last I shall be able to go to Amman to see my wife."

He must have noticed my look of surprise, for he smiled and added, "You see, I use my wife for fucking, but my friend for love."

*   *   *

Sudan and I had planned to leave the following morning at eight o'clock. At eight-thirty Sudan decided that my camel's saddle was lopsided, so he took it off and began to load Ashwa, as my camel was called, again. At nine we said goodbye to our friends at Jafer. As soon as we were out of sight of the fort, Sudan took off his army boots and socks and settled the folds of his khaki shirt comfortably in the saddle. Then he began to sing at the top of his voice:

> *Eliad Eliad Eliadill yemma al Baidiye*
> *Ya jorkh min fasalak lil helu sidriye*
> *Tintain wurden sawa winte khalawiye.*

> My darling, my darling, my darling of Baidiye,
> I envy the cloth that shapes your breasts.
> Two maidens are gone to the well to draw water,
> And you are alone.

"The slaves of domestic tyranny," Gibbon had said, "may vainly exult in their national independence: but the Arab is personally free."

No one who had heard Sudan singing would doubt for a moment that he felt personally free.

The grey desert stretched flat around us as far as we could see in all directions. It was a brilliant morning, fresh and not yet too warm. I felt very happy; I knew what people meant when they talked about 'Liberation of Spirit'. Secretly, I now hoped that I would be able to learn to live with the bedouin, for the desert soothed my nerves and uplifted my spirits.

At eleven we stopped to eat *arbud*—flat cakes of bread—and a tin of beans, washed down with tea. Sudan was in a great hurry to get started again.

"*Ishrab ya Bek.* Drink up. Drink up. Away. Away."

I refused to be hurried, and stroked Ashwa's fluffy ears before climbing on to the saddle. Compared to Gaude, Sudan's camel, she was slow and rather lazy. But she was taller and more firmly built and far more beautiful.

All through the heat of noon, Sudan urged me on.

"Beat her. Beat her. Make her get a move on."

"She's all right."

162

"No, no. Beat her."

I would dawdle happily along, meditating on the glorious emptiness of the desert.

Then: "*Ya Bek! Ya Bek!*"

"Yes."

"Catch up with me. Beat her."

At three o'clock I said, "Look here, this isn't a race."

"No, but we must hurry or we shan't have time to visit Sheikh Selman."

"Why should we visit Sheikh Selman?"

"That's where we must spend the night."

"But why?"

"He's a great friend of the Basha's."

"Are his tents far away?"

"Oh, yes. Very far."

"Do we have to go there?"

"For meat and water."

"But we've got water in the skins."

"Yes, but not meat."

"I've got meat in a tin. Ox meat."

"As you will," he said rather sulkily. "Why do you want to go to the tents of Sheikh Selman?"

"Because he's a friend of the Basha."

I gave up. I was sore and tired, and it was an effort to have to search for every word one wanted to say. By five o'clock I was exhausted. Sudan kept shouting to me to catch him up, but I was too annoyed to answer. After I had been silent for a while, he waited for Ashwa to draw level to Gaude. Then he looked at me.

"*Mabsut?*" he asked. "Are you happy?"

"*La.*"

"*Laish?* Why not?"

"Because I'm tired."

"We must go a long way farther if we want to visit Sheikh Selman."

"Fuck Sheikh Selman for a start," I said in English.

"What's that?"

"I said don't let's hurry. If we take four days to reach the next camp, who cares?"

Presently Sudan said, "*Ana mush mabsut.* I'm not happy."

"Why?"

"Because you're tired," he said, and smiled so sweetly I forgave him and smiled back. He burst into song again. Suddenly he stopped singing.

"Do you come from Lindin?"

"Yes. I come from London."

"Do you possess many girls in Lindin?"

"No."

"Are you married to many girls in Lindin?"

"No."

"Ali, my brother, has a little girl. You should marry her when we go to stay there. She's very little and ever so nice."

"Good."

"Perhaps you will find a girl in the bedouin tents tonight."

"How old is your wife, Sudan?"

"Sixteen."

"How long have you been married?"

"Four years. I have a son two years old. *Ya Bek*, you really should get married to a Howeitat girl and live with us. You and I and our wives. *Sawa, sawa.* Side by side."

To the south I could see the faint outlines of what I knew from my map and compass was Bir esh Shadiya, a station on the derelict railway which T. E. Lawrence had destroyed. The desert behind it was red in the setting sun.

We drank some tea and ate a little bread. There was no good camel-grass, and we spent a very cold evening on either side of a tiny fire. Sudan gave me most of the blankets and slept soundly. Ashwa chewed and dribbled and grunted in the moonlight. At last I fell asleep.

*   *   *

At dawn we drank tea and ate bread again. At seven we set off. I found riding very painful. The camp lay almost due south. But Sudan insisted on moving west-south-west. "For water," he said. At noon we stopped. I clambered stiffly down from the camel saddle. It was so hot that I stripped off my shirt and lay, half-naked, in the sand. I closed my eyes. Presently I felt a hand stroking me. I opened my eyes and looked up. Sudan was kneeling beside me. He gave me a cheerful smile of complete complicity. Instinctively, he had known that I was attracted to him. His hand was now moving softly over my body. But for once I felt certain that if I pulled his head down towards me and we lay together in the warm sand it would, in some way, spoil our relationship. I wanted us to be close friends. If we made love, it might unbalance the spontaneity of our friendship because the strength and quality of our passion were almost certain to be different. I could feel desire quickening in me, but I knew I must resist the temptation. So I smiled gently at Sudan. Then I turned away from him and stood up and walked towards Ashwa who was blowing out her tongue like a balloon, which was one of her habits.

We moved westward over a black limestone desert. Sudan rode his camel so neatly that from a distance he looked like a jockey on a race-horse.

*   *   *

When one is wounded in battle, the feeling of duty accomplished, and perhaps a certain glamour, assuage the pain. But there is nothing romantic about being very sore and stiff and tired so that each movement is an effort of will. I began inwardly to blame my body for being untrained and soft, to blame Ashwa for being slow and lazy, and to blame Sudan for being obstinate and incomprehensible. Above all, I blamed myself for being unable to rise above physical fatigue. And the more I blamed, the deeper I sank into the abyss of my pain.

"Tonight we find bedouin tents. And there, *Bek*, there will be camel's milk and a girl for you."

I turned over the pages of my pocket dictionary to the letter 'S' so that I could say, "I expect both will be sour." Then I chuckled and gave it up.

"Camel's milk and a young girl for you," Sudan repeated. "Do you want a girl tonight to marry?"

"No," I said. "But I do want some camel's milk."

"In the tent it will be nice and warm for the *Bek* to sleep tonight."

"Good," I said.

We moved steadily to the west. I could, of course, order him to go south-east, straight to the camp. But I reckoned I would learn more from him if I treated him as a guide and companion than if I spoke to him as an officer to a corporal.

At last we saw a flock of goats in the distance. Sudan began a long shouting match with the shepherd across the valley. Eventually he said, "The tents are to the south." It was evening, and the goats were being driven into the camp. The little black kids trotted meekly behind their mothers. Our camels stumbled along a narrow wadi with steep, stony sides until we reached five lowly bedouin tents pitched on the mountainside. A dozen curs rushed out at us barking, the kids bleated timorously, our camels groaned, men shouted at the dogs, and a middle-aged man with a beard, in tattered robes, greeted me and led me to his poor tent.

The Howeitat bedouin of these hills live on the margin of starvation. When Sudan produced the stale *arbud* from our previous meal, the haggard men round the fire snatched eagerly. Tiny bits were given to

165

the tousled children who tottered about the edge of the tent in different stages of nudity and development. Sudan also produced tea and sugar which were quickly popped into the kettle. As is customary after sundown, Arabs from the other tents came in to join the headman in his guest-tent (kinsmen kissed Sudan ceremoniously), until at last there was no more room round the small fire, and children were turned away to make room for newcomers. One child of about five years old, clad in a thin cotton smock, looked pitiably dejected when he was pushed out into the cold to make room for an evil-looking old man. I signed to the boy; and rather nervously he came and sat down beside me.

"What's your name?"

"My name's Smaer," he whispered shyly.

The first thing I could think of to amuse him was my compass. The illuminated dial fascinated him until he discovered my matches. He had never seen matches before. I had shown him how to strike a match, and he was on the point of making his first solo experiment, when his elder brother snatched the box from his hands and rushed out into the night. Smaer burst into tears. In despair I produced a pencil and a sheet of paper. He was amazed that he could make marks with the pencil.

Sudan tactfully mentioned that I was tired so that I could make my excuses and go to sleep early. As we rose to sit round the dish placed outside the tent, I heard the evil-looking old man mutter, "But if he's a soldier why is he tired?" Why, indeed! The dish was full of cold, greasy rice mixed with bread. In the middle of the rice was a well of dark, stale oil. The smell almost made me vomit. The oil, which I discovered later was melted butter, was evidently a luxury, because they kept dabbing it over the rice by my place at the dish. I smacked my lips and tried to look happy and to seem to eat more than I did. As the guest of honour I had to make sure that I went on eating until they had all done. For all of them would rise from the dish when they saw I had finished, and I did not want to spoil their meal.

We returned to the fire. The children were sent to bed, and blew me kisses as they left the tent. The coffee-cup was handed round. Sudan said loudly:

"Would you like to sleep now?"

"Yes, please."

"I'll make you a bed in front of the tent."

*   *   *

Primitive life must be governed by strict convention. If your only luxury is coffee, it is good to make a ritual of its preparation. If you can offer a visitor only bread to eat, it is well if you make a ceremony of your offering and he of his acceptance. If you have as your home only one small, low tent, divided by sacking into one side for you, your wife, and your lambs to feed in and sleep in, and another side in which to entertain, it is convenient if your friends know before they arrive that they must squat close together round the fire and ignore what happens in the dormitory. If your boy is growing fast and begins to cause trouble at night, it is expedient to marry him off to the most suitable girl available. Even if she is only twelve years old, they will mature together. Physical conditions are bound to influence a people's way of living. Convention may be described as the set of rules created in the course of time by a community in order to adapt itself to its environment. Generally, the more precarious the environment, the stricter the convention; the more secure the environment the less strict the convention.

Bedouin live on the edge of starvation. Drought may destroy whole tribes. Their code for living is rigid. But they can be bound by it and yet count themselves 'the kings of infinite space'. But I, the European, am not in this way personally free. Therefore this code, which does not confine the Arab, does confine me. And herein lies my mistake. I have confused three things: the Arabs, the bedouin way of life, and the desert. I am fond of the Arabs. I do not, however, enjoy the bedouin way of life, because a formal society tires me, whether sitting round drinking tea from a Dresden pot, cocktails from Lalique glass, or coffee from one tiny cup. But I love living in the desert; for so far it has always brought me peace. I still believe I could adapt myself to its conditions in my own way.

Having reached this conclusion I felt happier. I could now afford to examine my physical state. The sun had burned the skin off my nose, which was like a piece of raw meat. I was lousy; the semi-sedentary lice were bearable, but the nomadic ones, crawling over my stomach, kept me awake. My haunches and shoulders ached like a wound. And I felt sick.

"Very sick indeed," I said to myself in conclusion, and chuckled because it was all so utterly horrid. Then I turned over once again to try to find sleep, while the dogs barked, the camels groaned and a flow of conversation poured from the tent.

*   *   *

At dawn, a strangled coughing noise came from the sack in the corner of the tent. The top slowly opened, and something began to squirm slowly out of it. In the half light I could not see what it was. Then I perceived a claw-like hand and a grey robe. It was human. I wondered whether I should turn away, but I could not. I was fascinated with horror. My host threw some tinder on to the ashes which sprang up into flame and illuminated a face contorted by age and covered with mucus. The creature crawled to the opening of the tent where it stopped and lay trembling. My host went to it, and I turned away as I understood the reason it had left its bag. Presently it was carried to the fire. I could now see that it was an old man. Water dripped from his eyes and from his mouth; mucus dribbled from his nose. It seemed as if he could not close his mouth, for it was wide open and revealed two yellow teeth, long and tapering like fangs. A dirty robe fell loosely about his chest which was covered with thick white hairs like soiled wool. The men propped him up solicitously, and he knew what they did, for a high-pitched grunt came from him.

"He's very old indeed," Sudan whispered to me. "I think he's a hundred and fifty."

I looked at Sudan. He was not a bit horrified. His face was wrapt in awe. With his wide brown eyes and smooth skin he looked like a boy of sixteen. I wondered whether he would live a hundred and fifty years and be put in a sack and taken out to be cleaned and fed once a day.

"I pray to Allah you will live as long as him," said our host.

"*Enshallah*," we said in chorus.

"A sudden death for me," I thought.

*　　*　　*

The same cold dish of rice and rancid oil from the previous night was produced. I made a fair pretence of eating, though my inside heaved against it. At seven o'clock we rode away with thanks and Allah's blessing. We trotted up the winding wadi which was pleasantly splashed with clumps of bright green bushes. When we climbed up on to the plain, Sudan turned off due west.

The plain ended in a narrow tongue of ground. From the tip of this we beheld a different world. We were standing on the edge of the high limestone desert. A thousand feet below us, through a great, red gorge, we could see the sandstone desert sparkling in the sunshine with scarlet and orange rocks rising abruptly, like giants, from the yellow sea of sand. It was brilliantly unreal, like a country of dreams.

To spare Ashwa, who was stumbling with fatigue, I walked down the gorge, past clear-cut changes of strata in the cliffside. An hour later we reached a wadi carpeted with white and pink crocuses.

After we had been riding for an hour across the golden plain, Sudan stopped and said casually, "My home is not far from here. In fact, if we were on top of that mountain we could see the tents."

Then in a flash I understood. It was so obvious that I cursed myself for an idiot for not having guessed before now. I looked at my map to confirm. I was right. Ever since we had left Jafer we had been travelling steadfastly, true as an arrow from the bow, straight to the target—Sudan's young wife. The plan was so simple and impudent that all resentment at the forced marches of each day left me. If I had not used the map and compass, if I had not been suspicious of all navigation in the desert except my own, his plan might have succeeded, though I might have been rather surprised at the number of days it took to reach the camp.

"Rumm is a long way away," Sudan was saying. "We should spend the night in my brother's tent. Then we should travel to Rumm in the morning. *Ana awzha.* I need my wife this evening. I need her badly."

*   *   *

Towards sunset we met a wild, hairy shepherd. Sudan asked him the way to his home, which might, of course, have moved overnight. We turned through a narrow pass into a valley surrounded by steep mountains.

A few minutes later, Sudan burst out, "Look! Look! There it is. There it is."

He urged his camel to a stumbling trot over the stony ground. In a fold of the valley eight tents were dotted beside tall bushes of camel-grass. He beat Gauden's head to make her kneel.

"Look! Look!"

A lithe boy came running out to greet us. He led our camels to one of the nearest tents. As Ashwa, grunting and groaning in protest, fell to her knees, Sudan said casually, "This isn't Ali's home. This is the home of Sheikh Selman."

Then I understood why it was so important to visit Sheikh Selman. Sheikh Selman was Sudan's oldest brother.

He was a tiny little man with a neat, pointed beard and a black moustache. Even in a flowing burnous he looked trim and dapper. He fussed about putting down rugs and covers round the fire. At last we settled down happily, but he moved us again to lay down more blankets in case we were uncomfortable. Seeing me look like a village idiot when he nattered away at me in Arabic, he concluded I was deaf and began to make his remarks very slowly, which helped, and at the top of his voice, which did not. I had expected Sudan to rush to his wife. But there he was, sitting meekly by the fire, rising decorously to greet each kinsman with a kiss. There were now sixteen of us in the circle. The sheikh gave us coffee; Sudan offered them sugar and tea from our rations. Suddenly he sprang to his feet and ran into the other side of the tent. We heard rapturous kisses, and murmuring, while the old men smiled, and I tried to carry on a polite conversation with Sheikh Selman.

Half an hour later, Sudan returned with his two-year-old son, very sweet and solemn, whom I kissed dutifully. Then Sudan spied a *rubeyby* hanging from the side of the tent, and he began to play. He played so that its single string sounded not mournful and distressed, but like a quiet voice. It was the voice of a being who has seen all the goodness and all the evil in the world, and now recollects his life in tranquillity. Nostalgia was there, and pain. But above all, it seemed to me as I looked round the hairy, worn faces now relaxed in contemplation, the voice proclaimed with the quietness of certainty that all things in the world are one and that evil and goodness wash around us as the sea washes about the earth.

I think I shall remember Sudan as he was then. I shall see him in my mind as he sits in this circle of men on the sand round the fire. His face is raised to the mountain towering above the tent opening. By the firelight I can see that his features are in repose; for the pain of his desire has been assuaged, and in his slanting eyes are glistening tears of happiness.

A relation appeared, and the spell was broken. At that moment I noticed that a hole in the curtain separated us from the women and children. It was about two inches wide, and by turning my head a fraction to my left while Sheikh Selman bellowed politenesses at me I could just see a pair of hands resting on a lap. The hands were those of a young girl. I felt sure it was Sudan's wife. I shifted my position casually to get a closer view. But when I next turned my eyes towards the slit, the hands had vanished. All through the day I had wondered if I would catch a glimpse of Sudan's wife. I now began to yearn to know what she looked like.

The sun had dropped behind the tall mountains flanking the valley. The sheikh and his friends left the tent to say their evening prayers. This is the moment for one who is not a member of their faith to leave them in peace. So I wandered away from the camp and admired the evening. Wraiths of white cloud twisted about the twilight, and vast grey ghosts of mountains seemed to lean inward over the valley as if sheltering it from the world outside. Presently I found myself walking back to the tent from the north side, so that I would have to pass the opening where Sudan's wife, Ageyle, lay. My curiosity was now intense. But in front of the tent I met Sheikh Selman standing over the corpse

170

of a black lamb he had slaughtered in my honour. And I was so grateful and worried by this that I forgot to look.

For an hour or more I sat in my place of honour by the fire, smiling, I hoped naturally, but longing for the food to be finished so I could decently go to sleep. My arms ached from the strain of pinioning myself to Ashwa's saddle. Each time I refused, with polite gestures, another helping of sugary tea, my glass was refilled. They began discussing ages. I was amazed to learn that many of the haggard men were in their early thirties. The bedouin's life is hard; they wizen young. Not one of them was certain of his own age in the lunar years by which they counted. "Perhaps I am thirty-seven," said one; and, "I am thirty-four approximately," said another.

At last the little lamb was brought in, well roasted and neatly arranged in a bowl. We gathered round in a tight circle which shut out the firelight. Eating in the dark is tricky if you are as ignorant of anatomy as I am. However, most of what I ate tasted delicious. There was more conversation, more tea and coffee. Then Sudan said to me in a loud voice: "You want to go to sleep now, *Bek*, don't you?"

"Thank you, yes," I replied. "I expect you do, too."

Rugs were laid down in the sand at the back of the tent. Blankets were wrapped tenderly about me by Ali and Sudan, who said good-night to me and departed. For a while talk murmured round the fire, but soon men began to drift away to their tents. I lay awake, impatiently waiting for the last one to leave me alone, because the rugs were so placed that by sitting up in bed I could see through the slit, and from the shadows on the tent-top I knew that a fire was burning in the next compartment.

I looked round furtively. I was alone in the tent. Cautiously I sat up in bed. I began to bend my head towards the slit. Then I lay down again. Somehow I felt it would be wrong—not morally, just plain wrong, as a note can be wrong in music—to look through the slit. So I lay back in bed. Presently I fell asleep.

I awoke at three o'clock, and lay on my back, thinking. I was now at the farthest point of my journey. I had left belongings in London, some more in Cairo, some in Jerusalem, some in Amman, some at Jafer. Apart from my battledress I now had only a razor and a tooth-brush. Of what other than clothing had I stripped myself? Of skin, certainly; perhaps of a little conceit and an illusion. But for that one moment as I stared out at the starry night, I was stripped of desire. And I felt light as air.

*   *   *

In the morning I awoke in the gleam of a cold, blue dawn. Standing outside the tent with her face turned towards the mountains was a young black-clad girl. My heart leapt with excitement, for this must surely be Ageyle, Sudan's wife. But the dogs began barking; and she moved quickly away so that I had only a glimpse of her.

Sudan appeared while I was shaving, looking exhausted.

"You know my camel Gaude?" he said.

"Yes," I replied, thinking, "Only too well."

"I'm afraid she's very ill this morning, so we won't be able to travel to Rumm today."

This was the merest try-on. And both of us knew it.

"I'm leaving in an hour's time."

"Perhaps Ali might go with you."

"Perhaps. But you'll come as well."

"But Gaude's very ill."

However, I knew the form by now.

"I intend to leave at seven-thirty," I said, and went on shaving.

Sudan sighed very deeply. Then he left.

At seven he reappeared and suggested we open the last tin of beef sausages so we could all eat them for breakfast. This I did. Nothing more was said about leaving. But by seven-thirty he had saddled the camels and we left. I was sad to say goodbye to gentle Ali, who walked for a while beside my camel to postpone the moment of parting. Sudan and I rode on in silence. I supposed he was thinking of his wife, Ageyle. I was still wondering whether it was Ageyle I had seen outside the tent at dawn. Was this the girl for whom we had urged forward our camels every hour of the way from Jafer? Was this the girl for whom he would risk disgrace? Was this the target of our journey? For the girl I had glimpsed standing outside the tent was utterly hideous.

The ground over which we travelled was strewn with heavy stones, and the camels moved slowly. In the distance I could see a flock of black sheep being driven out to pasture. At last Sudan broke the silence.

"Do you see that girl over there?"

I looked towards the flock and saw another black-clad girl.

"Yes."

"That is my girl. My wife. Ageyle."

He drove the camel towards her. For a moment I hesitated. He beckoned me to follow. As we approached, she turned away shyly. But he said something to her softly, which I could not understand. Slowly she turned round and looked up at us. She was slim and small and very young. As she stood there with rosy cheeks and sparkling eyes, gazing up at her man, she was very beautiful. I could understand what he felt. And I was happy as I said farewell, and turned to leave them a moment together. But he followed after me immediately, without a word to her. Perhaps their eyes said all that was needed.

I expected Sudan to be sad as we rode on to Rumm. But he was in high spirits, and carolled most of the way, urging me to sing with him:

> *Eliad Eliad Eliadill yemma al Baidiye*
> *Ya jorkh min fasalak lil helu sidriye*
> *Tintain wurden sawa winte khalawiye.*

We stopped to make tea before we reached the fort. I intended to travel back to Maan by truck the next day, so this was our last trip together. I thanked him for the stay in his home, and gave him money to buy a present for his wife. I also gave him the small mirror I used for shaving, which I'd noticed he coveted. He observed his face in it frequently on the way.

*   *   *

That last evening as we drank tea round the fire in the fort at Rumm, I looked around the circle to press the scene on my memory. And as I looked at Sudan I saw that his eyes were full of tears.

*   *   *

If I could speak Sudan's tongue fluently, if I lived with the bedouin for many years, I wonder whether one day I should understand him. Perhaps I am still provincial, and expect my own reactions in other people. Exchange is complicated by different values; for I feel instinctively that though I could not trust him with a pound note, I could trust him with my life.

I found Sudan in the yard of the fort looking miserable, with his red *kafiyah* awry, and his circlet hanging down over his nose. In all, he said goodbye to me three times. Then he mounted Gaude and trotted away through the gate with the other two *gindi* who were travelling with him. As they moved abreast down the slope to the north, he turned round in his saddle and sadly waved goodbye. But soon after he was out of sight I heard, echoing along the valley, the joyous strains of his song:

> *Eliad Eliad Eliadill yemma al Baidiye*
> *Ya jorkh min fasalak lil helu sidriye*
> *Tintain wurden sawa winte khalawiye.*

*   *   *

My reason for telling the story of my journey with Sudan at length is that it has remained most wonderfully clear in my memory—perhaps because of Sudan's joyous sensual innocence and because of the seeming infinity of the desert.

*　　　*　　　*

Dressed as a major in the Arab Legion I could move about Palestine freely. But it soon became clear to me that whereas the moderates among both Arabs and Jews were prepared to agree to a partition of the land which, in her crass stupidity, England has granted to both of them, the politicians of both sides would become wildly intransigent as soon as it came to any form of conference. Moreover, it was the extremist politicians in Egypt who were urging the Arabs towards bloodshed. So I decided to return to Cairo.

*　　　*　　　*

In Cairo, I discovered a state of hopeless corruption and confusion. The courtiers of King Farouk had already seen that their days were numbered. Yet they were so out of touch with reality, so ignorant of the new political forces stirring in the Arab world—they were so insulated in their tiny enclave—that no member of the royal family had ever met the President of the Arab League. And it was I, a foreigner and an Englishman, who effected, at the last dinner-party I ever gave in Cairo, the introductions between the King of Egypt's sister, Princess Faiza, and Azzam Pasha, the President of the Arab League.

*　　　*　　　*

When I returned to London, Sir Edward Hulton, the Press magnate, asked me to dine privately with a handful of top-ranking Tories at his apartment in the Dorchester in order to inform them of the impending crisis in the Middle East. I had already been invited to address the Royal Institute of International Affairs and the Royal Empire Society, but it was thought that I might reveal more facts in private, so the dinner took place.

After the ladies had left us to our coffee and liqueurs, I made my brief report. King Farouk and his regime were done for, I stated. Helicopters were kept permanently warmed up at the royal palaces both in Cario and Alexandria. Farouk was prepared to escape at any moment. The insurrection against his regime would, I stated, most likely come from the extremist Moslem Brotherhood. There might be the possibility of a putsch from the Army. But this I thought unlikely. (And, of course, there I was wrong.) However, my main conclusion was that Farouk's regime was finished—for good and all.

If Sir Winston Churchill had been present at that meeting, things would have turned out differently. But as it was, the senior statesman present rounded on me. (I do not give his name, for he is now a sick man.) To suppose that the monarchy in Egypt was doomed was idiotic, he proclaimed. Anyone who had studied Egyptian history knew that the monarch was not only king of the land, he was also divine. Should any attempt be made to depose Farouk, the eighteen million fellahin of the Nile Valley would rise to a man in order to have their deity reinstated.

It was at that instant that I decided to abandon intelligence work and to give up my interest in Middle East politics generally. Suddenly I realised that if the top politicians could be so stupid as to disregard first-hand intelligence reports there was no point whatsoever in trying any more.

So I determined to try to become a good creative writer. My period of illusion had come to an end. Political activity was no longer my ambition.

But as a writer—from time to time—I still force myself to look ahead, however disquieting it may be . . .

There would be hope, I feel, if we could believe that a new code would be given to the world, a new morality by which mankind could live in happiness, a new creed which would change the way man lives to ways of love and beauty. For thousands of years commandments have been given to men; religions have been revealed; and all their prophets consider the individual, proclaiming that the spirit is more important than the flesh, putting freedom before wealth. Yet we daily contribute more power to the State, surrendering more of our liberty in the hope of greater comfort. Only a few are free to make the decision between freedom and comfort. Therein lies the most bitter inequality.

"The slaves of domestic tyranny," as Gibbon said, "may vainly exult in their national independence; but the Arab is personally free." In the choice between freedom and comfort, the bedouin chooses freedom. For the sake of his freedom he is willing to live barely; and the sheikh in his tent will turn his blue lips to the wind, saying, "That is my liberty."

Perhaps we, who have drawn our carpets and cathedrals from the desert, have forgotten the message of the voice crying in the wilderness: "For what shall it profit a man, if he shall gain the whole world, and lose his own soul?"

*   *   *

Soon afterwards I was invited to Chartwell. I walked with Churchill round the famous goldfish ponds, and he asked me to report on the state of the Middle East. And so I did. When I had finished he gazed down sadly at the fishponds.

"At the election," Churchill said, "I proclaimed that I would be no party to the dismemberment of the British Empire. And it may well prove that my defeat was a blessing in disguise." He paused and turned towards me, screwing up his face in a wry grin. "It was indeed *heavily* disguised," he concluded.

The next time I visited Chartwell was with Charles Fletcher-Cooke. Churchill was in high spirits. "I have spent the afternoon with the most well-instructed and erudite man," he told us. "His name is Mr. Gossage, and he informs me that in every public house throughout the length and breadth of the land the people are singing: 'A penny more on beer, a penny more on stout. You put them in, and you put them out.'"

He paused to light a cigar. "You may well be asking yourselves," he continued, "*who* is Mr. Gossage? And I can tell you. Mr. Gossage is the fish expert from Harrods. For when I came down from London last night it was to discover my goldfish positively *gasping* for breath and the pond empty. We have now devised a most intricate system whereby the water is pumped up to the top pool and thence can return to the swimming-pool by gravity—through the filter of course."

He turned and stared at me. His eyes twinkled, then he made a large dramatic gesture with his hand. "The price of limpidity," he announced, "is perpetual filtration." And he chuckled to himself.

*   *   *

The last time I visited Chartwell, Churchill took Mary and me to his studio where he sat on a huge chair placed on the top of a square box on wheels.

"I shall use this when I can no longer walk," he told me. He pushed on to the floor with his stick and propelled himself backwards and forwards. "I can advance to my paintings so," he informed me, "and I can withdraw to examine them thus."

He stared at a picture he had painted in Miami. "I have attempted a new technique to achieve brilliance of light," he told us. "I am now painting the park," he said, pointing to another picture. "I think I will now take this small canvas and draw in some of the trees."

I carried down a chair for him and put it in position. Then Mary and I left him to his painting and his thoughts.

I will end with one story about Churchill which Willie told me.

Robin Maugham as a trooper in the Inns of Court Regiment in 1939 (*front row, third from left*)

W. Somerset Maugham and Robin Maugham at Yemassee in 1944

Robin Maugham met at London Airport after the Agadir earthquake: with him are his sisters, Diana Marr-Johnson (*left*) and Honor Earl (*right*)

Robin Maugham with W. Somerset Maugham at a cocktail party

A married couple—friends of Lady Churchill—asked if they could take their son Tim, aged seven, to Chartwell one afternoon in order that he might be introduced to the great man so that in time he could tell his grandchildren that he had met Sir Winston Churchill.

Lady Churchill in her kindness invited the couple and their son Tim to lunch. As they drove to Chartwell, the wife turned to her son and said, "Now, at lunch you'll be meeting the greatest man alive in the world today."

But Lady Churchill met them at the door with the sad news that Churchill had had one of his attacks and had been told by his doctor he must remain in bed for the day.

"I'm very sorry," Lady Churchill said, "but at least we can show Tim the goldfish ponds."

So after lunch they strolled round the grounds, and Tim admired the famous ponds, and since the husband and wife were great friends of Lady Churchill they were soon absorbed in conversation and did not notice that little Tim had wandered off. However, they found him waiting by the car.

As they drove away, the mother turned to her son. "Tim," she said, "I'm awfully sorry you didn't meet the greatest man alive in the world today."

"Oh, but I did," Tim replied.

"No, dear," his mother said, "I mean Sir Winston Churchill."

"But I met him," Tim insisted. "While you were talking away around the ponds, I went back to the house and I climbed up a huge great flight of stairs and I walked along a huge great corridor, and I came to a great big door—and I opened it. And there, lying in bed, smoking a huge great cigar, was a very, very old man. So I said to him, 'Are you the greatest man alive in the world today?'

"And he looked up at me, and he said, 'Yes, I am—and now you bugger off.'"

*   *   *

Now that I was a full-time writer, two disparate events in my life fused together in my mind. I am often asked what idea or incident suggested some particular novel I've written. Since *The Servant* is one of my better-known novels and plays, I will put down its genesis.

The first event took place in Dorset, in the summer after the war. My parents' country house near Hartfield had been requisitioned first by a hospital and then by a tank regiment. It was now being restored, so I had moved to a small cottage to recover. One afternoon, when I was walking on a near-by common, a girl cantered by on a horse. The girl was very blonde, and the horse very black—perhaps it was this contrast that first attracted my attention. I looked at the girl's face— she was lovely, and about eighteen. I walked on the common each afternoon in the hope of seeing her again, but she never appeared. Then I found myself standing next to her in a queue at a bus-stop. I spoke to her, and we soon made friends. I will call her Vera, which is the name I gave to the character I used in my novel *The Servant*. I discovered that she was, in fact, only sixteen, but had already won several cups for riding. By now I was extremely attracted to her. She was wonderfully slim, and there was a sensual look about the lips of her wide mouth. However, I decided she was far too young for me to have an affair with her.

One evening she came to my cottage for supper. It was a warm night. After we had washed up, we went for a walk. We strolled through the woods until we came to a clearing. We stopped, and she lay down on a bank of grass. She beckoned to me to sit down next to her. I looked at the girl sprawled out beside me, all legs and arms. My desire was fierce, but I made no move. Then Vera began to speak. She told me that one day, when she was fourteen, her riding-master had taken her to this clearing and stopped because he'd said the horses were sweating.

"He lay down beside me," Vera said. "He began playing with me and he got me so excited that when he did it to me I didn't mind . . . We'd stop here every day he'd take me riding after that, and he'd have me. Then I got frightened that I was going to have a baby, so I told my mother. She was livid. But if we reported the riding-master to the police I'd have had to have gone into the witness-box. My mother didn't want that. So she went round to see him and frightened him off. He moved out of the county soon afterwards."

Vera paused and lay on her back, looking up at me.

"So you see, you needn't worry," she said.

As I stared down at her she stretched up her arms and drew me down to her.

*　　　*　　　*

The second event took place a year later.

When I returned from abroad I had rented from a friend a small house in Fulham, and there was a manservant to look after it. Again, I will call him Barrett as I did in the novel. Barrett was an excellent servant. Softly moving and soft-voiced, he would glide silently around the house. But there was something about him which made me shudder each time he'd come into a room. One evening Mary Churchill and I had been to a cinema and gone back to the house for a drink before I drove her home.

"If you've got such a thing," Mary said, when we reached the living-room, "I'd love a cold lager."

I remembered that there were two lagers in the fridge in the kitchen.

"I'll go downstairs and get some," I said.

There was no one in the kitchen, but the door of the servant's room, which led off the kitchen, was open and the lights were on. Lying spread-eagled and naked on the double bed was a boy of about fourteen. His beauty and slenderness reminded me of Drew when I had first met him at school. While I stared at this vision in astonishment, a soft voice spoke from behind me.

"I can see you are admiring my young nephew, sahr," Barrett said.

"Would you like me to send him up to you to say goodnight, sahr?"

At that moment I could see myself caught in the mesh of a smooth-voiced blackmailer. By this time I had taken the bottles of lager from the fridge. I pretended I had not heard a word he had said.

"Good night, Barrett," I said crisply, and walked up the stairs.

When I reached the living-room, Mary stared at me. "You look as if you've seen a ghost," she said.

I tried to smile. "I have," I answered and poured out our two lagers.

A year later I gave up the little house because, to use Willie's favourite word in relation to me, I was 'impoverished'. I moved back to my flat at the top of the family house in Cadogan Square.

*   *   *

The complimentary copies of *The Servant* arrived when I was having breakfast with my mother and father. Without thinking I opened the parcel. My mother was attracted by the cover of the book, my father was interested by the title, so I gave each of them a copy. That night at dinner, when I came down from my flat on the top floor, I realised by a warning look from my mother that all was not well.

"We have both of us read your novel," my father said, fixing in his monocle. "We both of us find it very unpleasant and wholly disgusting. And I cannot on any account allow it to be published."

"But it's already been printed," I explained to my father.

"Then you must pay back to the publisher the amount of money for printing expenses," my father said. "Be it even two or three thousand pounds. Whatever happens, you cannot publish that novel under our name."

After dinner I climbed back to my flat in despair. I phoned my friend and literary mentor, Harold Nicolson, who had become a kind

179

of godfather to me in my struggle to become a writer. I told him what had happened.

"Don't worry," Harold said. "I'll do my best to reason with your parents."

That very night he wrote a long letter to my father in which he said that, shocking and abhorrent as some of the scenes in my novel might be, the work would make my reputation as a writer. Reluctantly my parents withdrew their objection to publication. *The Servant* was published and received almost universally good reviews.

* * *

I shall always be grateful to Harold Nicolson for his help to me while I struggled to become a writer.

One evening I had dined happily at the Travellers' Club with him and we returned to my flat for a nightcap. My father and mother were already asleep, so we had crept gingerly up the steep winding stairs that led past their room. At about midnight Harold announced that he must go home. At the top of the staircase he turned.

"Don't bother to see me down," he said. "By now I know the way blindfold."

Unfortunately on the cue word 'blindfold' he somehow caught his foot in the carpet and fell headlong down the stairs, landing up finally with a crash against the door that led into my father's bedroom. Such was the force of the impact that the woodwork splintered, but the door remained closed. I rushed down the stairs, picked up my distinguished guest, and found that he was not seriously injured, so I was able to help him down the stairs and find him a taxi.

When I came down rather late to breakfast the next morning *The Times* was trembling violently in my father's hands—a sure omen of trouble.

"Good morning," I said brightly.

My mother nodded her head in my father's direction and gave me a warning wink. After I had helped myself to bacon and eggs from the hotplate and had taken my place at the table, my father lowered the paper.

"Now, Robin," my father began in a mournful tone of voice, "your mother and I have been having a long talk about you, and we have decided that it is high time you changed your present mode of life— and your present friends. Even before my discussion with your mother I had been giving the matter some considerable thought. Now, I personally would like to see you consort with people *older* than yourself instead of young flibbertigibbets. I would like to see you make friends with some important politician or someone who has won world renown in the world of letters rather than with common riff-raff. *Who*, for example, was the drunken young hooligan who crashed against my bedroom door last night?"

"Harold Nicolson," I replied truthfully.

* * *

As I have said, it was Harold who introduced me to Guy Burgess. In drink, Guy could be unpleasant and malicious, but his nature was essentially generous. In 1948, for instance, I was asked to address the Royal Empire Society about North Africa. At the end of my speech the chairman opened the meeting to questions. I had noticed that Guy was sitting with a boy-friend in the third row; I had also observed that he was drunk. To my horror he now lurched to his feet.

"The distinguished lecturer," he said in a slurred and ironical tone of voice, "has in his speech used the phrase: 'Fascism does not seem to matter so much in Spain.' But inasmuch as this meeting is being reported by the world Press, the lecturer might decide to qualify this statement in view of the fact that it might be quoted out of context."

I sighed with relief. I thanked him. Guy had been right in drawing my attention to my slip. With typical kindness he had done me a good turn.

Afterwards there was a small party at my sister Diana's house. Guy arrived with his young friend. By then he was very drunk indeed. His blue eyes were a little watery. His curly hair was dank. But with his inquisitive nose and sensual mouth he never lost his alert, fox-terrier expression—nor his energy. There he sprawled, burly and truculent, on the floor in front of the fireplace. He wore a very old tweed jacket with leather patches at the elbows, and very old, very dirty, grey flannel trousers. His shoes were cracked and dusty. His uncut fingernails were grimed with dirt. His talk was wild and extremely pro-Russian. Suddenly his conversation switched. He began to quote and requote E. M. Forster's dictum to the effect that if he had to choose between betraying his country and his friends, he hoped he would choose to betray his country.

"I believe Guy Burgess is a Communist," my sister Kate said to me later.

"Nonsense," I answered. "If he were a Communist surely he wouldn't *act* the part of a parlour Communist so obviously—with all that Communist talk and those filthy clothes and fingernails."

"Perhaps it's double bluff," Kate suggested.

I wondered. In fact, I wonder still.

Guy was four years older than I was, so I had not met him at Eton or Cambridge. Harold Nicolson admired Guy's rapid and acute mind and his fantastic vitality. So did I, but both of us knew by 1948 that this high-powered personality was running down. For a while the clock could be rewound by drink. But the machine became erratic. Then in May 1951, Guy Burgess, who had been recalled from the British Embassy in Washington for 'unsuitable behaviour', absconded with Donald Maclean, the career diplomat and blue-eyed boy of the Foreign Office. Guy—we now know—had driven down from London in a hired car to Donald Maclean's country house in Sussex. He had collected Maclean and driven fast to Southampton just in time to reach the cross-channel boat which left at midnight for Saint Malo.

"What about the car?" yelled a garage attendant.

"Back on Monday," Burgess cried out.

But they were not back on Monday. Gradually, over the years, the full story of the 'missing diplomats' and later of the 'third man', Kim Philby, came out. And then we learned that Guy Burgess and Kim Philby had been employed by the British Secret Intelligence Service (M.I.5) since 1940. It was further learned that all three of the 'defecting' diplomats had been recruited by the Russian Communist Secret Service since their undergraduate days at Cambridge. As more stories about the diplomats came to light it seemed wholly incredible that M.I.5 should ever have employed them, and still more incredible that, having employed them, they should not have got rid of them.

Guy Burgess, for instance, had a brilliantly fertile brain and great personal charm but in his cups he could be wildly indiscreet. At a large dinner-party in Tangier he startled all present by giving the names of the head of each Department of the British Secret Service. He was emotionally unstable and aggressively homosexual.

"I dined with Guy Burgess," Sir Harold Nicolson wrote in his diary on January 25th, 1950. "What a sad, sad thing this constant drinking is! Guy used to have one of the most rapid and acute minds I knew. Now he is just an imitation (and a pretty bad one) of what he once was."

Donald Maclean was equally emotionally unstable and equally unreliable. These two outrageous characters would never have lasted two months if they'd been working for some reputable business company. They would have been sacked. Why were they kept on by our intelligence service? Why? Because in those days our intelligence service was run by an 'Old Boy' network and backed up by an Establishment of crypto-queer ambassadors. All that has now changed. After the unveiling of the 'third man', Kim Philby, the whole of our intelligence service was reorganised.

Though Guy gave the impression of being extremely Left wing, he was in fact essentially a liberal-minded intellectual. The extraordinary thing is that he became a Communist and remained one. In the political climate of 1937 most intellectuals were Left wing. Many were Communist. But that doesn't explain why Guy seems to have remained a Communist. I think I know the explanation. Guy was quixotic and he was romantic. I think he genuinely believed that by betraying an American plan—of massive atomic retaliation, should Russia go too far—he was saving humanity. Guy was certainly a spy, but nowhere near such an important spy as was Kim Philby. Moreover, he was hesitant even on the very day that he drove down to Sussex to rescue Donald Maclean, who our intelligence had at last discovered was a Communist agent.

Guy, only that very morning, had rung up his old friend Wystan Auden in Ischia to ask him if he could go out to stay. However, we now know that Guy Burgess and Donald Maclean travelled from Saint Malo to Paris and took a plane to Prague. It was in Prague that the moment of decision for Guy came. He knew that he was about to be dismissed from the Foreign Office for his outrageous behaviour. He was like a child who has been smacked by his mother. He was resentful— and he was aware that he could cause a lot more trouble by defecting with Donald Maclean.

It took Guy only a few days in Moscow to realise his mistake. Soviet life repelled him. Guy was an intellectual: he liked conversation, music, literature, and art exhibitions. There was little of all this in Russia. A friend has told me that Guy was so bored in Moscow that he didn't even bother to learn the Russian language. Whenever he could, Guy would move south to Black Sea holiday-resorts—together with some young boy-friend. But Guy desperately longed for England and he very nearly came back. If he had returned to England, M.I.5 would have prosecuted him. But it is by no means certain that the prosecution would have succeeded.

In Moscow, Guy took refuge in drink and in sex.

"I have just had a wonderful session in a Turkish bath in Tiflis," he wrote to Harold Nicolson in a letter which he knew was bound to be opened by two censors. (Tiflis, now known as Tbilisi, is an ancient Georgian city in the south of Russia.)

The year before he died, Guy pleaded once again with the British authorities to let him visit England so that he could see his mother. The request was refused. During the next few months drink and sheer boredom killed him. His ashes now lie in a Hampshire churchyard where the Burgess family once lived.

But perhaps the strangest thing of all is this. Guy Burgess, Donald Maclean, Kim Philby, and Maclean's fellow-scholar at Trinity Hall, Dr. Nunn May, were all recruited as young men at Cambridge. The dose of Marxism which was injected into them in those years was, in fact, fatal.

Who injected the Marxism?

I believe there was a don who had been won over to the Communist cause in the 1920s. I believe, in fact, there was a *fifth* man—a man who may still be alive today.

*   *   *

I had upset my parents with the publication of *The Servant*. But I little thought that Willie would be bitterly angry about it.

By the time the American edition was published I was living in the Southern Highlands of Tanganyika, where I had gone on doctor's advice. The wide African sky, it was thought, would cure my claustrophobia; the simple life would improve my health. It would not be true to say that letters arrived in the crook of a stick carried by a native who had swum across crocodile-infested swamps. My little mud hut was so remote that I did not even know that *The Servant* had been published in the United States. But indeed it had. And James Stern, in the *New York Times* hailed it as 'a masterpiece of writing'. But then he had added the fatal words—'written with a skill and speed that the author's uncle might envy'. Other reviews made similar comparisons. And my enterprising American publishers had taken huge space in all the literary papers to quote every review of this nature.

My uncle was furious, thinking that I had done it on purpose. It was several years before he became friendly with me again.

*   *   *

While in Tanganyika, I had a telegram from my sisters to say that my mother was seriously ill. I flew back to London. By the time I arrived she had recovered; the doctors told me, however, that the illness might recur, and I decided to stay in England for some time.

From the age of seventeen I enjoyed a wonderfully close relationship with my mother. I remember her telling me that she believed my father had been fonder of her parents than of herself, and certainly the brief mentions of his wife in my father's long autobiography would appear to support that belief. But their marriage could never have been completely happy because of the sharp difference in their temperaments.

My father was quiet, dignified, reserved and solemn; my mother was a Romer—irrepressibly cheerful and high spirited. To use Cyril Asquith's words:

> . . . she had the secret of disengaging the kernel of fun or absurdity which often lurks within the most unpromising material and bringing it to the surface, a process warming to the cockles alike of the heart and of the mind. It was this, along with her unforced, unposed approach to people and things which made her one of the happiest human beings, and a potent and persuasive cause of happiness in others. In her presence shyness was disarmed, diffidence melted, spirits rose, dullness began to emit sparks, or to think it was doing so, while the most exacting were held, charmed and exhilarated.[2]

But my father was not exhilarated. What A. A. Milne described as my mother's 'ever-youthful spirits and sense of fun' were apt to irritate him; and while my mother "bubbled over . . . with an absurd travesty of everything which had been happening to her; illness, war troubles, domestic difficulties . . . an irresistible saga of nonsense", my father would sit tense and pale and silent at the other end of the table. I remember a large lunch-party when he was Lord Chancellor at which he had not said a word. But when his guests were drinking their second cup of coffee he suddenly leaned forward towards my mother. So impressive was his movement that the others stopped in mid-sentence to hear what they expected to be an important political or legal pronouncement.

"Will you kindly pass me the sugar, Nellie?" said my father and relapsed into silence.

*   *   *

The fame or notoriety of *The Servant* had been responsible for introducing me to people who shared the same inclinations as I did. I now began to lead a dual life. I found friends at whose parties I would sometimes find a boy with whom I could spend the night. But in my fatal, romantic way I yearned to find some boy with whom I could share a permanent relationship.

Over the last twenty-five years I have been lucky enough to find three boys who were prepared to share my life with me. All of them are still alive. To save them embarrassment—as I said I would in the preface to this book—I have fused their personalities together into a single character whom I shall call Jim.

*   *   *

[2] Written in *The Times*, October 1950, when Asquith was Lord of Appeal in Ordinary.

I was still nervous of going to homosexual clubs, but the strength of my need to find a permanent friend overcame my timidity—especially when I had been drinking all day.

On *that* particular evening I had been to a smart cocktail party given by the Anglo-Arab Association which I had helped to form under the presidency of General Spears. After I left the party I visited two or three pubs and, by ten o'clock, I was so drunk that I decided I could face a queer club. I took a taxi to Soho.

The inside of the club—with its crimson and white Regency striped curtains, chairs to match, crimson carpet, and prints on the walls—looked like a setting in the Ideal Homes Exhibition. About twenty men were clustered around the bar; at least another dozen men sat on the long, plush-covered banquette which ran along one wall. The atmosphere was as restrained as that of a church meeting. I went to the bar and ordered a large whisky. Standing next to me was a pleasant-faced, sad-looking boy of about twenty listening to a tall emaciated man on the other side of him who was dressed in a tight-fitting city suit and whom I supposed to be a stockbroker. I could hardly stop myself staring at the boy because, with his untidy blond hair, wide-set eyes and smooth, slightly fleshy face, he reminded me of Laurent. Nor could I help overhearing their conversation.

"Stop looking so gloomy," the man was saying to the boy.

"I'm sorry," the boy said. "I can't help it but I *feel* gloomy. I can't stand this place."

"What's wrong with the place?" the man asked petulantly. "It's supposed to be one of the best bars in London."

"You may be right," the boy said. "But I feel out of place here, it's too piss-elegant."

The tall man gave a little shiver of distaste.

"I've told you not to use that kind of language," he said sharply. "Be careful—or I'll make you very sorry when I take you home."

"I said 'piss-elegant' because that's what this place is. Piss-elegant and bloody boring."

I finished my drink and paid for it. I could see what was going to happen.

"If that's what you think," the man said, "there's nothing to stop you going. But you needn't come to me next time you're in trouble."

The boy gulped down his drink. "Right," he said, "I'm off."

Even as the boy spoke I slipped off the bar stool and walked quickly out into the street. For an instant I stood by the door of the club. It was a warm summer night. As the boy came out of the door, I smiled at him. "You're perfectly right," I said, "the place *is* 'piss-elegant'."

186

The boy looked startled. For a moment I thought he was going to walk off.

"Let's go and have a drink," I suggested. "There's still time."

The boy hesitated. "What's it all about?" he asked. "What d'you want?"

"Nothing, at the moment," I answered. "Nothing except a pint of bitter."

Suddenly the boy smiled. His teeth were small and very white. More than ever he now reminded me of Laurent.

"All right," he said. "I don't suppose a pint of bitter can do us any harm."

*   *   *

When we had settled down with our drinks in the pub I turned to the boy—I'd discovered his name by then—and said, "Tell me, Jim, what's the story?"

"What story?" he asked.

I was still drunk, but in addition to my drunkenness I felt wildly elated. Waves of happiness were lifting up my spirit, because I had an oddly strong instinct that, at last, I'd found the person whom I'd been seeking for so long. I smiled at Jim. "The story of your life," I said. "The story of how you came to be sitting just now at a queer bar with that man."

For a moment Jim hesitated. "Why do you want to know?" he asked.

"Because I'm interested," I answered. "Because I feel that one day we might be friends."

Jim stared at me, then he took a gulp of his drink. "Right," he said, "here goes."

Jim's story was a familiar one. I had heard it several times before. It was almost predictable—the father dead, the mother taking a second husband, the family arguments and scenes in the cramped prefab in Bristol where they lived, leading to Jim's decision to give up his job in a shipping supplies store, and to leave home; his search for a job in London, his failure to find work of any kind; suddenly finding himself penniless and unable to pay the rent of his room; his meeting with a boy of about his own age who initiated him into the ways of making quick money and who introduced him to the queer world in general and to the tall man, who, it turned out, was an insurance broker, in particular.

When Jim had finished his story it was closing time.

"Can we meet somewhere tomorrow?" I asked him.

"It's only eleven o'clock," Jim answered. "It's early yet."

"Where shall we go?"

Again Jim hesitated. "If you like we can go back to my place," he said. "I've got nearly half a bottle of gin, and I've got a key. But we'll have to let ourselves in quiet or the landlady will be after me for the rent."

* * *

An hour later I was sitting in Jim's bed-sitting-room on the fifth floor of a decrepit Victorian house in Fulham. On to the stained walls had been pasted photographs and coloured prints of sailing ships and motor yachts.

"My father was a sailor," Jim explained to me. "I've been mad about ships since I was a kid. But what about you?" he asked. "What were you doing in that queer club?"

Suddenly I felt that if I could manage to make Jim understand me I would gain his friendship. I told him about the war in the desert and about Nobby, I told him about the Arab Legion and about Sudan. Lastly, I explained to him the reason why I had gone to the club. Jim listened intently.

When I had finished he was silent for a moment. Suddenly he smiled at me. "It looks as if we're both on the wrong side of the fence, doesn't it?" he said.

"Listen, Jim," I said, "why don't we try and make a go of it together—and see what happens?"

"But where could we live?" Jim asked. "You wouldn't want to stay here, would you?"

As I looked around at the ships pasted on the wall of the shabby room the idea came to me. "We could live on a boat," I said.

Jim sprang to his feet. "D' you mean," he began, "d' you mean we could really have a boat to live on?"

"Yes," I answered. "I think so."

"That'd be great," Jim said. "It really would."

He picked up the bottle of gin and found it was empty. He smiled at me again, then looked towards the bed. He gave me a grin.

"P'raps we'd best be turning in," he said. "After all, we've got to begin sometime."

* * *

When I woke in the morning I found Jim was staring at me solemnly. "It's going to be fine," he said. "It's all going to be fine."

* * *

I wonder, now, what each of us expected and as we sat that morning in his bed-sitter, drinking coffee, and what each of us wanted from the other.

I suppose that above all I wanted a devoted friend with whom I could share my little triumphs and disappointments. I had been a rather lonely person until then; I wanted not only the passion but the comfort of a lover. Mixed with these feelings was a longing to help this strange boy with his clear, wide-set eyes which had an odd look of yearning in them. I wanted—as did Ewing, the hero of *The Wrong People* which I was to write several years later—I wanted to help him to appreciate all that I had discovered to be fine in civilisation. In my pathetic way, I hoped to teach him to understand painting and sculpture, I wanted to take him to see the works of El Greco and Praxiteles, I wanted to encourage him to appreciate Bach, Beethoven and Proust, I wanted to take the unhardened clay of his mind and mould it into a shape of beauty.

And what did Jim expect and want from me? Certainly he wanted loyalty and affection and constancy. His life had been insecure; I probably represented to him the safety he had lacked for so long. He was twenty and I was thirty-three. Though I was only thirteen years older than he was, I think he saw me, perhaps unconsciously, as a father figure. He needed security, and, as I had discovered the previous night, he enjoyed sex. I could give him both. Lastly—if our relationship prospered—I could sell my little house in Chelsea and buy a yacht for us to live on.

To put it in a phrase—I suppose that what almost every homosexual wants is a marriage with his friend.

*   *   *

I was very much aware that my relationship with Jim was illegal and could land me in prison. I was equally determined not to be a hypocrite. I agreed with Hawthorne's dictum: "Show freely to the world, if not your worst yet some trait whereby the worst may be inferred." I introduced my sisters and my close friends to Jim. Most of them liked him for his candour and his charm.

In a yachting journal, Jim and I found an old motor yacht called *Clio* for sale. The price asked was two thousand, seven hundred and fifty pounds. We looked up *Clio* in the Lloyd's Register for 1910. "1241: *Clio*: Wood: TwnSc: Tonnage 25·19: Dimensions 56·8; 12·15; 6·5: W. Fife & Son: Fairlie: 2 paraffin motors: W. R. & Mrs. W. R. Hutchinson: Glasgow."

We drove to Teddington to see the boat and immediately fell in love with her. She was of solid mahogany; all the fittings were opulent; she had obviously been built 'regardless of expense'. There was a solid Edwardian air about her and not a trace of dry rot. We bought *Clio* for two thousand five hundred pounds and lived on board her even while she was being refitted.

*   *   *

At lunch at Cadogan Square a few months later I noticed that my mother ate very little and seemed to be in pain. That afternoon the doctor came. Towards morning my mother was seldom conscious and an ambulance took her to the London Clinic. I now moved back to Cadogan Square in order to be close to my sisters. At six-thirty in the morning, two days later, they telephoned from the London Clinic and told me that my mother was dying. I rang up my sisters and then went downstairs to wake my father. Together we drove round to the Clinic. All five of us were with her when she died.

*   *   *

I now felt there was no longer any reason for me to stay in England. Jim and I took *Clio* to France, sailed up the Seine to Paris, travelled through innumerable locks to Marseilles and then on to Villefranche for a final refit in Voisin's Boatyard.

*   *   *

I took Jim to lunch at the Mauresque. Willie had changed very much since Gerald's death.

"There's no point in trying to change your essential nature," Willie had told me. But Willie had always tried to change. He was socially ambitious, and he kept up his heterosexual pretence in public to the end of his life. (This was displayed in its most unpleasant form in the sections of his autobiography which were published in the *Sunday Express* in England and in *Show* magazine in America. In it Willie dismissed Gerald with the words, 'I had found him a very useful companion', and he puts all the blame for the failure of his marriage on to Syrie.)

At this period Willie had somehow managed to persuade himself that he had never been queer.

Willie led a comfortable life at the Villa Mauresque. He was looked after by Alan Searle, who had been with him constantly since the end of the war. If ever the over-used words 'loyalty and devotion' meant anything, Alan Searle exemplified them. There were six servants and four gardeners. The villa ran smoothly. But Willie was an unhappy man; he had become withdrawn and censorious. He disapproved violently of my relationship with Jim. *Now*, I can understand his anger with me at that time because, after all, I had done precisely what he had told me not to do. Where was the heiress? Where was my seat in Parliament? How could I end up as the Governor of some colony while leading my present life? Indeed, what was I doing? In Willie's eyes, I was committing two crimes. I was living openly with a boy, and, far worse, I was writing novels which sold well.

Towards the end of lunch that first day Willie suddenly turned on Jim.

"You may think you're eating ger-gruel," Willie said to him. "But it is in fact *zabaglione*—and very expensive to make."

Jim made no reply. But the remark was unkind because he knew perfectly well he wasn't eating gruel and was enjoying the *zabaglione* very much. Years later Jim was to quote Willie's remark to me as being typical of the attitude of some of my friends towards him.

A few nights later I was invited alone to dine at the Villa Mauresque. After Gerald's death, Willie seldom gave large parties, but that night there were several guests. In the middle of dinner Willie turned on me in a sudden fit of rage.

"Yer-you're making a complete hash of your life," he said. "You'll never be a writer. And do you know how I see yer-your fer-future?" he stammered.

"No, Willie," I answered. "How?"

There was silence round the table. I could see that the guests were extremely embarrassed by Willie's rage.

"I see you as an ageing, impoverished viscount," he told me, "on the fer-fringes of literary society."

I smiled at him. "And do you know how *I* see my future?" I asked him.

To my delight Willie fell into the trap.

"No," he replied. "How do you see it?"

"Precisely the same," I answered.

The guests laughed, Willie glowered at me.

I was asked to lunch at the Mauresque a few days later. Once again I was told to come alone. After lunch, Alan left me with Willie. We were sitting on the sofa. Willie clasped and unclasped his hands.

"I have a few remarks to make to you," he announced.

I was silent. Willie lit a cigarette.

"I her-happen to know something about writing," he began. "I must tell you here and now that you'll never make a writer. I want you to ger-give up the attempt before you make a complete fool of yourself. I also wish you to discontinue your friendship with that common young man. He quite obviously doesn't care a rap for you. He's just out for what he can get."

For a while Willie was silent, then he turned to me once again.

"I realise that you're obstinate," he continued. "I know also that you're cer-conceited. So I don't expect that you'll listen very carefully to what I have to say. Ber-but I happen to know that you've got very little money apart from what you make from your novels and from journalism—and that can't be very much. Your young friend and your yacht are going to ruin you between them. So this is my proposal. If you do what I say—if you give up writing, if you abandon your ler-ludicrous affair with your boy-friend, if you per-promise me that you'll go back to England and marry and settle down to the career of a politician, then I will make over to you fifty thousand pounds."

"Thank you," I said. "I'm very grateful. But I'd like time to think your offer over."

Willie stubbed out his cigarette. "I have said all I intend to say," he told me. "And now I intend to go up to my room for my siesta."

He rose from the sofa and walked out of the room. Our meeting was at an end.

The following day Harold Nicolson came to stay with me on board *Clio*. Benign, generous and witty, he got on well with Jim. He was one of Jim's favourites among my friends. When I was alone with Harold I told him of Willie's offer.

"Why did you say that you'd think it over?" Harold asked. "Why didn't you tell him that you refuse to be bribed?"

"Perhaps I should have done," I answered. "But I just couldn't face a scene. Sometimes Willie frightens me."

"Well, he doesn't frighten *me*," Harold said, laughing. "I find his hypocrisy rather unpleasant. Did you tell him that I was coming to stay?"

"No," I answered.

"Then *don't* tell him," Harold said. "I don't want to see him."

But Willie heard that Harold had been staying on my yacht. He was enraged that Harold hadn't called on him. Once again I was summoned to the Mauresque.

"I mer-must tell you," Willie said, when we were alone, "that your affair with *that boy* is causing a scandal in Villefranche. In the bars he frequents he fer-flaunts his relationship with you. Everybody in Ville-franche knows that you are my nephew, and you're getting me a bad reputation."

Terry Thomas with Robin Maugham

Robin Maugham and Honor Earl

Gerald Hamilton

Robin Maugham with Noël Coward

I said nothing. Willie was silent. I looked at him. His yellowish eyes were glaring at me. He was a very different person from the man who had lain on my bed in Yemassee sobbing that, now Gerald was dead, I was the most important person in his life.

"I mer-may also tell you that it's only a question of time before your sainted father hears about the life you're leading. And I certainly wouldn't like to be responsible for the consequences," Willie concluded.

The threat was quite obvious.

*　　　*　　　*

By now, *Clio* had been refitted. Two days later Jim and I sailed out of Villefranche harbour. I did not say goodbye to Willie.

PART

FIVE

I FELT DEPRESSED BY MY UNCLE'S OBVIOUS DISAPPROVAL
of me; I admired him so very much as a writer. I was sad that he
thought I was heading for ruin; I was sad that he now seemed
to dislike me. But in this, apparently, I was wrong—I quote from
Beverley Nichols' book:

Willie spared nobody in his letters. No—there was one exception;
he never wrote anything disagreeable about his nephew Robin. He
appreciated his worth, not only as a gallant young officer whose
charm and sparkle enlivened the dullest party—some of the parties
at the Mauresque were very heavy-going—but as a brilliant story-
teller in his own right. "I suppose we must grant Robin a touch of
g-g-genius," he once said to me, and he obviously meant it. "And I
suppose that if it hadn't been for me his genius would have been
more widely recognised." In this, he was stating an obvious truth.[1]

*   *   *

Travelling with us on board the *Clio* was Michael Davidson. I had
first met him when David Astor had asked me to contact him in Tangier
where he was *The Observer* special correspondent. That had been in 1947,

[1] Beverley Nichols, *A Case of Human Bondage*, Secker and Warburg, London, 1966.

when I was preparing to cross Africa from coast to coast. From the articles of his that I had read in *The Observer* I had imagined a squat man with a severe face and a stiff collar. But not at all; I discovered Michael to be a slender man, usually dressed in open-necked shirts, and well-cut but shabby tweeds. He had a lean knobbly face with a large nose and very light blue eyes beneath heavy eyelids. His lined neck was set at an odd angle on his stooping shoulders. He looked like a humorous camel. We have been friends ever since.

Mike had been working in the Far East, but he had asked *The Observer* for three or four months' leave.

We decided to sail to Capri to make a pilgrimage to Norman Douglas because we felt he was the last and most distinguished of a marvellous breed of authors. We found him drinking a Negroni outside the Café Victoria on the cliff behind the piazzetta. His white hair was parted in the middle, his deep-set blue eyes were soft but searching, his face was surprisingly firm. He was dressed like a clerk on a Saturday afternoon. His baggy grey trousers were unbuttoned at the top, he wore rather frayed braces, an open shirt and a shabby coat. Standing behind his chair was a little round-eyed boy called Paolo whose curly hair fell over his forehead. The boy was immaculately dressed in orange velvet shorts and a light blue shirt.

"Do you know why the drinks we've got are called Negronis?" Norman Douglas asked us.

We shook our heads.

"Well," Norman said, "in Florence there was a Count Negroni who used to sit each day in the same café at the same table, drinking the same drink which was compounded of Campari bitters, sweet vermouth and gin. Each day he would have this very selfsame drink prepared for him. Then one day his chair was empty. The count had died of heart failure. But the drink—and his name—lived on. He never did a stroke of work in all his life, yet he has achieved immortality."

Norman took a sip of his drink.

"Let *that* be a moral lesson to you," Norman said.

He saw me glancing at little Paolo and smiled. "I've always loved a very large possession attached to a very small boy," he murmured.

We began to talk about literature. Norman talked of the old Bloomsbury days. "You must let writing ferment," he said to us.

At that moment a bearded sailor with a gnarled face approached us, knelt down in front of Norman and kissed his hand. Norman ruffled the man's grey hair.

"You wouldn't believe it," he said after the sailor had gone, "but thirty years ago he was the prettiest creature on the piazza."

Suddenly he turned round and noticed that Paolo had slipped away. "Where's that boy gone?" he asked.

"Shall I go and look for him?" Michael suggested.

"No, no," Norman said. "He'll come back."

But Norman's Augustan face had grown sad, and presently, leaning on his stick, for he was over eighty, he tottered from the Victoria towards the piazza. Michael and I had another Negroni. Norman returned, and called for Giorgio, the waiter.

"*Sono in disperazione*," he told him.

So Giorgio went off in search of the boy. But he returned alone. Norman then summoned the proprietor.

"*Sono in disperazione*," he repeated. So the proprietor went off in search of Paolo.

Meanwhile, Norman fumbled with his right hand in his pockets for his snuff-box—until he found he was holding it in his left hand.

"It's that wretched aunt of Paolo's again," he announced. "Paolo never goes off with other boys. He's as brave as a lion. But he simply hasn't the guts to stand up to that terrible aunt of his."

Obviously Paolo had disappeared for the night, so we took Norman off to dine at a small trattoria that he loved and where he was loved.

"Perhaps *one* more glass," he kept saying at the end of the meal.

As Michael says in his book,[2] Norman was brimming with fun and wit—'very old on his legs but youthful in mind.'

"You know," Norman said, "I left Europe under a cloud." Then he paused for effect. "A cloud no bigger than a boy's hand."

"Do you think the people at the table next door are English?" I asked him.

"Hope they are," he said glaring at them. "Do them good . . . Did I tell you that my son Robin was born as the result of a bottle of *strega*?"

His conversation was becoming rather incoherent. He now began to worry about getting home. He called for the waiter. "Go and find me a boy," he told him. "One waiter here's a shit," he informed us in a loud aside. "But the other one's good."

The waiter returned without a boy. "*That* one was the shit," Norman told us. Then he leaned forward to us. "I'm afraid I shall have to ask you to help me home," he said. "I may die of heart failure at any moment; I must have someone with me."

It was as Michael and I got up from the table that we realised that the wine of Capri doesn't go to one's head; it goes to one's legs. We

[2] Michael Davidson, *The World, The Flesh and Myself*, Arthur Barker, London, 1962.

swayed up the hillside with Norman leaning on our arms until finally we reached the villa in which he was staying.

The following morning his son Robin, a congenial business man from Chicago, came down to the yacht.

"I have to warn you," he told us over a pink gin, "that another evening like last night may well kill my father."

"But he's invited us to dine tonight," we said in dismay. "Should we cancel or what?"

"Go," Robin said firmly. "It's on a happy evening with friends like you that he wants to die. I'm only warning you in case he does die tonight and you have a terrible conscience about it."

Three months after we left Capri, Norman Douglas died. I hope that those festive days with us didn't hasten his death; but, if they did—as Michael Davidson says—Norman certainly enjoyed them.

＊　　　＊　　　＊

In Ischia we met Robert Clarke, the head of Associated British Pictures, drinking coffee at the Diana Bar in the narrow main street of the little port. I was all the more pleased to meet him because his company had been considering making a film of my story, *The Black Tent*. The following day he came on board *Clio*.

"I don't want you to be too optimistic about *The Black Tent*,"[3] he told me. "I can see difficulties ahead. But meanwhile, why don't you come and work for me as my assistant? It would teach you a lot about film-making."

I liked Robert Clarke and I liked the idea.

"When I get back to England I'd love to," I said.

Robert's Scottish face creased into a smile. "You may well return to England before you think," he said. "I can see that this yacht's going to ruin you."

As he spoke, Robert Siodmak,[4] who was directing *The Crimson Pirate* in Ischia, together with Burt Lancaster and his wife and a vast entourage, streamed over the gangplank on to my little yacht.

"You see what I mean?" Robert said.

＊　　　＊　　　＊

Crossing the channel to Malta from Port Augusta in Sicily, *Clio* nearly sank. We had stupidly allowed the level of one of the diesel

[3] In fact *The Black Tent* was made into a film three years later by the Rank Organisation, and directed by Brian Desmond Hurst.

[4] Robert Siodmak later directed the film of my novel *The Rough and the Smooth*.

tanks to fall low before we refilled, and the muck from the bottom of the tank had blocked the filters from one of the engines which broke down completely. Presently a storm arose. Two hours later we were down to one cylinder of one engine. The bilge pumps failed, the engine-room was flooded, the ship was in darkness, we had no navigation lights. When I staggered up into the wheelhouse Jim was at the wheel. His lips were moving and, at first, I thought that he was trying to say something to me above the roar of the storm and the crashing of huge waves over our decks. Then I realised that he was praying.

Shortly before dawn we sighted Malta. *Clio* crawled along a creek. In the darkness we saw the outlines of a huge naval ship and realised the creek must be Sliema which was out-of-bounds for all vessels except those of the Royal Navy. We found a stern-buoy and made fast to it before falling exhausted into our bunks.

In the morning, Captain Trevor Lean, D.S.O., the captain of *Manxman*, was making his morning rounds with his first lieutenant. He happened to look over his stern-rail. Way below him lay a white, bedraggled little object still fastened to his buoy.

"Good God!" he exclaimed. "I've laid an egg."

By noon we were drinking pink gin with him.

While in Malta I had leisure to examine my financial position. *The Black Tent* had still not been sold. My novel, *The Rough and the Smooth*, had been given wonderful reviews and had sold out within a week, but unfortunately the publishers could not make arrangements for an immediate reprint. At each port of call *Clio* seemed to need some form of mechanical attention—which was always extremely expensive. In fact, Robert Clarke had been right: *Clio* had ruined me, and, moreover—as I said to Mike—'the weather's broke, and *I'm* broke'.

I cabled to Robert Clarke. Immediately I received a cable back instructing me to fly straight to London. Mike sailed with Trevor Lean in *Manxman* to Suez. Jim stayed behind for a while to look after the yacht until she was sold. I flew back to England.

*   *   *

I found the people whom I met in the film industry kinder and more intelligent than I had supposed. But beneath their pleasantness I soon perceived that there lay uncertainty and the incessant effort and struggle to maintain or improve their position. After I had worked for the Associated British Picture Corporation for some time, Robert Clarke decided to make a film of my novel *Line On Ginger*.[5] He introduced me

[5] *Line on Ginger* was eventually filmed by British Lion under the title *The Intruder*. Jack Hawkins starred and the film was directed by Guy Hamilton.

to Ivan Foxwell, who became the producer, and to Jackie Hunter, who worked with me on the film script. We got on well together.

I had sold the yacht in Malta, and Jim came back to England. Now that my mother was dead, my father seldom left his study, and Jim came to live in my flat on the top floor of Cadogan Square. Jim missed the yacht, but I had bought a new car; he enjoyed driving it; and he had learned touch-typing so that he could help me with my various scenarios and plays. I was as fond of him as ever, but now and again I sensed a kind of restlessness about him. I began to feel guilty because I had not persuaded him to adopt any definite career.

*   *   *

After the success of my first three films I gradually drifted away from the industry, and I began to write novels again. Whereas I enjoy writing a film script with a collaborator, while I am writing a novel there are long periods when I need to shut myself up in a room alone. I would leave Jim in London with the friends he'd made of his own age, and I would go down and stay in a wing of Boxley, the beautiful house Diana and Kim, my sister and brother-in-law, had bought near Maidstone. I was very grateful for the peace they gave me.

*   *   *

One winter I revisited Ischia with Michael Davidson and Jim. As Mike tells in his book, he had known Wystan Auden as a boy of sixteen —"Tall and gangling, with fair hair limp across a pale forehead and clumsy limbs apt to go adrift; and an old, cogitative face that was frighteningly unboyish." Mike now introduced us to Wystan, who was living in Forio. We walked up a twisting cobbled side-street one afternoon. Wystan Auden opened the door and showed us into his living-room. We sat on deck-chairs beside a gas-stove which was fed by a giant cylinder. Behind us were two modern side-tables littered with books, letters, documents and ashtrays. I was unprepared for Wystan's heavily lined face and pronounced American accent; I was equally unprepared for his humour and his charm.

"Forio has been invaded by Limey lushes," he told us. "I've only got the lease of this house till 1960 by which time, I'm afraid, Forio will have become impossible. I like it best here in the winter. You see, I don't like sunshine. I would like a Mediterranean life in a northern climate. I work in the mornings, I take the dog for a walk in the afternoons, I work till it's time for a cocktail, I eat at seven and then go down to Maria's bar for a coffee.

"I love Italian," he continued. "It's the most beautiful language to write in, but terribly hard for writers because you can't tell when you've written nonsense. In English you know right away."

He spoke of the libretto of a new opera he wanted to write.

"The great difficulty is to get open vowel sounds in English. There are no dactyls in English. But I dislike French as a language. Even Racine's Alexandrines sound to English ears like 'The Assyrian came down like a wolf on the fold'. The metre is comic.

"When I went back to Oxford," he told us later, "I just found I didn't belong. I said to them: 'It's all fine, but where's the gravy?' In America I won't open my mouth for less than three hundred dollars. In England I found people expected me to speak for five pounds. I found them provincial. A don at the House asked me whether Eisenhower was a Democrat or a Republican. So I gave him a little lecture on the American electoral system. But I feel he ought to have known, don't you? England *is* terribly provincial—it's all this *family* business. I know exactly why Guy Burgess went to Moscow. It wasn't enough to be a queer and a drunk. He had to revolt still more to break away from it all. That's just what I've done by becoming an American citizen. You can become an Italian or a French citizen—and that's all right. But become an American citizen and you've crossed to the wrong side of the tracks. I found even the nicest people in Oxford tried to forget I'd ever done such a thing. I had to keep reminding them by starting sentences with 'Speaking as an alien . . .' I also find criticism in England very provincial. In the literary world in England, you have to know who's married to whom, and who's slept with whom and who hasn't. It's a tiny jungle. America's so much larger. Critics may live in New York, but the writers don't."

I met Wystan quite often that winter. I was fascinated by the mixture of the gay hedonist and the strict schoolmaster, between the outrageous rebel and the didactic puritan. He would talk about sex; then suddenly he would check himself: "Sex is a part of life but only a part of it," he would say. "I think people are a bore who can think of nothing but sex."

He gave me valuable advice about the novel I was writing; he also advised me to try to meet Gerald Hamilton. "Christopher Isherwood used him as a character called Arthur Norris in Mr. *Norris Changes Trains*," he told me. "But there's a great deal more material hidden in *that* man."

*   *   *

Jim and I flew to Tangier where Gerald Hamilton was living at that time.

I had already heard a little about Gerald Hamilton's background. His father had been a Shanghai merchant called Frank Souter. Gerald was born in Shanghai on November 1st, 1890. He was sent back to England to be educated—first at a preparatory school, and then, in January 1905, he entered the famous public school at Rugby. He left in 1908. His father found him a job with a commercial firm back in Shanghai. He settled down in a comfortable house with several servants, and began—to use his own words—'to live like a prince'. He also shocked the European community by wearing Chinese clothes. He travelled around the Orient attended by his Chinese servants, and drifted, by way of Egypt, Russia, Germany and Italy, back to England, where he took a large house in Westminster, and began to lead the life of a rich young man about town. Stage stars and countesses, lords and layabouts, flocked to his apartment with its Chinese scrolls and lacquer ornaments, and peeped in awe at his Louis XV bedroom upholstered in rose damask.

By now the dashing young man had changed his name by deed poll to Gerald Hamilton, and he was hinting at aristocratic connections. But the life that he was leading needed money, and by the time he was thirty he had been cut off by his father because of his idleness and dissipation. And Gerald soon ran through the allowance he got from an indulgent aunt. He was always living in a world in which he was surrounded by money. When he travelled in Europe he was constantly courting rich people and living in luxurious suites at the most expensive hotels. With his wit and facile charm, he was such good company that certain people were always prepared to pay to have him around. But by now he was in the hands of the money-lenders.

It was at this stage, I already knew, that Gerald's life of crime began, but I had no idea of the enormity of his misdeeds.

I met Gerald Hamilton at Dean's Bar. For at Dean's Bar gathered the bogus barons and furtive bankers, the tipsy journalists and sober Jewish business men, the young diplomats and glamorous spies, the slender French and Moroccan girls, the English self-styled colonels and their friends, the foreign agents—the highly coloured collection of fake and genuine, cruel and kind, which formed the international society of Tangier.

Behind the bar was Dean himself, full of elegance and wit, mixing— as Mike once said—'a dry Martini with the air of a member of the Borgia family preparing a loving cup', and with 'a heart made of honey and, often, a tongue like a scorpion's sting'. It was Dean who introduced me to Gerald Hamilton, who was then approaching seventy. He was completely bald, immensely fat, with a twisted mouth and blubber lips.

He was fastidiously dressed. But his appearance was not enhanced by the fact that he was suffering from gout and supported himself on two crutches. To cure his erysipelas a Tangerine doctor had placed a thick bandage all round his neck and this reached up to his chin. He was one of the most unprepossessing people I'd ever met—until he began to talk. Then one forgot about his appearance and became aware only of his strange wit and charm.

He invited us to dinner at an expensive restaurant. When Gerald had settled himself down at the table in the restaurant that evening his distinguished manner and exquisite French impressed the head waiter. He ordered food and the most excellent wines in the solemn voice of a priest intoning Mass. After the waiter had left us, with a small bow of admiration, Gerald suddenly raised a well-manicured finger, placed it on his lower lip, and simpered at Jim and me coyly. "I have the most terrible confession to make," he said. "I seem to have left my wallet behind at the hotel." Then he leaned forward and smiled at us benignly. "But I must admit," he added, "that even if I had brought my wallet with me it would have been empty."

I always like people who behave 'in character', and I could see that Jim was already fascinated by Gerald. By the time we had reached the third bottle of wine, Gerald was in a loquacious mood.

"I've heard you described as the greatest con-man in the world," I told him.

Once again, Gerald lifted his finger to his lower lip and simpered so violently that his whole body quivered like a jelly.

"I think that's an overstatement," he tittered. "But I must admit I've had my moments."

He took a gulp of his wine.

"I once knew a wealthy industrialist who was insanely keen to be given the *Légion d'Honneur*," he said. "But unfortunately he'd laid himself open to a scandal with an under-age girl. The man knew I had friends in the right places in French society. So he offered me vast sums of money to see that the matter was hushed up and didn't reach the Press, and so ruin his chances of getting the *Légion d'Honneur*."

Suddenly the right-hand corner of his mouth lifted in a kind of snarl. "He was the type of man one could only treat like dirt," Gerald continued. "I didn't lift a finger to help him get his *Légion d'Honneur*. Eventually I only pretended to be helping him. I kept up a show of intrigue for over a year and he paid me handsomely, the idiot. Eventually, the wretched man *did* get his *Légion d'Honneur*—through no help of mine—and he was extremely grateful to me." Gerald simpered. "Of course I didn't care to disillusion him."

"Who is the wickedest man you'd ever met?" I asked.

Gerald fluttered his eyelids. "What blunt questions you do ask," he exclaimed. "And if you insist on an answer I suggest you should allow me to order another bottle of Pommard which attunes so pleasantly with this *tournedos* . . . Well, there's no difficulty in my answer. It's Dean, of Dean's Bar, without any doubt. His real name isn't Dean anyhow. It's Donald Kimfull. He's a naughty baggage, and he always was. I first met him in London in about 1913. He was then a gigolo about town. We formed quite a profitable partnership. Once, when I was due to travel with a millionaire—a Greek one this time—on the Blue Train to Monte Carlo, I gave Dean the tip-off that the millionaire had his wife's jewel-case amongst the hand-luggage. Dean booked himself on the same train and travelled in a separate compartment. When the Blue Train stopped in Marseilles on its way to Monte Carlo, Dean got off and bought a ticket from Marseilles back to Paris. The Paris train was on the track right alongside the Blue Train. So all I had to do was hand the jewel-case out of the window to Dean, who popped it under his arm and took it back to Paris. When the Blue Train reached Monte Carlo, the loss of the jewel-case was discovered. There was a great hue-and-cry. But I knew that even if they searched my luggage they would have found nothing because Dean was already on his way back to Paris with the loot."

Gerald lay comfortably back in his chair and folded his hands across his stomach. "But that Dean's a naughty baggage," he repeated. "He took far more than his fair share." Gerald gave a sigh and wiped his lips with a large bandana handkerchief.

"What was your greatest coup with royalty?" I asked.

"Undoubtedly the Khedive of Egypt, Abbas Hilmi," he replied. "He would toss over ten thousand pounds to me as anyone else might hand out ten shillings. I was intriguing for him all the time. I must have got almost one hundred thousand pounds out of him altogether."

Gerald sighed heavily and took a long drink of his wine.

"If only I hadn't been so extravagant throughout my life," he said. "Of course, Spain was the greatest place for bribery," he continued. "I remember when it was essential I should get a certain document signed by King Alfonso XIII. So I invited one of the King's private secretaries to lunch with me at my apartment in the Ritz Hotel, Madrid, where I was staying. The man noticed that I had a copy of Carlyle's *The French Revolution* and asked me to lend it to him. 'With pleasure,' I replied. 'I'll send it by my servant to the palace after lunch.' So I stuck several one-thousand-peseta notes between the leaves and sent off the book. A few hours later the telephone rang. It was my friend the secretary. 'Thank you *so* much for lending me the book,' he said. 'But I notice that you've only sent me the first volume—and there are two volumes.' 'I'm so sorry,' I replied. 'I'll send the second volume across this evening'—which I did, stuffed with yet more one-thousand-peseta notes. Needless to say, my important document was signed by the King the next morning."

At that moment the waiter advanced with a pitcher of water. Gerald brushed him away.

"I *seldom* touch water," Gerald told us. "But my good friend Prince Nicholas of Rumania *never* does. I once asked him what he did about cleaning his teeth—if he never used water. 'Oh,' he replied, 'I find a light Chablis suffices.'"

By now we had drunk quite a lot of wine, and Gerald was becoming even more loquacious. I noticed that far from feeling any remorse about his exploits he seemed to revel in them.

"The *cleverest* confidence trick I ever used was one summer in Monte Carlo," he told us. "I'd sit at a roulette-table, and when I saw a rich-looking American I'd push back my chair and get into conversation with him. 'I'm tired of playing tonight,' I'd tell him. 'Besides, they'll get suspicious if I win every time.' This remark would intrigue the American and I'd invite him for a drink. Over a bottle of champagne I'd explain my system to him. 'It's quite simple,' I'd tell him. You see half the croupiers in this place are crooks, and there's one who's a close friend of mine. He can spin the ball so that it falls into the red or the black—whichever he chooses. All I have to do is wait for a certain signal from him, and then I back black heavily.' By this time the American would be fascinated. He'd suggest coming in on the deal with me. 'Fine,' I'd answer. 'But, of course, I have to pay the croupier fifty per cent and—I must confess—I would like ten per cent for my services.' The American would agree, and I'd take him to a table at which some completely innocent croupier was presiding. I'd watch the croupier like a lynx. Eventually he was bound to make some slightly unusual gesture. He'd stroke his head, touch his cheek, or put his finger to his mouth. At that moment I'd nudge my companion. 'Put everything you've got on black,' I'd tell him. And he'd do so."

Gerald's upper lip suddenly lifted once again in his alarming snarl. Until then his expression had been benign, almost torpid. But now he looked quite savage. He reminded me of an old lion in a cage at a circus who has seen another lion moving towards the choicest piece of meat. An instant later his face was serene again.

"You see the joy of it," Gerald said to us. "When black came up

I'd get sixty per cent of the man's winnings. And you'd be surprised how often black would appear."

"But what if red turned up?" Jim asked him.

Gerald tittered to himself as he sipped his brandy. "Oh, well," he said, "then it was quite easy. I'd just tell the American I'd mistaken the signal, and I'd slide away. What could the poor dope do about it?"

"How many times have you been in prison?" I asked.

Gerald simpered bashfully as he stared down at his brandy glass. His finger rose to his lower lip. "I can't count after dinner," he said.

I soon discovered that Gerald was a collector of people. He was remarkably ubiquitous. When I lived in Chelsea, he established himself in Dartrey Road, the next street, which he christened 'Dirty Dartrey', where he zealously pursued a series of intrigues which at once risked his being sent to prison but which never brought him in a penny. When I flew to Tenerife to stay with some friends it was to discover that Gerald had already arrived and borrowed money from each person whom he could accost on the island. He would sit in the living-room, glowering at us in silence if we were late going in to lunch—until at last hunger overcame him and he would tap his stick on the tiled floor and cry out, "Poor fucking Gerald wants his beans." When I went to Madrid, it was to discover that Gerald was well-installed, flattered by Franco and intriguing to restore to their thrones every single one of the ex-royalties who gave him a free meal. And wherever he was, Gerald had the gift of making himself supremely comfortable and of being able to amuse all his friends. And once you formed part of his collection you were there for life.

*   *   *

The atmosphere is strong in Tangier. It seems to drift into everything, pervading all the Moors; seeping even into Europeans if they live out there long enough. Sometimes I try to analyse the smell: burning charcoal and dung—they are mixed in it; incense and sweat, and the pungent sweet smell of *kif*. The atmosphere drifts everywhere. It is sometimes exhilarating; sometimes it can be lethal.

Gerald was too involved in his devious schemes to be much affected by the atmosphere. But Jim and I suffered. Each day the place demoralised us still more. We were both drinking too much, and Jim had now formed the habit of going round the bars till dawn. He would appear at the flat we had taken, pale and trembling with exhaustion, his fair hair damp on his forehead, and his blue eyes staring vacantly. The following day he would be bad-tempered; for the first time, we began to quarrel. I was as much to blame as he was, for I too was depressed and short-tempered. The book I was working on, *The Man with Two Shadows*, which was an attempt to present disassociation of personality in novel form, was going slowly—even though I had set the last half in Tangier.

*   *   *

At that period I had a letter from Willie who was staying at the Dorchester. "Robin dear," he wrote, "I went with Alan to see your play *Odd Man In*[6] on Saturday and greatly enjoyed it. Like everyone else I laughed a great deal . . . I don't see why the play should not run for ever."

I accepted this letter as an olive branch. I reminded myself that Willie was now an old man and that, after all, I had been devoted to him. So I wrote him a letter of thanks. Shortly afterwards I received an invitation to stay at the Mauresque.

*   *   *

When I arrived at the Mauresque it was obvious that Willie had now reconciled himself to my way of life and to the fact that I meant to go on writing. He seemed far more concerned to discuss what he described as the 'odiousness' of my father.

"It may have escaped your notice," Willie said that first night during dinner, "but during your absence abroad your sainted father deigned to spend a fortnight as a guest in this house."

"Did he?" I exclaimed in surprise.

"Indeed he did," Willie said. "And he managed to spend fourteen days beneath this roof without passing one single civil remark."

Success over the years mellowed both my father and Willie sufficiently for the two brothers to meet on odd occasions with interest and a certain admiration for their mutual longevity, combined with a solicitude for their health.

"We must face it," Willie said to his brother, when my father was ninety and Willie was eighty-three, "we must face it that both of us were endowed with very frail constitutions."

But though they sometimes met quite affably, my father's disapproval of Willie persisted, and my uncle's resentment of my father's attitude grew to a violent dislike. Unfortunately neither brother was capable of appreciating the full extent of the other's success—and for this reason: my father was convinced that if he had stooped so low as to

[6] *Odd Man In* was adapted from *Monsieur Masure* by Claude Magnier. It was presented at the St. Martin's Theatre, London by Henry Sherek. Also see Henry Sherek, *Not in Front of the Children*, Heinemann, London, 1959.

adopt the career of a professional writer he would have written far nobler and more eloquent works than Willie; whereas Willie was calmly certain that if he had decided to adopt a political career he would have done better than end up as Lord Chancellor for a year or two. These convictions did nothing to improve the relationship between the two old and distinguished brothers.

My father's visit, I discovered, had been a failure from the very beginning. In those days Willie knew three princesses in Monte Carlo, and when he wanted to impress a guest, Jean, his chauffeur, was sent off to collect them for lunch. They were fetched for my father's benefit, and Annette, who had the reputation of being the finest cook on the Riviera, was given special instructions for the lunch-party.

"Tell me, Lord Maugham," said the youngest princess, aged seventy, towards the end of a luxurious meal, "tell me, how do you find the Riviera suits you?"

My father took out his monocle, raised it with a trembling hand to his right eye, looked at the princess for an instant without speaking, and then let the monocle drop from his eye. The dignity with which this ploy was accomplished was such that it reduced the whole table to silence—which was precisely its purpose.

"Does the Riviera suit you?" the princess quavered.

"Yes," replied my father. "I find this plain cooking agrees with me."

The remark did not endear him to his host. Then, while Willie was still silent, the eldest princess addressed my father.

"Your nose is exactly like your brother's," she remarked.

"You mean my brother's nose resembles mine," he corrected.

After lunch Willie had news that an empire table he had recently bought in Paris for a high price was being delivered during the afternoon, and he determined to invite a few friends up to the villa for a drink to celebrate its arrival. By now he realised that my father's presence would dampen the party, so he suggested to his brother that he should rest in his room until it was time to dress for dinner.

"You're looking very pale and tired," Willie said firmly. "A long rest would do you good."

My father departed rather sadly to his room. Willie's friends were invited. But in the evening, as they stood admiring the new piece of furniture, suddenly the door into the long living-room was flung open and there stood my father looking quite stricken. Willie did not know that for the last twenty years of his life my father could look like King Lear on the blasted heath at the drop of a hat. Willie moved forward nervously and introduced my father to his friends. My father did not speak.

"I asked a few people in to celebrate the arrival of this new piece," Willie said, pointing to the carved gilded table in its place of honour at the far end of the room.

Slowly my father raised his monocle up to his eye. Then he spoke. "Rather florid, isn't it?" he remarked.

To the end of his life my father resolutely ignored my uncle's increasing fame, although at various times, such as Willie's eightieth birthday, it became quite difficult to do so. One day my father received a letter addressed to Viscount Somerset Maugham. He opened the letter and found that it was intended for Willie, so he sent it to the Villa Mauresque with a tart covering note.

I was greatly disturbed by the letter you sent on to me [Willie replied by the next post]. I know exactly what it is going to be. Shakespeare and Bacon all over again. Posterity will say that as an eminent lawyer and Lord Chancellor it was impossible for you to acknowledge that you had written plays and novels under your own name, so they were produced and published under the insignificant name of your younger brother.

I was in my father's sitting-room when this letter arrived.

"I detect a distinctly unpleasant flavour about Willie's remarks," my father commented. "I think I shall feel myself obliged to make some suitable reply."

And indeed he did reply—in words to this effect:

Dear Willie,
        You may well be right in thinking that you write like Shakespeare. Certainly I have noticed during these last few months an adulation of your name in the more vulgar portions of the popular press. But one word of brotherly advice. *Do not attempt the sonnets.*

*   *   *

I still lived with Jim in the top flat of Cadogan Square. The floor below was completely empty because the two servants who were the only survivors of the dozen who had once looked after my parents were so old that they would not climb the stairs. A visitor to the house would ring the front door bell and could hear it echoing in the cavernous basement. There would be time to read a few pages of a paper or magazine before the door was opened by one of the subterranean basement-dwellers—blinking at the light like a pit pony—and the guest would be admitted in silence into the cobweb-hung hall. The stained-glass windows had not been cleaned for many a year. Light filtered in dimly between grimy chinks. One of the aged troglodytes was apt to develop fits of cramp, and the visitor would be appalled to see her standing, contorted and immobile, in an alcove. The visitor would then be admitted into my father's study to find that my father had forgotten the invitation and also forgotten the person's name.

Meanwhile, my father was immersed in writing his autobiography which he called *At the End of the Day*.[7] Unfortunately the autobiographical passages occupy less than a seventh of a very long book. During the last years of his life my father became obsessed with the campaigns that had been waged in the two world wars he had lived through. Why he became so absorbed in grand strategy I shall never know. He had no first-hand knowledge of military problems; he had never fought in a battle. But he became determined to give his balanced judgement on complicated plans and manipulations of forces that have baffled most historians. The result was unhappy, for while he devoted only twenty pages to a description of his early days, thirty pages to Cambridge, and thirty-seven to the Bar, his account of the beginning of the First World War, the Dardanelles Campaign, the battles of 1915, Jutland, Verdun, and of the Somme runs to nearly a hundred pages. As R. F. V. Heuston says, when writing of my father: "the account is, as with everything Maugham wrote, clearly written and trenchantly argued. It is certainly a remarkable performance for a man aged eighty-eight years, but the verdict must be that it is not a permanent contribution to military history."[8]

One morning, when my father had been at work for three years on his voluminous memoirs, he summoned me downstairs to his sitting-room.

"I have a question to put to you," he said. "It is this. Do you think people would consider it odd if, in the autobiography I am now engaged in writing, I made no mention of my immediate family?"

For once my father had asked me a question to which I could give a short and simple answer.

"Yes," I replied.

My father gazed at me mournfully with his large brown eyes.

"I was afraid you would say that," he said. "But I have already written nearly a quarter of a million words, and so I'm afraid I can't

[7] Rt. Hon. Viscount Maugham, *At the End of the Day*, Heinemann, London, 1954.
[8] R. F. V. Heuston, *Lives of the Lord Chancellors: 1885–1940*, O.U.P., London, 1964.

spare the family very much space. I must therefore ask you to write out for me a brief description of your three sisters and of yourself and of my brother Willie—*in that order*."

"How brief?" I asked.

"Four lines," my father replied. "I can't spare more than four lines in all. And you will kindly bring me those four lines before lunch."

My father turned his attention back to revising his intricate description of the Battle of the Somme, which had been troubling him for some months. The interview was at an end. I went upstairs to my little flat and began my task. The time was half past twelve.

"My daughter Kate Mary Bruce is a novelist and playwright," I wrote. And that took one line. "My daughter Honor Earl is a well-known portrait painter." That was another line. "My daughter Diana Marr-Johnson is a novelist, playwright and short-story writer." And there went the third line, leaving only one line for Willie and me to share. And my orders were to put my name next. "My son, Robin, writes novels, plays and stories." And that was all of half a line gone. How in heaven's name could I describe Willie in six words? I was still trying to solve the ghastly problem when the gong rang for lunch. "My son, Robin, writes novels, plays and stories," I repeated frantically to myself.

"And so does my brother Willie," I scrawled in despair and went downstairs to hand over my homework.

"That will do very nicely," my father said after he had read the four lines through.

And thus, in the main, it appears in the book—except that my father changed "And so does my brother Willie" to the colder-sounding "I need not describe the works of my brother William Somerset Maugham." Willie gets only three brief mentions by name in all the five hundred and eighty-seven pages of the book.

*   *   *

Meanwhile my relations with my father were fast deteriorating. On one occasion, he discovered that my sister Kate was drinking cocktails in my flat upstairs. This evidently threw him into a violent fit of jealousy. I had a separate telephone number; suddenly my phone rang; I answered it. My father's voice was trembling with anger, "I will not have you inviting *my* guests to *my* house and taking them upstairs without *my* permission," he told me. "You will send Kate downstairs immediately."

Kate gave me a wink, shrugged her shoulders and went downstairs.

For Kate had somehow managed to establish a closer relationship with my father than any other of his four children.

*   *   *

I realise only too well that I was a disappointment to my father. I know so well the kind of son he would have liked to have had. "One of the best specimens of the all-round-man"—to quote from *The Granta's* description of my father in 1889—a magnificent games player, a brilliant scholar, and eventually a famous lawyer. I was none of these things. Moreover, I believe that my father had found out about my friendship with Jim—although they had never met. One afternoon I was summoned once again to the study. My father was surrounded by a dozen books about the Battle of the Somme; he looked very grim.

"My income has sadly diminished," he told me. This did not impress me as I knew what shares he had, and in addition the government gave him, as an ex-Lord Chancellor, a pension of five thousand pounds a year. "So I must make economies," he continued. "I have decided to let the top flat of the house, and the one beneath it as well. I must ask you to leave the house within a week."

I left the house a few days later and moved down to Brighton with Jim.

However, I like to believe that my father forgave me my short-comings before his death, for when he was dying he sent for me. I walked through the dimly lit, gloomy hall of his house and entered his bedroom which was now on the ground floor. The room looked out on to a narrow lawn, sparsely covered with grass like a threadbare carpet. My father was lying in a small bed propped up by pillows. He did not appear to recognise me. I sat down in the chair beside the bed. After a while I thought he had gone to sleep, but presently he stirred and turned towards me. He looked up at me with watery eyes.

"Hullo, my boy," he said. Slowly he stretched out an arm and took my hand. I stayed with him until he went to sleep again. Soon afterwards he died.

*   *   *

My father's death and Willie's increasing senility made me feel that the shadows were leaving me. How little I knew! The shadows were only growing longer.

*   *   *

In his will my father divided his money between his four children.

214

My share was just enough to buy a decrepit little house in Seaton Street, off the King's Road in London.

*   *   *

I have often wondered what made my father such a strange and a sad man.

All four of us children adored my mother and we were fond of each other. The deep and happy relationship we enjoyed was bound to make my father feel cut off and hurt and jealous. Though his wife's high spirits and robust humour frequently annoyed him, my father was, in his own reticent way, intensely devoted to her; he remained so all his life. When he saw his wife's emotions almost entirely absorbed by her children, he was deeply resentful, and as we grew older and unconsciously made it clear that we were not only united in love for our mother but devoted to one another, his jealousy increased. These emotions of his, combined with his bitter struggle to succeed as a lawyer and the long hours of work 'late every night', were probably responsible for turning him back into himself and into the 'shy and lonely' person he had said in his autobiography he had been before he found friends and affection during his days at Cambridge.

It was the tragedy of my father's life that a seemingly ill-suited marriage, almost constant worries about money, and a neurotically violent jealousy allied to an intensely personal ambition did in the end sour his whole existence. He withdrew into his cloak of loneliness and seldom, if ever, emerged again.

*   *   *

Looking back on it, I think my father's life was pathetic. By his almost ceaseless effort to make money to keep his wife and children in comfort he dried up the sources of humour and of love in his own character. In his autobiography my father wrote:

'The necessity of getting briefs, especially if one has a wife and children to support, is of a very poignant kind . . . A day, sometimes a whole week, would go by without any of those glorious sheets of paper tied up with red tape arriving with my name on the back. The waiting for work is a terrible drawback to a young barrister's life and tends to sour his whole existence. I shall never forget those unhappy days.

But I have reason to believe that my father had another cause for his unhappiness. I believe that when my two elder sisters were young my

215

father fell in love with a young girl who was a friend of theirs. He was an extremely conventional man; he was also loyal to my mother. The experience of being in love with a girl so many years younger than himself must have distressed him terribly. One can only hope that this relationship—which lasted almost until the moment he was made Lord Chancellor—afforded him occasional happiness to atone for the grief.

*   *   *

I now lived partly in my little house in Seaton Street and partly in a flat in Brunswick Terrace on the Brighton side of Hove. My flat was on the top floor of a large Regency house which belonged to the Durnford family who ran one of the largest preparatory schools in London and came to Brighton for weekends and holidays. I had been told that when the Durnfords arrived for weekends they needed complete rest and I must be extremely quiet. Indeed, I moved up and down the stairs so noiselessly for the first two weeks that I never met a single one of them. Then, one day, as I descended from my flat, an impressive, well-dressed, red-haired lady came out of her bedroom on to the landing. I was so startled by her sudden appearance that I gaped at her in awe and said apologetically, "I'm Robin Maugham."

"Well, I'm Winifred Durnford," she replied.

Suddenly—for some reason—we both burst out laughing.

"I *do* hope we didn't keep you up last night," Winifred said. "I'm afraid our last guest didn't leave till four this morning. Come down to the drawing-room and have a drink."

Such was the beginning of my friendship with Winifred, her husband Dudley, headmaster of St. David's School, and their son John, the assistant headmaster. They became a kind of second family to me. Jim moved into a flat of his own—half way up the house—which also contained an office for my excellent and good-natured secretary Jeanne Francis. I stayed in Brunswick Terrace until I went to live abroad. Those were the happiest years of my life. Brighton is only an hour away from London by train, so friends could come down and visit me when they felt like it. Some Sundays my housekeeper and Winifred's would cope with a large lunch-party in the dining-room downstairs—which ran the length of the house.

I already had several friends living in or near Brighton : Enid Bagnold, Terence Rattigan, who had lived next door to me in Ischia when I rented a tiny villa from William Walton and his wife; Hector Bolitho and Derek Peel.[9] More people would come down for the day from

---

[9] Derek Peel was my research assistant on *Somerset and All the Maughams*, Longmans and Heinemann, London, 1966.

London—usually one of my sisters, my nephew David Bruce, who had become more like a brother to me than a nephew, Hermione Baddeley, Joan Assheton-Smith, Keith Monk, Pamela Frankau, Marguerite Steen, Graham Greene, Cuthbert Worsley and Johnny Luscombe, Beverley Nichols—the list is almost endless. And generally dominating the lunch-table would be Gilbert Harding.

*   *   *

When I read the obituaries about Gilbert I felt that most of them had missed the essential point about him, which surely was that he was great fun. His personality was brilliant—so brilliant that when he died a light went out in Brighton, and the place seemed quite dim.

Of course, the brightness varied—like a ray that swung haphazardly around the town like the erratic beam of an unreliable lighthouse. But between its all too frequent occlusions when a dark glass—or too many dark glasses—would obscure the beam until the following morning, the ray shone clear and vivid, illuminating smart villas on high crescents or low pubs down on the front, sparkling in spacious drawing-rooms or cramped little flats, radiating warmth and comfort to old and young, rich and poor, good or unrepentantly wicked.

Now that the light has been extinguished, there seems to be very little left—only a faint glow in the memory, and that is all. His books don't give the essence of Gilbert's personality. He couldn't quite get across his personality on paper. His finest performances occurred only when he was surrounded by close friends. Unfortunately, too little of his virtuosity has been recorded. Much of Gilbert has been lost.

*   *   *

One summer in Brighton, Gilbert decided to tell me the story of his life.

"It will take me some time," he said, glaring at me firmly as if he expected me to contradict him. "In fact, I've calculated it will take all of twelve hours. I shall therefore arrive in my car to collect you at six p.m. It may be dawn before my story is concluded. But my driver will be at the wheel, so you need have no fear. You'd better get into training. Shall we make it next Wednesday?"

"Let's," I said enthusiastically.

Punctually at six the following Wednesday Gilbert arrived at Brunswick Terrace to collect me. He was brisk, determined and sober. No occlusion. The light shone clearly, without even a flicker. It was a warm summer evening; I felt I was going to enjoy myself.

"I've always promised to my conscience that one day I'd tell the whole story of my life to someone," Gilbert said as we got into the back of his Mercedes. "You're now going to have to listen to me perhaps for twelve solid hours. But I've mapped out quite a pleasant tour of Sussex. I don't think you'll be bored."

Bored? I was spellbound.

Seven o'clock found us in a pub at Poynings, and Gilbert was five years old. Four whiskies-and-sodas and two pubs later we were in Worthing, and Gilbert was ten. His years of puberty were spent in Littlehampton and Angmering between the hours of nine and ten p.m. I think we spent his schooldays in Henfield—but my recollection becomes a little confused at this stage. However, we must have been heading eastward because we arrived at the White Hart in Lewes where Gilbert had ordered supper. It was very late, and the dining-room had been closed an hour ago. However, Gilbert, being Gilbert, persuaded the most kind and forbearing management to bring us cold food and wine to 'the residents' lounge'. Thus we were surrounded by the hotel guests of the White Hart as we entered Gilbert's years at university. We couldn't have chosen a more unfortunate period of his life for the residents' lounge. His face was known to all of them from television. Gilbert was already very drunk and emotional. But as he talked about Cambridge and as we drank our wine he became even more drunk and even more emotional. Grief, however, did not quieten him. On the contrary. It seemed to make him all the more noisy. Though tears poured down his cheeks, his voice was stentorian. Several residents glared at us. Others muttered disapprovingly. I began to be afraid that at any moment we would be turned out. There was, it is true, a welcome period of rest when Gilbert went to sleep with his head in his plate of ham. But his snores were disconcertingly violent and he woke up again, poured himself another glass of wine, and back we were again on the Cambridge campus. It seemed a long time before we reeled into the Mercedes and were driven home to Brighton by his patient chauffeur.

As soon as we reached his house in Montpelier Villas, the chauffeur went to bed and we went to the kitchen and opened a bottle of Chablis —which helped us over Gilbert's experiences in Cyprus and his war years in Canada. Dawn was breaking as we embarked on a crate of beer and reached the present day. The milk had been delivered and children were bicycling to school when I was finally released and tottered down the street to Brunswick Terrace.

I spent the next day in bed. I was exhausted. I had listened to him for over twelve hours. That is why I know too much.

If I have concentrated on the lighter aspects of that evening it is because, even now, I cannot bear to think of the story he told me that night. I shall always respect his confidence in me. But without going into any details, I can say this. If ever a man had difficulties of character and temperament to contend with it was Gilbert. The trouble was that he was fastidiously honest with himself and his standards were extremely high. The result was that he disliked various aspects of his own nature and despised what he called his 'telenotoriety'.

Gilbert would have liked to have been a very good and highly moral man. He would have liked to have been a distinguished writer or a famous artist. But he believed that he was none of these things. So he was in constant conflict with himself. Hence the drunkenness. Hence the fits of rage and irritability.

The sad thing is he underrated himself. For, in many ways, Gilbert *was* a good man. He was extremely kind and he was very generous. He would put himself to fantastic inconvenience to help someone in distress. He always backed the weaker side. He was a champion of the downtrodden or oppressed. He was supremely honest. And as a private entertainer, as a virtuoso performer at a lunch-party, he poured out recklessly all the vitality he had to give. His wit was superb, his memory prodigious, his energy astonishing. At his best, he was terrific—and that's how I prefer to remember him; not as a tortured, insecure man longing for the final release from human bondage, but the Gilbert we knew and loved, the most brilliant raconteur of our day, with four or five old friends around him and four or five whiskies-and-sodas inside him, launching into a long diatribe perhaps against some man whom he had decided to dislike for at least ten minutes and whom he would probably help with a loan the next day.

"There he sits," Gilbert is saying in my memory, speaking of a journalist he disliked, his eyes glittering behind his spectacles, glaring round Winifred's lunch-table, as if to defy anyone to interrupt him, "there he sits, day after day, chewing the remains of an etiolated chocolate between his yellow fangs which are insufficiently closely disposed around his mouth to prevent a brown dribble from trickling down his treble chins and falling on to his greasy shirt—a garment already so drenched in vegetable matter that if wrung out it would provide ample sustenance for the starving masses in the soup-kitchens of Prague."

No one else carries on as Gilbert did. Certainly no one that I know has ever had a crueller burden to bear on his way through life—or bore it more gallantly.

*   *   *

I enjoyed the life I was leading—half in Brunswick Terrace and half in Seaton Street. It was a pleasantly hedonistic life, full of friends, dinner-parties, theatres, films—and, alas, drink. I began to feel guilty that I seemed to have abandoned the high ideals which I had once held: "Gird yourself with a sword of resolution," I had written on the last page of my war book, Come to Dust, "and return to the arena to fight for the family of mankind." But there I was basking in amiability and wallowing in alcohol. Moreover, apart from a film script or two, I was doing little work. I resolved to try to reform, for at last I'd found another cause to fight for.

A friend of mine had been attached to the Trucial Oman Scouts who captured the Buraimi Oasis from the Saudi Arabian forces during the autumn of 1955. In one of the outlying villages on the uncertain frontier between Saudi Arabia and Oman he discovered young children in fetters. They were sitting in a corner on the market place, and there were shackles round their ankles. They were slaves in transit for the slave market at Riyadh. They had been bought by Arab dealers from their parents in Baluchistan, smuggled across the Gulf by dhow and carried by caravans of camels across the desert to the Buraimi Oasis whence they would be taken by air to the capital of Saudi Arabia. The story disturbed me. I wanted to find out more. I approached the Anti-Slavery Society in London; I met other officers from the Trucial Oman Scouts; I met travellers who had recently visited the area and read their books together with every report I could find. All these sources confirmed that the largest market for slaves lay in Saudi Arabia. There appeared to be two main slave routes into Saudi Arabia: one led from West Africa— from villages in the French Sudan, the High Volta, the Niger Provinces and the region of Timbuktu. I decided to go to Timbuktu and buy a slave to prove that slavery still existed.

The information about slavery had been reported to the Foreign Office, but no mention of it was made during the Buraimi frontier dispute in October 1955—or, indeed, since. In fact, no positive action had been taken about slavery in Saudi Arabia for political and economic reasons, arising from American influences in that country. When I began to approach newspaper editors, I discovered to my surprise that even some of those steely-eyed tycoons were frightened of the 'political implications', as they put it, of the material I might obtain. The steel of their eyes grew tarnished at the very prospect. However, at last I found the right editor. Stuart Campbell, editor of The People, commissioned two articles as a gamble.

Jim was not anxious to make a long trip to Africa. Luckily, Michael Davidson was in London and he agreed to make the journey with me.[10]

[10] Robin Maugham, The Slaves of Timbuktu.

We bought a Land-Rover in Dakar and made the long trek to Timbuktu. In the desert outside the town we bought a Bela slave of about twenty from his Tuareg master, and we gave the boy his freedom. It was an arduous but most satisfying exploit.

After my father's death, I had taken my seat in the House of Lords. In July 1960, I made my maiden speech on the subject of slavery.[11] It attracted headlines in newspapers all over the world; it also attracted an Italian documentary film company who, now that I had put the whole subject in the public domain, went off to Africa and made a film based on my speech.[12] The film-makers came to London to run the film through for me when it was completed; I agreed to appear on the screen to do an introduction.

*   *   *

However, my interest in slavery persisted. Through the Anti-Slavery Society and other sources I now learned that the slave trade was still flourishing between Southern Morocco and Mauritania. Here was something for me to investigate. Again Jim preferred to remain in England with his friends in London. As my companion and driver I took Keith Gossop, a young man I had met two or three years previously.

In Tangier we bought a car. We drove south to Marrakesh, the lovely city that Churchill called 'the Paris of the Sahara', where we dined with T. S. Eliot and his wife at the Mamounia. It was pleasant to see Eliot sitting beside his wife and holding her hand throughout the meal. For some reason he was extremely interested in all the songs I had learned as a trooper during the war, so I recited as many as I could remember. "They are the stuff of real poetry," he said.

Frail, wise, yet pleasantly inquisitive, T. S. Eliot was, I found, a most understanding character. His kindness, incidentally, nearly lost me my life. The next place at which Keith and I were stopping on the way down south was Agadir. We had booked ourselves two rooms in the Hotel Mauritania.

"You won't like the Mauritania," T. S. Eliot told me. "My wife and I stayed at the Hotel Saada which is far nicer. It's a new hotel right on the beach. We'll send the hall porter here to fix you reservations."

On the morning of March 1st, 1960, I called on the Governor of Agadir to obtain permission to drive farther south. At noon when Keith and I returned to the Hotel Saada there was a tremor. But no one

[11] The complete text of my maiden speech is given in Appendix IV.

[12] The film called *The Slave Trade Today*, was produced by Maleno Malenotti and directed by Folco Quilici.

seemed to worry. Tremors did occur now and again in Agadir. I had an odd apprehension, but I felt that I would despise myself if I left a town merely because of an intuition; and we had planned to stay another two days. That evening, at about seven o'clock, my literary agent Eric Glass rang through to me from London concerning the film rights of *The Man with Two Shadows*. However, the line was so indistinct and the crackling so loud that I could not hear a word he said, and the local Agadir operator told me that Eric would telephone again later in the evening. At dinner in the huge dining-room on the ground floor, Keith offered to stay in with me to wait for the telephone call.

"There's no point in both of us having our evening spoiled," I told him. "You go out. If my call comes through I'll join you at midnight at the bar we visited last night."

When we had finished our coffee I went up to my room on the second floor which communicated, through a bathroom, with Keith's room. By eleven o'clock there had been no call. I was feeling pleasantly tired; I undressed slowly and got into bed. I started to re-read Wilkie Collins' *The Moonstone*.

Suddenly I looked up. There was a great rumbling noise. I hadn't drawn the curtains; I stared at the clear sky outside my bedroom window. To my consternation it seemed as if the stars were sweeping across the window. (I now realise, of course, that the stars were not moving, but that the whole hotel was swaying from side to side.) Even as I stared, abruptly, there was total darkness. It was as if some stage electrician had cut off all the lights in the theatre. My bed now seemed to be swaying and floating in the air. Then I was deafened by a tremendous crash. From everywhere came the noise of concrete blocks splitting, beams snapping, glass breaking, and the whole ceiling of my room seemed to crumple. Great hunks of concrete were tumbling down all around me and smashing through the floor. I had an eerie sensation of falling—and falling. Yet I was still in my bed. With an abrupt jerk, I came to rest. At the same moment I became conscious of terrible pain. I opened my eyes. It was pitch black all round me; I could see nothing. And there wasn't a sound. I could hear nothing—not a scream for help, not a voice, nor the blare of a car horn or the crash of more concrete. I now know that this silence was the silence of the tomb, for when the earthquake occurred the Hotel Saada had literally sunk into the sand.

Perhaps I was unconscious for a few minutes—I don't know, but gradually I came to realise my position. Something was pressing against my chest making it hard for me to breathe. Both my legs were somehow pinioned to the mattress; I couldn't move them an inch. I could move nothing except my left wrist. I was trapped. The shock had numbed me, but as the pain increased I began to cry out for help, limiting my screams because I was afraid of using up such little air as there might be in my tomb. "Help," I cried out. There was no reply, only that uncanny silence. I told myself I must keep calm; I must work out what had happened. The hotel was five storeys high, and I had been on the second floor. Clearly the whole hotel had collapsed, so on top of me there must be the rubble of two more floors. My right arm was now growing numb, I could feel blood trickling down my chest and legs. The pain was growing worse. Suddenly—it seemed to come from many miles away—I heard Keith's voice.

"Robin!" he was crying. "Robin!"

The shock came at about a quarter to twelve, when Keith was in the bar at which we had arranged to meet. When the building began to shake he ran out into the street. He rushed back to the hotel. As he turned a corner he saw that the sign HOTEL SAADA from the roof was level with the marble steps. At that moment he was certain I must be dead; but he remembered that my room had been on the left-hand corner of the hotel overlooking the beach. He clambered over the rubble and reached the corner, then he cupped his hands together and shouted into the ruins. "Robin!" he shouted. Then—to his amazement—from far away he heard my voice. "I'm trapped," I bellowed.

"Wait and I'll bring help," Keith called back.

In my confused state I didn't understand why he had to bring help. I still couldn't appreciate how difficult it was going to be to rescue me.

I waited. I could feel the blood drying on my legs. I gasped from the pain; sweat was pouring from me. Then came a second quake. But all that happened was that the concrete pressing against me shifted slightly and crushed me more closely. The pain increased. I felt despair spreading through me. I began to make promises—not to Providence, for Providence cannot be bribed, but to myself. If I were an eighteenth-century squire lost in a blizzard on a moor, I told myself, I would vow to build a church if I reached safety. But with my overdraft as extended as it was there was no question of building a church. Then I had a thought. If I survived it would mean there would be other survivors from the disaster, so I promised myself I would give a thousand pounds to an Agadir Relief Fund.

I had lost all sense of time. In order to try to forget my pain I made myself consider my life from childhood to the present day. At that instant, faced with death, I must record that I felt no regret for any of the stupid and idiotic things I had done. I did not regret lovers or parties or drinking bouts; I only regretted the dull and boring things of my existence—such as becoming a Barrister-at-Law.

The pain was growing worse. I began to wonder if Keith's voice had not been an hallucination. I longed to die; I wanted the agony to end. Suddenly—for the first time in hours—I heard a voice. It was screaming wildly. Then, to my horror, I realised that it was my own voice I could hear. I began to think I was going mad. I was afraid that Tommy would take over once again. Anyone who has fought in tanks is apt to be claustrophobic. I was so claustrophobic that I could not even travel on the underground or sit in the centre of a row of seats in a theatre. My worst nightmares were of being shut in a prison cell; but this was worse than any nightmare, for I had been buried alive.

Suddenly I felt there was only one way of escape. I could still move my left wrist; now I began to scrape it against a jagged edge of concrete that I could feel. I moved my wrist painfully to and fro, knowing that eventually I would cut the vein and bleed quietly to death. I began to twist my wrist in an effort to try to find the sharpest point of the concrete. Then I heard a distant voice. For an instant I even forgot my pain. *"On vient,"* I heard faintly. *"On vient.* We're coming."

At first I was afraid that my imagination might have played some trick. I could still see nothing; I had no idea where the voice was coming from. But I shouted back: *"Au secours!* Help!" Then I saw a gleam of light. It came from a torch and filtered dimly down to where I lay. From my right-hand side there now came a blessed sound—the noise of rubble and plaster being moved.

Keith had found a troop of men from the French Aero-Naval Base which had not been damaged by the earthquake. He had brought them to the Hotel Saada with him. An officer had joined the men and had taken charge of the rescue operation. He made car drivers focus their headlamps through the clouds of dust at the wreckage.

Soon, light reached my tomb. I could now see the situation I was in. Just above my head was poised a beam of concrete weighing several tons. By some freak, this beam was supported by the headboard of the bed in which I lay. If the headboard cracked I would be crushed to death. My rescuers could also see this. They worked with infinite caution. The ceiling of my room—or what was left of it—was only a couple of feet above my head and they had to crawl in sideways like miners working in a three-foot seam. As they moved, the rubble above us all was continually shifting and groaning. They were risking their lives. The officer in charge crawled towards me. He insisted on being the first in taking the risk. He was a brave man. Somehow they managed to pull away the rubble from on top of me. But, of course, they could not shift the beam. Both my legs were crushed—one was actually trapped by the beam.

Gerald Haxton in 1934

W. Somerset Maugham

The Villa Mauresque

The exterior of Robin Maugham's villa on Ibiza

"*Il faudra lui couper le pied*," the officer said. "We'll have to cut off his leg."

I was already in agony, and they had no morphine. I forced myself to remain calm and to think quickly. Obviously the springs of the bed had been broken. Then I noticed that some of the men had clasp knives. This gave me the idea.

"Cut out the flock from the mattress," I told them.

Rapidly they ripped open the mattress and began pulling out great wads of stuffing. This, of course, lowered me by several inches.

"Now," I said to them, "take hold of my arms and shoulders and pull—don't mind how much I scream."

With a ghastly wrench they pulled—and my foot came free. They carried me gently, moving me through the rubble from man to man. At last I was out into the coolness of the night. I was alive, and the sky was above me.

I was driven to the emergency hospital at the Aero-Naval Base. I was terrified that they were going to put me in a bed inside the building. I needn't have worried; the hospital was already full. I was laid down in the open on a stretcher alongside several hundred other casualties. On the stretcher next to me was a French boy of about twelve who was screaming in anguish. I found out from the orderly who was bandaging me that the boy's legs were both broken.

"You must give him morphine," I said.

"There isn't any left," the orderly answered. "We've run out."

At last a doctor came by.

"If you don't give that boy morphine," I told him, "he's going to die from sheer pain."

The doctor nodded and came back with perhaps the last syringe of morphine.

A woman was wandering from stretcher to stretcher. Her head was swathed in bandages. "Have you seen my little boy?" she would ask each person. "He's only three years old, but he looks four. He has blond hair, and we call him Coco."

Nobody had seen him.

The road to Casablanca had been cut by the earthquake so it was impossible to send in medical supplies by land. But the French colonel in charge of the military hospital at Casablanca had got five medical units airborne within an hour of hearing the news of the disaster. The bombers began to land. The doctors had brought large supplies of morphine, so, at last, I was given an injection. I was unconscious most of that day. I can remember Keith coming to visit me, and I can remember thanking him for having saved my life. Twenty thousand people had been killed, he told me, the Mauritania was the only hotel left standing, and he was working with a rescue team.

"All stretcher cases are going to be flown to Casablanca," I told him. "They'll put us on the bombers in accordance with the urgency of our injuries. I don't want to give them my name here in case they make a fuss of me. But if you can possibly get a message through to the Mamounia in Marrakesh, please tell T. S. Eliot that we're both alive— I don't want him to think we're both dead."

The next morning my stretcher was put on board a bomber. A very young Moroccan girl was on the stretcher next to mine. Her head had been horribly cut about, and she was in the last stages of pregnancy. Obviously she had never flown before; probably she'd never even been in a car. As soon as the engine started she began to tremble with fear. On board was a young French orderly—a boy of about eighteen who was doing his military service. He knelt down beside the girl and put his hand on her forehead and murmured to her gently, trying to calm her. Suddenly she looked up at him and realised that she was unveiled; she pushed his hand away. But the young orderly understood and was patient. He began stroking her forehead, quietening her as he might have done some injured wild bird. At last she understood that he meant her no harm. He eased her head on to his lap. Presently she went to sleep. In his kneeling position the boy began to suffer from cramp, but he would not move for fear of waking her. Twenty minutes after we reached the hospital in Casablanca, her child was born. Both survived.

Now that I was in hospital and in safety I remembered the promise I had made to myself. I was heavily overdrawn at the bank; obviously my best way to make a thousand pounds was to sell my story of the Agadir earthquake to a Sunday newspaper. The editor I knew best was Stuart Campbell of *The People*, so I decided to cable him. It was now Thursday. I knew that if I did not produce my story in time for the Sunday edition it would be dead. This meant I must reach London the very next day. Obviously there was no question of priority on the planes because half the seats were empty. My problem was to get out of the hospital.

The British consul was walking round the wards with the colonel in charge. When they stopped by my bed I said I must leave at once.

"The man's a lunatic," the colonel said. "His legs are crushed; he can't be moved for at least three weeks."

I pleaded with them both, but in vain. I then, for the first and only time in my life, used an expression I had once read in an old phrase-book and which I had always longed to find an opportunity to use. "In that case," I said, "pray will you fetch me the British ambassador."

Luckily I had already met Sir Charles Duke; luckily he had both wisdom and a sense of humour. I explained to him why I had to reach London on the following day and he understood.

"Don't worry," he said. "I'll go and see the colonel myself." Then he paused and looked down at me. "However," he added, "I don't quite think you can be allowed to return to London in your present attire."

It was then that I realised that apart from my bandages I was stark naked. However, the British authorities in Casablanca had already started to organise clothes for the injured. I was lent a great-coat by one kind man, grey flannel trousers by another, and shoes by a third; the hospital gave me a thick crutch to help me walk on to the plane.

At London Airport I was met by my three sisters and numbers of photographers. We drove to Kate's flat where two stenographers from *The People* were waiting. I dictated my article without pausing for an instant. Then I was driven straight to hospital—the Lindo Wing of St. Mary's, Paddington—where I remained for a month and was visited regularly by Jim. Stuart Campbell printed my article word for word as I'd dictated it; he paid me a thousand pounds which I gave to room the Agadir Relief Fund.

*   *   *

After I had come out of hospital, I went down to Brighton and stayed there as long as I could to recuperate. One evening I returned unexpectedly to London. I had tried to ring Jim to let him know I was coming but there had been no answer. I took a taxi from the station. It was a fine summer night. The lights were on in my bedroom, but this did not surprise me. When I was away Jim often slept in my double-bed upstairs because both telephones rang in that room. I let myself in with my latchkey and I walked upstairs. I opened my bed-door.

Jim was lying naked on my bed. Beside him was a boy of about seventeen. Then I began to notice details—the bottle of whisky on the dressing-table, the two glasses by the bed, the tattoos on the boy's arms, the glazed look in Jim's eyes, the tube of ointment on the sheets, the discarded towel on the floor. Neither of them spoke.

I went down to the living-room and poured myself a drink. A moment later Jim came in. He'd wrapped a towel round his waist. At thirty-three he was still extremely attractive, with his smooth skin, broad shoulders and tousled blond hair. He moved unsteadily to the drinks table and poured himself a whisky.

"Are you very angry?" Jim asked.

"Yes," I said. "But perhaps not for the reasons that you think. Has this happened often?"

Jim grinned at me, but his eyes were sullen. "Now and then," he answered. "You don't suppose that I went without it all those months you were in Africa?"

"I did ask you to come with me."

"I know you did. I just didn't want to come."

"Who's the boy?"

"His name's Gary—if you want to know. He's in the Merchant Navy."

"When did you meet him?"

"Four nights ago."

"Where?"

"At a gay club." Jim took a gulp of his drink. "I do *go* to queer clubs—much as it may surprise you."

"Don't you think it rather unwise to invite back to this house a boy whom you hardly know?"

"Wasn't it rather unwise for you to come back to my room the night we first met—when you were thirty-three and I was only that boy's age?" Jim demanded.

"Yes," I said. "Probably."

"So what are you worried about?"

"Theft. Blackmail. You can't tell. For all you know the boy's wanted by the police."

Jim took a step back and leaned against the mantelpiece. "So now we're getting it," he said. "We're getting the real reason at last. You're not jealous. You don't care that I've never left that boy's side since the moment we met. All you care about is your precious reputation. Shall I tell you something? You think you don't mind being queer, but let me tell you that you do! You mind like hell. You resent it every moment of every day. And shall I tell you why? Because at heart you don't care a fuck about me and my friends. It's only your own crew that you're interested in. Why? Because you're a bloody great snob."

The young boy, Gary, opened the door of the living-room. "I'll wait for you downstairs," he said to Jim, and closed the door.

I stared at Jim. "You're *not* leaving with him?" I asked.

"Yes," he answered. "We'll spend the rest of the night in some hotel."

Until then I supposed that the situation, though difficult, was not desperate. I had felt that I was sailing across a rough sea, but at least my ship was under control and in open waters. Now, suddenly, I saw the reefs ahead.

"Then give me a ring tomorrow morning," I said to Jim.

"I expect so," Jim answered. "I'll have to come back some time to collect my gear."

I gaped at him. "You're leaving for good?"

Jim took a step towards me. "Can you *still* not understand?" he asked. "I've told you, I haven't left that boy's side from the moment we first met. Can't you remember *anything*? Can't you remember how you and I were when *we* first met—before you dragged me round to meet all your smart friends and eat *zabaglione*, or whatever you call it? Can't you remember how quickly *we* fell in love? Well, that's how it is with Gary and me. We're in love. Gary's going to try to fix it so I can get into the Merchant Navy and we can go off together. Good night, Robin. Don't worry too much—there are plenty of other boys in London."

*　　*　　*

There were indeed other boys. But I could never fall in love with any of them. I still missed Jim. I knew he had managed to join the Merchant Navy, and I knew he was on a ship sailing for Australia. I never heard from him again.

*　　*　　*

A few months later, a film company bought the outline of a novel I had written which was set in Fiji. I flew to Suva and chartered a small schooner to sail around the islands. When I returned from Samoa I heard that my sister Kate had had a heart attack and was dangerously ill. I booked on the first flight. By the time I reached New York she was dead.

When Kate, at the age of twenty-two, sent Willie her first novel he wrote to say that he found 'the humour delightful and the whole story ... carried through with vivacity, high spirits and verve'. The words might well be used to describe Kate's character. He concluded: "You have a natural humour which is very valuable and a power of sincere observation which is admirable ... but do not think success can be achieved without hard work. It is because they will not work that women on the whole write less well than men. It is for you to decide whether you think it worthwhile to take an infinite amount of pains. Personally I think it is."

But Kate, bless her heart, did not. To Kate, with her vitality and her wonderful capacity for friendship and sympathy, the business of living to the full each day was an excitement more rewarding than the labour of constructing a book. A date for lunch was worth more than a chapter; a friend's troubles poured out into the telephone took precedence over

229

an afternoon's work. Although these distractions did not affect her short poems, some of her novels suffered in consequence. Kate enjoyed herself when she could and gave happiness to her family and to all her friends until the day she died.

*   *   *

"I shall never get over her death," Willie said to me when I was staying at the Mauresque a few months later.

I was surprised, because until then I had not realised he was so devoted to Kate. Then, as he went on talking, I realised from the context of his words that he was thinking of his mother who had been dead for over eighty years.

Willie was now very old. His face was lined and the colour of parchment. His fading eyes looked out on the world without any illusion and without much interest, for he had seen it all so many times before. His hands and feet were small, and he seemed somehow to have shrivelled, but he moved with dignity and his gestures were full of authority. In the evening, when he had changed into a double-breasted, quilted smoking-jacket and black trousers, and put on his black velvet shoes with his monogram stitched on the toes in gold braid, he looked like a Chinese mandarin—ancient, fragile, wise, and benign, and—you would have thought to look at him—wholly detached from the trivial problems of the world.

But Willie was not detached, and he did not wish to leave the world; he was afraid of death. He made every effort to keep alive; he sometimes went to a clinic in Switzerland where he was injected with goat hormones.

"Ner-now, Noël Coward is coming to stay tomorrow," he told me one morning. "And I der-don't want him to know I've had a goat."

"There's no reason why he should know," I replied comfortingly.

That night at dinner Noël leaned forward to me. "I must tell you that your uncle really is a remarkable man," he said. "This afternoon he took me for a walk up the mountainside, and there he was hopping and skipping from boulder to boulder like a mountain goat."

There was an awkward silence.

A few months later I was staying with Willie at the Beau Rivage Hotel in Lausanne. Alan was sorting out fan letters; Willie seemed to be dozing in an armchair. Suddenly he looked up at me. "Your father was a brilliant lawyer," he said. "The trouble was that he didn't like the human race. And he'd got no patience with fools. Most human beings *are* fools, and there's nothing we can do about it."

Willie was silent. At that moment the main door leading to his suite

230

was flung open. Willie looked up anxiously, then he smiled with pleasure as he saw that his visitor was Noël, for he could still enjoy the company of an old friend. Noël walked swiftly across to Willie and embraced him. "My darling Willie," he cried. "*Cher maître*"

"What a surprise," Willie said, as Noël greeted Alan and me.

"Well, I was passing in front of the very gate of this hotel, so I thought I'd just pop in," Noël said. "You may *suppose* that I've only come in for five minutes."

"That's what I was hoping, Noël," Willie answered.

"Well I haven't. I've come for a whole hour," Noël said. "I intend to enliven your poor, dreary old life by teaching you a brand new game of patience—not that childish one you play. Now, come to the table."

Obediently we sat down at the card-table.

"We need two packs—and you've got two packs," Noël said. "Splendid. Now these are the rules. The ace of spades is wild and so are the three of hearts and the eight of clubs. Right? . . . Now you deal out seven cards face-down—thus." Noël dealt out the cards quickly. "Seven cards upwards, and seven cards face-downwards," he said.

Suddenly Willie turned to him. "Yer-you know, Noël," he said, "it's very ker-kind of you to invite me to stay in your villa for three months."

Noël gazed at him in astonishment. "Now whatever crossed your strange little Chinese mind to suppose that I should issue such an invitation?" he asked. "And may I add that if ever, at some unguarded moment, such an invitation escaped my lips, it is promptly withdrawn. But what makes you imagine that I *should* ask you to stay—and for three months?"

"Wer-well it's going to take you three months to teach me this patience," Willie said. "And I'd far rather learn it at *your* expense than at *mine* . . ." He paused. Then he added: "You see, my dear Noël, it may have escaped your attention—but I am in fact a thoroughly stupid man."

"Escaped my attention!" Noël exclaimed. "*What* did I say to myself when I first clapped eyes on you half a century ago? '*There*,' I said to myself, 'goes a thoroughly stupid man!' And fifty years have only confirmed me in my opinion."

Willie laughed. He stretched out his hand for a moment and touched Noël's arm. "Fifty years," he said. "It's a very long time."

*   *   *

I wish I could leave Willie as he sat there that morning at the card-table, cheerful and benign. But I cannot.

For centuries it has been a convention among biographers to suppress the unpleasant traits in their subject's character and to extol the virtues. They have tried to hide the real character and to present to posterity only his public image. Thus Dickens' cruelty to his wife was disguised, and until recent times General Gordon of Khartoum was held up to the public gaze as a pure, innocent-minded, religious man without an ignoble thought in his head. A recent biography of Ronald Firbank even attempted to ignore his homosexuality. But why? Why should the public and posterity be cheated? Surely it is better that we who are alive today should know that many of the great men in the past suffered and sometimes succumbed to the same temptations as afflict us, rather than that we should suppose them to have been so far removed from our common humanity as to have been unaffected by desire, impervious to envy and jealousy, and insensitive to lust?

*   *   *

We had dined alone together one evening at the Mauresque towards the end of Willie's life. The butler had come into the drawing-room to clear away our coffee cups and say good-night. Willie had been silent for a while. I looked up and saw tears flowing down his wrinkled cheeks.

"I've been such a fool," he cried. "And the awful thing is that if I had my life all over again I'd probably make exactly the same mistakes."

"What mistakes?" I asked.

"Mer-my greatest one was this," he stammered. "I tried to persuade myself that I was three-quarters normal and that only a quarter of me was queer—whereas really it was the other way round."

Towards the end of his life Willie's mind appeared to be tormented by remorse.

"I've been a horrible and evil man," he once said to me. "Every single one of the few people who have ever got to know me well has ended up by hating me."

Restless and distraught, he would wander past the marble-and-gilt furniture in the high-ceilinged rooms and drift like a shaking ghost through the whitewashed patios. On the way out to the terrace after lunch one day, he leaned his head against the wall at the top of the steps and burst into tears.

"I'm so miserable," he said. "Why can't they let me die?"

His grief was heart-rending, yet later that afternoon he was making plans to visit the famous clinic in Switzerland that gave him life-preserving injections. Some part of his nature clung to life. And his wit never altogether left him.

"Dying," he said to me, "is a very dull, dreary affair." Suddenly he smiled. "And my advice to you is to have nothing whatever to do with it," he added.

*　　　*　　　*

Willie died on December 16th, 1965.

*　　　*　　　*

"No man is of one piece," Willie used to say to me. "He's made up of selfishness and generosity, cruelty and kindness."

I believe that the originality and strength of Willie's writing is due to the precision with which he explored the diversity of instincts and emotions in almost every single one of his characters. The brilliance with which he created his characters—especially in his short stories—amounts in my opinion to genius. Yet for long periods of his life Willie was either treated with condescension or ignored. Only a few critics such as Cyril Connolly, who called Willie 'the greatest living short-story writer', considered that he was an important, underrated literary figure.

I am convinced that the area in which we have freedom of choice in our lives is limited, for—as Willie said—we are the product of the genes and chromosomes of our parents, and that product is in its turn shaped or twisted by our early environment. Therefore I am sure that the Arabs who accept that the story of their lives is *mektub*—in fact, written in advance—are closer to the truth than the Christians who think that by an exercise of will-power they can go to heaven or to hell.

Willie's nature was determined by his parents: he believed, for instance, that homosexuality was always hereditary, and he has yet to be proved wrong. The cruelty in his character was, I feel, caused by the misery of his childhood—a poor, stammering orphan flung at the age of ten from the security of his life at the Avenue d'Antin into the strange bleak world of a vicarage in Whitstable. And Willie was aware of the cruel streak in him. He knew that mankind was compounded of good and evil because he had analysed his own nature mercilessly. He had rid himself of cant; he had examined himself with the precision of a surgeon. He knew each foible, and he knew each defect within him. Having explored himself, he turned the harsh searchlight of his examination on to the characters around him, and in them discovered a similar diversity of impulses. It is this coldly objective examination of all his characters that makes *Cakes and Ale* a masterpiece. It may shock Willie's readers to think that in his private life he was at times a sadistic queer. I must confess that I believe that if he hadn't been tortured by desires which in his heart he despised, he wouldn't have written as he did, and he wouldn't have written as excitingly.

*   *   *

Now that both Willie and my father were dead I thought I was rid of their two shadows. I was wrong. I had written, as I have said, a book about my family which I had called, taking the words with his permission from one of Noël's lyrics, *Somerset and All the Maughams*.[13] Embassy Pictures bought the film rights of the book, and I flew over to Hollywood to work on the script with George Schaefer who was to direct the film. My arrival coincided with the American publication of my novel *The Second Window*. Interviewers from all media insisted on comparing me—favourably or unfavourably—to Willie. Critics compared my novel to his work. "Robin fails to stand up to Somerset," one headline would read. "Robin wipes the floor with Somerset," said another. But I didn't want to stand up to W. Somerset Maugham, and I certainly didn't want to wipe the floor with him. I wanted to be accepted as a writer irrespective of my relationship to him. However, the novel sold well; and I enjoyed working with George Schaefer. On my way back, Gloria Vanderbilt and her husband Wyatt Cooper gave a splendid dinner-party in my honour at which I met old friends such as Terry Rattigan and Peter Glenville. My life both in Hollywood and New York was wonderfully unreal, but I was happy, and I had almost managed to forget about Jim.

[13] . . . All well-known writers in swarms do it,
Somerset and all the Maughams do it . . .
Noël Coward

PART

SIX

I 'EMIGRATED' FROM ENGLAND IN 1966 FOR MUCH THE SAME
reasons as Willie had left England in 1926. I thought I would feel
more free abroad; I believed that away from England I would rid
myself of what Harold Nicolson had described as 'the nursery governess
peering over my shoulder'. I also, of course, wished to avoid paying
English taxes each year. Willie had left me only a very small annuity;
I had no capital to live on; and I knew only too well that my income
could diminish alarmingly if my energy and success as a writer should be
menaced by ill-health in the years ahead of me. With the money I
had received from Embassy Pictures I bought a villa outside Santa
Eulalia in the Balearic island of Ibiza. The rooms were large and well
proportioned, and a garden with a lovely mixture of pines and palm
trees, roses and oleanders, bougainvillaeas and cactus, ran down to the
sea. For month after month I was happy there; I already had friends
on the island such as Laurel and Gerry Albertini; I had friends in
Madrid such as Luis Escobar who put on a brilliant production of my
play *The Servant* at the Teatro Infanta Isabel; I made new friends among
the actors and actresses who, like moths around a flame, seemed to
flutter around the bar in Santa Eulalia run by my friend Sandy Pratt.
Sandy travelled with me to Australia where I spent some of the
happiest months of my life while I was searching for material for my

novel, *The Link*. Never have I known such wonderful hospitality; I was almost overwhelmed by the help and kindness I received. Later, I sailed to Mexico to continue with my research. Then I settled down in a small *hacienda* outside Taxco to write the novel itself.

Suddenly my good fortune changed. I had gone to stay with Diana and Kim in Majorca. I was on the wagon at the time. When Diana saw me drinking beaker after beaker of water she remembered the symptoms she had observed in our sister Kate. "You've got diabetes," she said.

I went back to Ibiza where a test was made; the evidence was positive; I had got the disease. By the time I reached London I was in agony from cramps. Once again I was admitted to the Lindo Wing of St. Mary's Hospital. By then I had also developed severe pancreatitis and other stomach pains. I was very ill indeed. After a serious operation I became dangerously thin. I went first to Brighton to convalesce and then to stay with Noël Coward at Les Avants, in Switzerland. There I consulted a diabetic expert who told me I would have to inject myself with insulin twice a day. All the doctors concerned with my health advised that I should leave Ibiza and live close to a well-equipped hospital where I could receive treatment. So I made plans to become a resident of Switzerland, but I could not bear the prospect of giving up my villa by the sea. Perhaps at the back of my mind lay the pathetic hope that I could find another Jim who would share my life with me. Indeed, in a nightclub in Madrid, I did meet someone whom I sincerely believed could become another Jim. But the young man made it clear that though he would love to come and spend the summer in my villa he would never stay permanently in Ibiza.

I had remained alone during the two years that I spent writing *The Second Window*, and I had not felt lonely. Now, suddenly, loneliness descended on me like a fog, covering my mind so completely that I could no longer see the mimosa trees, nor the palms and the umbrella-pines trembling over the shining sea. And as my loneliness increased I began to think almost constantly about Jim. I could see the pale hair falling down over his forehead and the rather sad look of yearning in his eyes. I could remember the fierceness of his love and his tenderness. I began to blame myself harshly for the break-up of our relationship. If I had been less selfish, I told myself, if I had been less drunken, if I had cared more about his welfare, if I had given more of myself to him and with less reserve, if I had made more effort to understand and get on with his friends—so that he could not have called me a snob; if I had been a stronger character and able to persuade him to be more interested in reading than in the nightly tittle-tattle of gay clubs, then Jim would still have been with me. I now felt I was wholly and completely to blame. Some part of my nature had managed to destroy my one chance in life of finding happiness.

One day I drove across the island to dine with Laurel and Gerry Albertini in their splendid villa overlooking the bay of San Antonio. It was a wonderful spring evening. Small fluffy clouds hung immobile in the wide, clear sky. The quality of light in Ibiza is very beautiful, and at each turn in the road I wished that Jim were sitting beside me to share the fresh loveliness that each bend disclosed. For once, even the warmth with which I was greeted at the Albertinis' villa could not dispel my sense of being alone. Before dinner, I drank a lot in order to appear cheerful and to forget my sorrow, and soon I reached the state that every alcoholic knows—when I felt nothing could harm me. Half way through dinner, after several glasses of the strong red wine called Marqués de Riscal, I had reached a perfect condition. My spirit and my heart had been lifted by drink and had swung away from the dinner-table to reach a mountain from which I could gaze down at my poor self with detachment. Yet my mind seemed quite clear: I could listen to the conversation round the table; I could even join in with it happily. But I was aware that I could remain in this state of happiness, poised on my mountain-peak, only so long as I continued to drink. I drank with the stealth of an alcoholic throughout the evening. Then I said good-night to Laurel and Gerry. As I drove home, my mind was still perfectly clear. I was even able to admire, from my mountain fastness, the moon shining through the clouds. When I reached my villa, the servants had long since gone to bed. I knew the place where they always left the key for me. I unlocked the door and switched on the lights. I was still up in the security of the mountains. As I came into the long, high-ceilinged living-room, in which the curtains had already been drawn, I saw the old Spanish cabinet in which drinks and glasses were kept, illuminated straight ahead of me. I had driven for half an hour; I was afraid of sliding down the declivity from my mountain-peak into a dangerous valley where doubt and loneliness were awaiting me. I went to the cabinet; I poured myself out a large whisky. As I drank it, I was still in the security of the mountain, but the fluffy clouds I had seen previously on my drive now seemed to be stretching out like an uneven carpet of white flock below the peak so that I could no longer see the valley below. My mind now swerved between the mountain-peak and the living-room in which I was standing with the glass clasped in my hand. I know that I finished the drink. I can remember walking out of the living-room and along the corridor into the bathroom where I injected myself with insulin. It was at that moment, I think, that my black-out must have begun. Only vaguely can I remember walking back into the living-room and helping myself to another drink. I had a strange presentiment that someone was about to appear—someone who would wish to take me away from my villa for ever.

In my confusion I tried to make myself concentrate on the furniture I had brought out from England and on the paintings around the walls; I made myself memorise them carefully so that I should have the strength to resist the temptation of leaving my home for ever. I walked back along the corridor and into my bedroom where the shutters were closed and locked. I think I still had a glass of whisky in my hand. Slowly, I began to take off my clothes. Then I walked to my bedside-table on which lay the sleeping-pills I had taken ever since the shrapnel entered my head. I swallowed my ordinary dose of pills. Then I hesitated. I was afraid. I was afraid because I had left the mountain. I was plunged into the murky darkness of the valley once again. The bedroom now held fear for me. I walked back into the living-room; I refilled my glass; I sat down in an armchair. The picture-lights were still on; I tried to make myself concentrate on one particular painting by de Belleroche: it was of a woman, his wife in fact, playing on an upright piano in a room whose walls were covered with drawings and sketches— one of them was by Degas. I tried to make myself remember how much I had loved this painting and how happy Jim had been on the evening I bought it from the painter's son, Willie de Belleroche. My mind now swung back into the past, and I thought of all my friends—like Willie de Belleroche—who were dead. I remembered, for some reason, the last time I had met Dorothy Parker. As I came into her apartment, she had embraced me, then had stood back looking at me. "I can't think," she said, "who I'd rather the Almighty sent through this door." Then she paused and looked at me solemnly. "Or do you think that in the case of the Almighty," she had asked, "it would be *whom* he had sent through this door?" And I'd known that Dottie was on form, yet again. "Whom," I kept repeating to myself, "whom the Almighty had sent through this door." But the idea of sending anyone through a door had aroused my fears again. I knew that somehow I was in great danger. I tried to make myself remember the names of the friends I had in the world. I went to the bookcase; I tried to gain comfort from the two dozen books or plays I had had published, and from all the translations in Hebrew and Arabic, in Japanese and Scandinavian, in almost every language of the world. But this ridiculous exercise could not dispel my fear. I knew that in the bedroom, someone was waiting for me—and I could tell his name. I filled my glass once again. Then I walked back into my bedroom. And there he stood.

For the first time I saw Tommy with my own eyes. He was standing

The garden of Robin Maugham's villa on Ibiza

Robin Maugham and W. Somerset Maugham at the Villa Mauresque

by the bedside-table. As I came into the room he looked up at me. For the first time I saw his face. Deep violet eyes gleamed from below a tawny forehead and thickly clustered dark hair. Below the high cheek-bones his face was unshaven. There was something very sensual about his broad mouth. His body was slender, his hands and fingers were delicate, yet he gave the impression of being coarse and brutal. His body might remind me of a faun yet there was a gross sensuality about him. He resembled no one I had ever seen before. As he looked up at me, he smiled, then moved slowly across the room to the door and locked it.

"I've come to help you," he said. "I've come to help you—as I have before."

For a while I was silent. I was so astonished at the vision of him that I could think of nothing to say. Tommy took a pill from each bottle on the table.

"First you must take your evening sleeping draught," he said.

I stared at him. "I've taken it already," I said.

Tommy grinned at me. "Then you must take it again, mustn't you," he murmured.

I gazed at him, and as I stared into his eyes I realised that Tommy—who had usually been extrovert, sometimes wild, callous and completely heterosexual—had changed. As he held out the two large bottles of pills, I realised that tonight Tommy had only one object in his mind. He wanted oblivion. He wanted to try to destroy both of us—once and for all. Nothing was worthwhile to *him* any more. He could regard the villa with complete indifference. The books I had written, or had intended to write, had no importance. Far above sadness, far more intense than grief or love or friendship, was the desire for permanent oblivion.

Then I can't remember clearly what happened. For an instant mist covered the scene. During that short period my mind had an occlusion like a lighthouse. But suddenly the mist lifted, and I could see Tommy standing beside the bed. I could sense the vitality of his body; I could see, at those last moments, the wildness of his beauty and the ruthless-ness of his design. He poured out a glass of water. Suddenly I could see him with complete detachment. I knew his intention, and I no longer cared. I watched him. I said nothing. Tommy smiled at me. It was a smile of such complicity and friendship that I knew that if he could have inhabited another body I would have found in him the person for whom I had sought all my life. But through the clouds that now seemed to soothe a part of my mind, through the piercing pain of the shrapnel I could once more feel stabbing into my brain, I could understand that I would never be able to see him and love him as a separate person. The desolation of this thought numbed me, so that I could no longer move or think. In silence—as if I were mesmerised—I watched Tommy as he tilted the remaining contents of the first bottle of pills into the palm of his hand. Once again he gave me a look of complicity, as if to join me in his act, then he swallowed the pills in a quick gulp. He put down the bottle; he grinned at me. He stood looking at me as if he expected me to make some protest. But I could not move. As I watched him, for the first time I became fully aware that he was as naked as I was. With one hand he lifted the glass of water into the air. With a deliberate slowness he poured some pills from the second bottle into his hand. With an abrupt tilt of his head, he swallowed them. Then he smiled at me for the last time. Without any hurry, he stretched himself out on my bed, and lay there, naked, his hands clasped together above the smooth skin of his chest, waiting—waiting, as I perceived at that moment—waiting for the oblivion of death.

As I stood there, watching the person whom I now knew I loved most of all—far more than Jim—I was drawn towards him without any volition, until, presently, I found myself lying beside him, and our limbs melted together.

*   *   *

In the morning my secretary in Ibiza, Nancy Hosegood, arrived at eleven and was surprised that I was not in the living-room. At noon she knocked on my bedroom door. When there was no reply she turned the handle and found it was locked. She knocked loudly on the door and called out my name. I answered in a faint voice. She then realised I was ill.

"You must unlock the door," she said. "Please try."

Presently she heard the sound of the key being moved in the lock, but the door would still not open.

"I can't do it," she heard me say. "I'm trying hard, but I can't."

Luckily there were some builders working on the roof. Nancy called them down and made them break open the door. By then I was lying unconscious beside my bed. Nancy at once telephoned for an ambulance and took me to a clinic in the town of Ibiza.

I recovered consciousness at about seven o'clock that evening. Laurel's face was peering down at me anxiously. "How are you, darling?" she asked. I was still very far away, but already I was strong enough to know that I had survived.

Next day Laurel and Gerry took me to stay with them until I was well enough to fly back to England. Once again I was put in the Lindo Wing. An encephalogram was taken of my head to make sure that the shrapnel in my brain had not moved. The following day Michael

Kremer came to see me, and I told him what had happened. Immediately I was given special drugs—which I've been taking ever since.

*   *   *

During the last two years I have spent as much time as I could in my villa in Ibiza. In the library of the villa, a long room on the first floor, I have written this book. Sometimes I glance up from a page to enjoy the bougainvillaea climbing across the balcony. My eyes follow the sweep of the gravel path between the pines and wild scrub that leads to the sea. I have been aware that my tenure of the house was transitory. Because of the heart condition I have now developed, as many diabetics do, the doctors who look after me have urged me to move from Ibiza, and to live closer to some hospital where I can get specialist treatment.

In these last three years I have produced more work than I did in the previous seven. The tranquillity of this house has helped me. Its rooms are filled with furniture, paintings, and bibelots. Each one of them is a relic of my past—of my flats in Cadogan Square and in Brighton, of my little house in Seaton Street, and of the journeys I have made abroad. At first I could not abide the prospect of having to leave it all behind. But I could not possibly afford to live in this place on my private income, and I am afraid that a heart attack might cripple me completely so that I could no longer write. My common sense tells me that I have been wise to put the house on the market; my emotions urge me to stay on here as long as I can.

But although the philosopher in me occupies, alas, a very small part of my nature, I can perceive that as one grows older one should seek to escape from the captivity of physical belongings. For, in a way, all things are lent to us—possessions, friends, lovers. We can never completely own them. Even Time is only lent to us.

My own future is very uncertain, but I am used to that condition. I don't even know where I am going to live. I recognise that without Jim I shall be very lonely at times. But loneliness is the inevitable price the writer must pay—whatever his nature or talent may be. I will try to be grateful for each day that is lent to me. I will try not to forget the visions of friendship and unselfishness which I have sometimes been allowed to glimpse in the wildness of my life. "Do not weep for the dead," I wrote in my war diary nearly thirty years ago. "Keep all your love for the living, and weep for those who are starving or tortured and for those who are dying in spirit while they live. Then dry your tears and go away from the vibration of people, from the clatter of conversation; go away quietly and alone into the wilderness, each man by

243

himself. You will not find peace, for it is too early, but as the dope of screen and paper is drained from your head you will begin to see that all things are so related that the torture of a child in the East affects all the world. You will see men as they are and as they can be. You have seen that comradeship and sacrifice can spring from the heart to meet a common danger. You will see that a greater comradeship and sacrifice can spring into the adventure of building a new world. Look hard and long at the vision of what can be, for you are mortal and the vision fades quickly. Then take up the shield of independence so that contempt and scandal cannot harm you nor desire of success weaken you."

I am very well aware that only sporadically have I been able to live up to those ideals that I once set myself. But there may be time yet for me to go back to the desert which then inspired me.

Memories of Jim are mercifully beginning to fade from my mind. With my departure from my villa, I feel that I shall finally be moving away from the shadows across my life, and I honestly believe that as I write the last sentence of this book, all the shadows will creep back into the mists of time. Even Tommy has vanished: I believe that when Tommy swallowed the sleeping-pills, in some strange way he may have killed himself, for I have not sensed his presence since that evening.

*   *   *

I sleep with my windows open. I awake in the hour before dawn, dazed with sleep. At first the streaks of light are menacing. Across the horizon, crawling slowly like beetles, come the enemy tanks, grinding towards my private world. Then, as I awake a little more, I stare towards the windows and become aware that streaks of light are sweeping across the horizon of pine and sea. Suddenly, I am frightened because I know that daylight can bring danger and assault. But by now the tanks have moved beneath the horizon. Now at last—without any fear and without any shadows spread out in the space before me—now, at last, I can stretch out my arms and reach towards the delivering sun.

Appendices

Appendix I

Select Bibliography of Robin Maugham's work
by Peter Burton.

All books were first published in London, unless otherwise stated,
when American and European editions are listed before the British.

Novels

1 *The Servant*. Falcon Press, 1948. Paperback edition, Ace Books,
   1961. Heinemann, 1964.
2 *Line on Ginger*. Chapman and Hall, 1949. Paperback edition, as
   The Intruder: Ace Books, 1960. New English Library, 1968.
3 *The Rough and the Smooth*. Chapman and Hall, 1951. Paperback
   edition, Ace Books, 1961. New English Library, 1967.
4 *Cheque Au Porteur* (comprising *Le Serviteur—The Servant, Le Rouquin
   —Line on Ginger*, and *Cheque Au Porteur—Pay Bearer £20*).[1] This
   volume is the first to publish *Pay Bearer £20* in book form. Presses
   De La Cité, Paris, 1951.
5 *Behind the Mirror*. Harcourt, Brace and Company, New York,
   April 1955. Longmans, October 1955, Paperback edition, Ace
   Books, 1961. New English Library, 1968.
6 *The Man with Two Shadows*. Longmans, 1958. Paperback edition,
   Ace Books, 1961. New English Library, 1967.

[1] *Pay Bearer £20* was serialised in England in *Chambers' Journal* under the title
'Desert Bond'. *Pay Bearer £20* was the alternative English title. The story was filmed
in 1955, under the title *The Black Tent*, and this is the title which it appears under in
The Black Tent and Other Stories—see entry under Short Stories.

7   *November Reef.* Longmans, 1962. Paperback edition, Panther Books, 1965.
8   *The Green Shade.* New American Library, New York, June 1966. Heinemann, July 1966. Paperback edition, New English Library, 1968.
9   *The Second Window.* McGraw-Hill, New York, September 1968. Heinemann, October 1968. Paperback edition, Pan Books, 1970.
10 *The Link.* McGraw-Hill, New York, September 1969. Heinemann, November 1969. Paperback edition, Pan Books, 1970.
11 *The Wrong People* (originally published as *The Wrong People* under the pseudonym David Griffin, Paperback Library Inc., New York, 1967). Published as *Anders Als Die Andern*: Wilhelm Heyne Verlag, Munich, 1969. Revised edition, Heinemann, 1970 (with a preface by Cyril Connolly).
12 *The Last Encounter.* W. H. Allen, 1972.

Short Stories

13 *Das Kleine Weisse Pferd* (comprising *Das Kleine Weisse Pferd—Broken Cellophane, Die Botschaft—The Messenger,* and *Der verlorene Sohn—The Prodigal Son*). This is the first volume to publish these three stories in book form. Claudius Verlag, Munich, 1958.[2]
14 *Testament: Cairo 1898.* De Hartington. An edition limited to 150 signed copies, and printed in the style of the period. 1972.
15 *The Black Tent and Other Stories* (edited and selected by Peter Burton). W. H. Allen.

Travel

16 *Come to Dust* (a war diary). Chapman and Hall, 1945. Paperback edition, Ace Books, 1961. New English Library, 1968.
17 *Nomad.* Chapman and Hall, 1947.
18 *Approach to Palestine.* Forum Books, Falcon Press, 1947.
19 *North African Notebook.* Chapman and Hall, 1948.
20 *Journey to Siwa* (with photographs by Dimitri Papadimou). Chapman and Hall, 1950.
21 *The Slaves of Timbuktu.* Longmans, 1961. Paperback edition, Consul Books, 1964. Sphere Books, 1967.
22 *The Joyita Mystery.* Max Parrish, 1962.

Biography

23 *Somerset and All the Maughams.* Longmans and Heinemann, 1966.

---

[2] *Broken Cellophane, The Messenger* and *The Prodigal Son* achieve first English book publication in *The Black Tent and Other Stories.*

Autobiography

24 *Escape from the Shadows*. Hodder and Stoughton, 1972.

Plays

25 *Odd Man In* (adapted from *Monsieur Masure* by Claude Magnier). Samuel French, 1958.
26 *The Lonesome Road* (with Philip King). Samuel French, 1959.
27 *Mister Lear*. English Theatre Guild, 1963.
28 *El Criado* (adapted from the novel *The Servant*). Ediciones Alfil, Madrid, 1967.
29 *Enemy!* In *Plays of the Year: Volume 39, 1969–70*, edited by J. C. Trewin, Elek Books, 1971. Acting edition, Samuel French, 1971.

Dramatic Work

In each case, the date of first production is listed, followed by the first British production—where the two differ—and by the date of the first London production.

30 *Thirteen for Dinner*. A. D. C. Theatre, Cambridge, February 11th, 1935.
31 *The Walking Stick* (included in an evening of one-act plays). Duke of York's, London, December 19th, 1935.
32 *The Leopard*. Connaught Theatre, Worthing, May 22nd, 1955.
33 *The Rising Heifer*. Margo Jones' '52 Theatre, Dallas, Texas, December 23rd, 1952. First British production, Intimate Theatre, High Wycombe, November 28th, 1955.
34 *Mister Lear* (now called *Just in Time*). Connaught Theatre, Worthing, September 24th, 1956.
35 *The Last Hero*. Strand Theatre, London, June 16th, 1957.
36 *Odd Man In* (adapted from *Monsieur Masure* by Claude Magnier). St. Martin's, London, July 16th, 1957.
37 *The Lonesome Road* (with Philip King). Arts, London, August 28th, 1957.
38 *The Servant* (from the novel of the same title). Connaught, Worthing, April 28th, 1958.
39 *The Hermit* (with Philip King). Opera House, Harrogate, May 18th, 1959.
40 *It's In the Bag* (adapted from *Oscar* by Claude Magnier). Theatre Royal, Brighton, April 4th, 1960; Duke of York's, London, May 25th, 1960.
41 *The Two Wise Virgins of Hove*. Independent Television, December 22nd, 1960.

42 *Azouk* (with Willis Hall, adapted from *Azouk* by Alexandre Rive-male). Flora Robson Playhouse, Newcastle-upon-Tyne, September 11th, 1962.

43 *The Claimant.* Connaught, Worthing, October 29th, 1962; Comedy, London, April 30th, 1964.

44 *Winter in Ischia.* Connaught, Worthing, January 27th, 1964.

45 *The Servant* (from the novel of the same title. A new version of the play, which differs extensively from the version seen in 1958). Yvonne Arnaud, Guildford, September 27th, 1966.

46 *Enemy!* Yvonne Arnaud, Guildford, October 7th, 1969; Saville, London, December 17th, 1969.

47 *A.D. 20.* Written 1969. Not yet produced.

48 *The Last Hero.* Written 1970. Not yet produced.

49 *The Wrong People* (from the novel of the same title). Written 1970. Not yet produced.

Film Scripts

Film scripts which have been produced are listed with the names of the producer, the director and the name of the distributing company, and the year of distribution. All other film scripts are listed with *only* the name of the production company which owns them *at the time of going to press*, and the date of writing.

50 *The Intruder* (based upon *Line on Ginger*). Written with John Hunter. Produced by Ivan Foxwell. Directed by Guy Hamilton. Distributed by British Lion, 1953.

51 *Speaker's Corner* (with Rodney Ackland comprising *Broken Cellophane* and *The Prodigal Son*, script by Robin Maugham, and *The Man Who Could Hypnotise Racehorses*, script by Rodney Ackland. These three stories appear in the volume *The Black Tent and Other Stories*). Owned by A.B.P.C. and N.F.C. 1954.

52 *The Black Tent* (based upon *Desert Bond*). Written with Bryan Forbes. Produced by William Macquitty. Directed by Brian Desmond Hurst. Distributed by Rank Organisation.1956.

53 *The Man with Two Shadows* (based upon the novel of the same name). Written for Hammer Films, now owned by Columbia Pictures. 1960.

54 *The Joyita Mystery* (based upon the book of the same name). All rights owned by Robin Maugham. 1962.

55 *November Reef* (based upon the novel of the same name). All rights owned by Robin Maugham. 1962.

56 *Willie* (based upon *Somerset and All the Maughams*). Owned by Embassy Pictures. 1968.

57 *The Carrier* (based upon *How Are You Johnnie?*). A play by Philip King 1969.
58 *School Curtains* (based upon the short story of the same name which appears in the volume *The Black Tent and Other Stories*). Owned by Triarch Productions. 1969.
59 *Cakes and Ale* (based upon the novel of the same name by W. Somerset Maugham). Carter De Haven. 1970.
60 *The Barrier* (with five sonnets by John Betjeman). Owned by Triarch Productions. 1971.
61 *The Wrong People* (from the novel of the same name). Owned by Serpentine Productions. 1971.

Journalism

Only major journalism is listed. It is not the purpose of this bibliography to indicate every written word by Robin Maugham, only those of importance. Thus, in this section, only passing mention will be made of magazines with which Robin Maugham has been associated editorially. These include, *Sixpenny*, Eton, 1933, *The Silver Crescent*, Cambridge, 1935/6, *Spark*, with an editorial board including Pamela Frankau, but which never actually appeared because of the advent of war, 1939, and the seven issues of *Convoy* which appeared between 1943 and 1947. No details at all will be given of undergraduate journalism—for example, in *The Granta*, and only series of articles will be listed. Single items, for papers like the *Daily Telegraph*, *The People*, and *The Scotsman*, would consume too much space in this present volume.

62 *Bought—One Man* (the series which later formed the basis for *The Slaves of Timbuktu*). *The People*. September 27th–October 25th, 1959.
63 *Hong Kong*. *The People*. July 9th–July 30th, 1961.
64 *Slavery 1963*. *The People*. October 20th–November 10th, 1963.
65 *Slavery Now—The Final Proof*. *The People*. May 3rd–May 17th, 1964.
66 *Gerald Hamilton Confesses*. *The People*. January 16th–February 13th, 1966.
67 *Somerset Maugham*. *The Sunday Telegraph*. January 16th–January 30th, 1966.
68 *My Life in Six Articles*. *Sydney Morning Herald* (Australia). January 20th–February 24th, 1968.
69 *Extraordinary Characters* (Noël Coward, La Marquise de St. Innocent, Somerset Maugham, Guy Burgess and Glubb Pasha). *The People*. February 22nd–March 22nd, 1970.

Contributions to Books

70   *Final Release.* In *Gilbert Harding, By His Friends.* Edited by Stephen Grenfell, Andre Deutsch, 1961.

Miscellaneous

71   *The 1946 MS.* War Facts Press, 1943.

This title is of particular interest for several reasons which are briefly explained below. *The 1946 MS* is a fictional piece, running to nearly fifteen thousand words. It would, thus, seem to belong with either Novels or Short Stories (though at such a wordage it would more properly be described as a *nouvelle*). However, it has been placed in a separate category as it is something more than either a novel or a short story. It was written during the Second World War as a prophetic warning about what could happen if a military leader were able to take control of Great Britain. The publishers, War Facts Press, printed manuscripts which were 'a contribution to the social, literary or economic future of Great Britain', and which were written by authors with 'something to say about the World of Tomorrow'. At the time of publication *The 1946 MS* was to be serialised in the *Sunday Chronicle*. Shortly before the paper went to press, on the first week, *The 1946 MS* was censored. The editor of the *Sunday Chronicle*, James W. Drawbell, remonstrated with the powers-that-be, and, the following week *The 1946 MS* appeared. It is interesting to note, however, that no copy was allowed in the Eighth Army area. Thus, more than a purely fictional piece, it must be considered as a semi-propagandist work, doubly interesting as it contains the pattern for all of Robin Maugham's later work. In fact, though themes occur which are used throughout his later books, *The 1946 MS* —his first important publication—is most directly the parent of *The Man With Two Shadows.*

Appendix II

National Service Memorandum: May 15th, 1939

NATIONAL SERVICE

1. I think that National Service at the moment is narrow in scope and negative in spirit. In spite of efforts to the contrary, the effect of the campaign has been to say to the people, "Join National Service so that this country or one of our Allies shan't be attacked, so that we shan't be bombed, so that your friends shan't think you're shirking," and the people feeling that they are living in troubled times, if they join National Service, join sadly from a sense of duty to defend their country, regarding their National Service as a necessary evil.

Owing to its narrow scope and negative spirit, the National Service Campaign has been forced to stress constantly the immediate danger of war to obtain enrolments. It has accordingly portrayed the horrors of war and its most inspired message has been that if this country is prepared war may not come or if it does come may not be so unpleasant. "We've got to be prepared," it has proclaimed, and the passer-by regarding the proclamation adds to himself "For War".

One result of this is that the number of enrolments per week is dependent upon the condition of the political barometer (see paragraph 5).

The other result of the campaign's defeatist spirit is more serious. Though fear of war may be a temporary stimulant to enrolment, like other stimulants it weakens in the long run. There is always a reaction. And the reaction in this case is none the less dangerous for being imperceptible. Throughout the last year of crisis the people of this country have known that quite soon there might be war. The National Service Campaign has played upon that fear. But the long period of fears and alarms has taken its toll by undermining their nerves and their confidence.

If war is declared in the next few weeks the Campaign's policy will be vindicated; but if this period of crisis continues, as it may well do for another three or four months, the policy will be proved to have been short-sighted. For if the people have to live for another three or four months in the shadows of war, with their fears reawakened by each new crisis, and with no positive spirit, it is unpleasant to envisage the extent to which their confidence may not be damaged and their spirit destroyed. Moreover under the present scope of National Service only a small proportion of the country will be in a position to be helping actively during that period. And there is no doubt that those who are National Service workers will be less affected by the period than those who can only sit and wait.

2. A positive spirit is needed, a broader aim than Defence.

The entire basis of National Service should be broadened to include and deal with the Unemployed, the Refugees, and 'the condition of Britain'.

1. THE UNEMPLOYED

(a) The existing organisations such as the National Council of Social Service and the Subsistence Productions Experiment should be co-ordinated with, and controlled by the Ministry of Labour and become part of National Service. Work for such organisations would then become one of the Civilian Services in the National Service Handbook for which training might be required. Though conscription will lessen unemployment the evil will still flourish.

(b) At the moment, in so far as Government grants are needed, the above organisations come indirectly under the aegis of the Ministry of Labour through the Unemployment Assistance Board, but only in respect of the work they do for the unemployed. Such segregation of the unemployed has many bad psychological effects which have a deep practical significance. Community centres which make no distinction between the employed and the unemployed should be started. Work for such centres would become one of the Civilian Services. The superior force of the co-ordinated organisations suggested above should be able to disentangle the difficulties about national and local finance involved.

(c) An appeal should be made to the young men throughout the country and especially to the young unemployed to *volunteer* for six months' National Service which while being of a semi-military nature should aim at being enjoyable and above all healthy and instructive.

(The last paragraph was written in memo 1 before conscription was introduced. But I think it could still apply to young men before or after their period of conscription. The training might well attempt to fit them for their future occupations.)

2. THE REFUGEES

(*a*) The existing refugee organisations are understaffed and over-worked. They are proceeding in a flabby fashion and lack co-ordination. Such organisations should become part of National Service. They would greatly benefit from the stiffening influence of a government department. The work for such organisations would become one of the Civilian Services for which training might be necessary.

(*b*) A Home Legion should be formed from the refugees to develop the land in this country, roughly 300 acres of which 'run to bracken' every week. The refugees will need experience of agriculture when they emigrate to colonies.

3. 'THE CONDITION OF BRITAIN'

All organisations official and private whose aim it is to alleviate poverty, sickness and distress (e.g. Slum Clearance Schemes and Boys Clubs in the slums) and all organisations official and private whose aim it is to improve the health of the nation (e.g. National Fitness Council) should be co-ordinated and become part of National Service.

Work for such organisations technical and non-technical would become one of the Civilian Services.

It is not conceived that National Service will solve these problems but it is thought that the bad results arising from them will be lessened. Co-operation with the trades unions would be a prerequisite.

3a. RESULT

If these things were done a different spirit could immediately prevail. The words 'National Service' would take on a new significance. People would be joining National Service not only to make the country bomb-proof or to be in a position to help should war break out, or to save their skins and honour, but they would also join National Service to help the unemployed, the poor, and the refugees. They would join to make Britain a better place to live in and by so doing, to make Britain strong so that her influence for peace and freedom may be real and effective.

4. In the present scope of National Service relatively few more enrolments are required; but the campaign to obtain those few is vast and expensive. We are using a megaphone to attract a mouse. If the scope of National Service were broadened the audience of the campaign would be increased, and there would be room for greater and more varied endeavour.

5. Since at the moment people are joining National Service because they feel they should be in a position to help their country should war break out, every time the Press announces a prospect of peace their enthusiasm for National Service quite logically wanes. If the scope of National Service were broadened and more positive spirit prevailed, the

work would continue irrespective of the waverings of the Press or the fluctuations of the political barometer; for even if it seemed likely that there would be a prolonged period of peace there would be no reason to stop improving Britain.

6. So far the National Service Campaign has tried to make people realise that we are living in danger of war and that we've got to be prepared. It has stated a fact and told the people that it's up to them. It has sought to inculcate and to explain to them a situation rather than to draw out of them something already latent *by means of an appeal*.

The ordinary person is a compound of pettiness and nobility and it is possible by means of an effective appeal to pierce through layers of apathy and selfishness to touch the streak of nobility that lies submerged.

7. An appeal should be made to all people to sacrifice their comfort and leisure to make our country a better place to live in. The appeal should ask every man and woman in this country to review their weekly calendar to see how many hours they could give to National Service in its broader sense, and, if they are unemployed by misfortune or choice, to review their lives.

8. Only a small proportion of the potential voluntary effort in this country has been used.

9. It may well be that this plan could be combined with the present agitation for a National Register.

The National Register could not only have reference to the existing National Services but could also include the Services suggested above.

10. There is no reason why the plan, if it were brought into effect, would lessen enrolment into the existing National Services (for example, the Territorial Army, which would still be of primary importance).

11. Much concrete good would arise from the above plan. Better health certainly would be considerable. But of far greater importance would be the positive spirit which might prevail and might unite the country in one common effort.

12. If war is to be declared within the next three weeks, obviously the above plan is useless. But if there is going to be no war for another three or four months, a positive spirit is essential, and the plan can operate until war breaks out.

If there is no war at all, the present National Service organisation should not be allowed to vanish into thin air, but should be harnessed to the work of reconstruction to make our country a better place to live in.

Appendix III

First Editorial for *Convoy*: February 1944

Convoy No. 1 is the first of a series of booklets which the house of Collins hopes to publish from time to time. If we can get the requisite licence and paper quota then this will become the first number of a national monthly paper with wide circulation at home and abroad for young men and women in civilian life and in the Fighting Services.

WHY IS A NEW PAPER NEEDED NOW?

A gulf lies between civilian life and the Fighting Services. Often some of us in the Western Desert, though proud of our tank, felt bitterness against the men and women in Britain who made that tank. We could envy their cash and comfort. Perhaps they envied our excitement and reputation.

The gulf between civilian life and the Fighting Services only exists because we do not understand each other. We are fighting the same battle, but our jobs separate us. We seldom meet as we used to. We only hear about each other second-hand through the Press. This is not good enough. We have got to get together and understand each other. Otherwise the gulf will grow wider, bitterness and distrust will increase, the period of demobilisation will be more difficult, and the great influence of all the young people in civilian life and the Services who have struggled to win this war will be dispersed and weakened when the time comes to make the peace.

Our jobs separate us. One way we can meet is in a paper. If we can write to each other in this paper we shall understand each other, and perhaps we shall find that just as we are fighting the same war now, so after the war we will want to fight the same battle for a better world. That is the first reason for this paper.

Therefore *Convoy* will print short stories, poems and articles by young men and women in the Forces and in civilian jobs.

We are fighting against evil things. A measure of that same evil exists on our own side and in ourselves, and it may be that the war on the Home Front will one day prove the most bitter. If we want freedom to survive we must believe in Democracy as strongly as our enemies believe in Fascism. But how can we believe in Democracy if Democracy means no more to us than part of the patter of politicians? We can ouly believe in Democracy if we understand the institutions won by toil and blood which form the fabric of our freedom.

During this war a sense of hopelessness and frustration sometimes invades a young person's heart because he wants a better world after the war, but he does not see what he himself can do to help make that better world; around him he sees authority or political power which do not seem to heed his effort.

Convoy will try to persuade/produce a belief in Democracy by explaining the fabric of our freedom and by an insistence on the responsibility of citizenship which can only come from a study of present institutions. *Convoy* will explain the full use every citizen can make of his rights.

We who are on the side of freedom and equality need more than brute force to defeat the creed of brute force. We need a faith. It has not yet come. We believe that an understanding of the message of Christianity will produce that faith. This paper will not expound that hearty form of Christianity which apologises for the Church by insistence upon the sporting nature of parsons.

Convoy will remember the teachings of Jesus Christ and will strive to make them understood.

The troops and civilian workers of Britain, the Dominions and the United States, are divided by differences in pay and outlook. Their one common bond is their stake in the future.

Convoy will try to bring about a better understanding between young people of all nations.

WHAT MORE DOES *CONVOY* WANT TO DO?

Perhaps the hardest to explain.

Although we will defeat Fascism, we may lose the struggle against evil in the long run because of the great price we set on material things. Our political parties concentrate on material interests to the exclusion of mind and spirit. It is hard to have a soul on an empty stomach. So the slum child has small chance of finding beauty and truth. We must have good food, clean air and decent houses for all, before we can expect spiritual development. A sick body may cause a sick mind. Therefore we should cure the body of our country by removing the slums and malnutrition. But that is only the beginning. One third of the country has long enjoyed good food, clean air and decent houses. Yet their minds and their souls are often sick.

Between the two wars these people, and the politicians they created, forgot that the spirit is more important than the flesh. They put their comfort and safety first, their duty second.

And what did young people do?

Those who were interested in politics lived in the slit trenches of their party, blue or red. They only studied the publications of their party, and if other literature came their way they cried 'Gas' and popped down still farther into their trench. In consequence their opinions were narrow and inaccurate; and because there was no place in the trench for other values, their opinions were materialistic.

Convoy is not concerned with/to boost any particular political party. Nor would it like to see the end of the division between the great political parties which is essential to our democracy. *Convoy* wants a square deal for all. But it wants more than that. It wants a new spirit born from our past and present suffering to inspire the future of this country, so that there is an improvement in government and a change of heart.

WHY TRY TO START A PAPER DURING THE WAR?

Why not wait until the war is won?

During the last war it was thought that with victory there would at once dawn a better world fit for heroes to live in. The Allies won; and within two years, while the people looked on with trust or indifference, the foundations had been laid for peace. Those foundations were rotten.

This time we know that on Armistice Day the first round will have been won but the struggle against evil and stupidity on the Home Front will only be starting. If rotten foundations are laid for a new world order, it is we who are young today who will pay for it. We and our children. It is our task to see that a good peace is made. Whether we are fighting at the front or working at home, it is our task to begin thinking NOW about the future which belongs to us. If we wait until the end of the war it will be too late.

Good intentions and kindly feelings are useless without accurate thought and concrete action. Sacrifice must be allied to thought, thought to deed. First we must train for the struggle as best we can, each in his own way by thought and study. We will not forget the strength of our tradition nor the value of experience and age. But no reactionary and selfish interest shall bar our way. We must be ruthless. Where the wood is rotten it must be cut down. Then, though divided by allegiance to different political parties, yet united by understanding in a common purpose, we will go forward together to help build a better world.

Why is this paper called *Convoy*?

If you made an operational flight with Coastal Command, when you reached the convoy the patrol was to protect, there below in the far distance you would see spread out long rows of vessels. Small and neat they look, like toy ships on a grey tablecloth. At that instant you could see a complete picture of the war effort. There in this picture are the ships of the Merchant Navy carrying troops and equipment bound for battle, protected by ships of the Royal Navy and by planes of the Royal Air Force. All this is made possible by work in the factories and mines and dockyards. The picture of united effort is complete.

If *Convoy* becomes a national monthly paper it is hoped that the three Fighting Services and the civilian workers of this country will be represented on the Editorial Board.

*　　*　　*

Convoy's intentions may sound ambitious; and it is certain that these intentions cannot be fulfilled until *Convoy* has been going for some time. It depends on you. This number is only the beginning. *Convoy* will become what you make it as well as what we make it. *Convoy* is for young people. It will be written not only by young people but by those of any age who can help us.

We have set sail and our compass is set.

ARE YOU WITH US?

WILL YOU JOIN OUR CONVOY?

Appendix IV

My Lords, I must beg that indulgence which is bestowed by your Lordships on those addressing you for the first time. Recently I read an article which seemed to me relevant to the question of my noble friend Lord Shackleton. It said:

> Among the calamities of war may be justly numbered the diminution of the love of truth, by the falsehoods which interest dictates, and credulity encourages. A peace will equally leave the warrior and relator of wars destitute of employment; and I know not whether more is to be dreaded from streets filled with soldiers accustomed to plunder, or from garrets filled with scribblers accustomed to lie.

The magazine was *The Idler*, dated November 11th, 1758, and the author—as I expect your Lordships will have guessed—was Dr. Johnson. Times have changed since then, and I am glad to say that we no longer have anything to fear from the soldiers in our streets, or, come to that, from the scribblers in our garrets. And I am all the more glad to say this because I was once a soldier and I now most definitely am a scribbler.

But the relevance of this quotation is this: in war and in cold war truth is the first casualty, because both sides use propaganda. And propaganda is a boomerang which recoils upon the person who uses it. A government puts out a distorted version of the truth and ends by accepting its own lies, and believing in them. The relevance of this to our present problem is this. Her Majesty's Government in general, and the Foreign Office in particular, have managed to convince themselves that slavery does not exist; and therefore, in the end, they have managed even to persuade the public that it is practically non-existent.

Why do the Foreign Office want to believe that slavery does not exist? Your Lordships have heard from the noble Lord, Lord Shackleton, that Saudi Arabia is the greatest slave-buying area in the world; and there are over half a million slaves there today. The main oil company operating in Saudi Arabia is the Arabian-American oil company—Aramco—and if it were known that children are enslaved in Saudi Arabia this might be taken as a criticism of Aramco's general moral influence over the country. Moreover, Aramco wields considerable influence in Washington; and the Foreign Office do not want to embarrass the government of Britain's largest ally.

A friend of mine was attached to the Trucial Oman levies who in the autumn of 1955 captured the Buraimi Oasis from the Saudi Arabian forces. In one of the outlying villages in that uncertain frontier between Oman and Saudi Arabia, he discovered children in fetters. There they were, in a corner of the market place, and there were shackles on their ankles. This story haunted me, and so I approached the Anti-Slavery Society in London; I met more officers from the Trucial Oman levies; I consulted travellers; and all the sources confirmed what we have already been told, that Saudi Arabia is the main and largest market. And as the wealth has increased so, of course, the demand for slaves has risen, because a man is known by the number of slaves he has; it is a form of snobbery out there—like having a Cadillac. Whereas formerly an able-bodied man slave cost £50, he now costs £150. Whereas formerly an attractive girl cost £150, she now costs anything between £400 and £700.

There are two main slave routes into Saudi Arabia. The first comes from West Africa. It goes from the high Volta, through the Niger provinces and the region of Timbuktu, across Africa to the Port of Suakin, and across the Red Sea, by dhow to Lith, a port south of Jedda. The other goes from Iraq and Persia and Baluchistan across the Gulf and then, by caravans of camels, across to Riyadh. The children taken on this route are generally children bought from poor parents in these countries, but quite often they have been kidnapped. What happens to these slaves after they have reached the slave markets? Arabists have told us time and time again that, in fact, the lot of a slave is really not all that bad; that, after all, he is valuable property, and so it is worth while looking after him and feeding him and clothing him. Certainly when I crossed the frontier into Saudi Arabia with Sir John Glubb in 1943 to visit the Emir Abdul el Sidar at Kaf, I saw no sign of ill treatment of the slaves there.

But, my Lords, conditions in Arabia have been changing and, as the noble Lord has said, the new wealth has undermined many of the ancient and respectable traditions. Western goods, Cadillacs and canned foods, refrigerators and radios, and western ideas (which also come in cans, in the form of films) have undermined the old sanction of Koranic law, and sanctions of morality have crumbled. Vice is unrestrained and the means to gratify unusual lusts can easily be procured with money. There are now sheikhs who can obtain sexual satisfaction only with very young children. Slaves are often horribly abused for pleasure or mutilated as a punishment and the castration of young boys is practised. The operation is performed on boys between the ages of ten and fourteen, and the amputation is done radically, both the penis and the scrotum being cut away.

My Lords, the children in shackles in the Buraimi Oasis were destined for Riyadh. The boys might be castrated and the girls bought by any merchant who fancied them. One of the British representatives there in the Buraimi Oasis noticed caravans and lorries coming into a little village called Hamasso at night, and when he tried to visit the houses he was denied admittance. So he began to watch the departure of Saudi aeroplanes. I should say that the planes were all Dakotas and, with the exception of one pilot, all the air crews were American. Shortly before the take-off a lorry would drive on to the airstrip and the children would be literally pushed and herded into the plane. My friend (I am sorry to have to keep saying 'my friend' but he does not want his name to be used) then spoke to one of the American pilots and asked him into his house for a drink. He said to him, "Do you realise that you are carrying children into captivity?" And the man answered, "When I took on this job I was told to keep my eyes shut and my ears shut as to what was going on around here. And that is the way it is going to be. Another seven years of flying for King Saud and I'll have earned enough money to retire for life."

This information, in point of fact, I happen to know was reported to the Foreign Office. It was never used at the time of the Buraimi frontier dispute, nor since. Why? Because the Foreign Office do not wish to embarrass a powerful ally. Nor, I may say, is it only the Foreign Office who do not want to embarrass a powerful ally. When I tried to interest various editors in this matter, some of these steely-eyed despots were alarmed at the matter which they thought might be revealed by my enquiries. The very steel of their eyes grew tarnished at the prospect. However, at last I found an editor who was prepared to back me. I then found that I was given no visas to enter any of the countries of the Trucial Coast. But since I could not get into the coast and could not get into Saudi Arabia, I decided to examine the alternative route. And last year I travelled in a Land-Rover from the Gambia, through Senegal and Mauritania, into what was then the French Sudan and to the legendary city of Timbuktu, where I lived for a month making various enquiries. I then moved out into the Sahara. And there I bought a slave from his Tuareg master, like one buys a piece of mat. I paid for him 25,000 A.O.F. francs, which is the equivalent of £37.10s. 0d. His name was Ibrahaim. He was twenty years old. I gave him his freedom and he now works as a free man in Timbuktu. My

Lords, I bought this man and photographed the money changing hands with the master and took the number of the notes and so forth, entirely in order to come back with the actual proof that slavery exists in the Sahara.

The Tuareg are a nomadic tribesmen, fair-skinned, who have a slave caste known as the Bela. These Bela, men, women and children, belong body and soul to their masters. I have lived in these Tuareg camps, and I have seen these slave girls and slave women working from dawn to dusk. I should explain that among the Tuareg women fatness is considered a sign of great beauty, and so the Tuareg women are not allowed to do any work, even if they want to. So there they lay, rather like sea-lions in the zoo after feeding time, watching their slaves from behind the folds of their indigo veils, and doing nothing. Moreover, the Tuareg caste of nobles refer to and think of themselves as nobles; and nobles do no work—nobles in the Sahara I mean to say! No Tuareg noble would think of handling a spade, erecting a tent or carrying a gourd of water. And so they have these great herds of slaves, exactly as they have always had great herds of sheep; and in the great wastes of the Sahara they have been able to preserve this institution of slavery some sixty-five years after the French occupation put an end to slavery.

I have lived in these camps and seen these little skinny boys, with bellies horribly distended from malnutrition, going out in the morning, before dawn, with the herds; and I have known that, until they come back in the evening, they would be in the desert without anything to eat or drink. And when they got back in the evening, after the Tuareg nobles had eaten, and after their wives had their ration of milk, if there was anything left they would get it. I have seen the marks of cruelty on their bodies. If they are disobedient, or if they lose an animal by neglect, they are tied to a tree and lashed until they lose consciousness—and sometimes they do not recover and are just left to die.

I have met, and know well, a little girl—Timolud is her name—who is sixteen years old. At the age of eleven she was raped by her master. She has already had two children. The first was still-born, and the second was left behind when they moved camp because it was sick; and they told her to leave it in the desert. Long before these girls reach maturity, they are used by their masters; and if, as a result of rape, a child is born, that child is born a slave unless the master happens to wish, by some quirk of his own, to acknowledge it; but that happens very seldom. So when I gave Ibrahaim his freedom, it meant not only that he could escape from the persecution of his master, and not only, as your Lordships have heard the noble Lord say, that his master could take him to Mecca with him on a pilgrimage (and I have met a sheikh who went to Mecca with six children and returned with none because he had sold them all, like a human traveller's cheque) but also that he could marry the girl he loved and that the children of that union would be born free.

My Lords, slavery exists throughout West Africa, concealed behind a legal code that asserts it has been abolished, like a cancer the doctors refuse to diagnose. French and British authorities are trying hard, and have tried hard, to stamp out slavery in the areas that are under their control. But as these African countries, one by one, gain their independence they are going to be forced to deal with the problems themselves. Now I believe in West Africa, certainly, the problem is largely, or certainly partly, one of education—that is to say, the Tuareg noble has been brought up to believe that the Bela is his slave, and the Bela has been brought up to believe that the Tuareg is his master; to such an extent that a Bela slave who has left the camp but is still working in Timbuktu, when he has made enough money, will come back and buy his freedom from his master, even though he knows that, from the point of view of the law, he is a free man. So it is a question of education. But can these newly independent countries, such as Mauritania, Mali or Nigeria, afford this mass education? They have neither the money nor the people to do it. One might think that the answer was that the former tutelary power should provide the experts. That, I think, would be disastrous; because, unfortunately, the tides of nationalism have tinged the peoples of Africa with a deep suspicion of the colonialist powers. A group of English educational experts would therefore be immediately suspect in Nigeria, and a group of French experts—people well equipped to deal with the psychological problem of the Tuareg and their Bela—would be very suspect in Mali.

My Lords, what is the solution? I think it can only be, as we have heard from my noble friend Lord Shackleton, through the United Nations. I should like to stress what he has said: that international conventions are useless unless they have the machinery for supervising their application. An international convention is a mere piece of paper if no agency exists for translating its terms into action. I believe that there should be a committee of experts to advise the Economic and Social Council of the United Nations on the decisions they take about slavery each year. The members of this committee—no more than nine or ten—should be of different nationalities, and preferably not of the nationality of the former tutelary power. They should be chosen for their knowledge of the problems concerned, and they should be there for an indefinite period to ensure continuity. They would be only advisory: the final decisions would still rest with the Economic and Social Council.

Lastly, I believe that everyone of the experts and technicians and advisers needed by African countries should be sent to them by the United Nations. These people should be international not only in outlook but in fact—white or black, red, yellow or brown—and they should owe allegiance directly to the United Nations. I think they should go to the Africans as friends, not as patrons. Because, in the final analysis, to the Africans as well as to the Arabs, policies are less important than personalities; and, deep down, political equality is less important than social equality and friendship.

Index

Index